Korea's Great Buddhist-Confucian Debate

KOREAN CLASSICS LIBRARY: PHILOSOPHY AND RELIGION

Korea's Great Buddhist-Confucian Debate

The Treatises of Chŏng Tojŏn (Sambong)
and Hamhŏ Tŭkt'ong (Kihwa)

translated and with an introduction by

A. Charles Muller

University of Hawai'i Press/Honolulu
Korean Classics Library

20 19 18 17 16 15   6 5 4 3 2 1

Library of Congress Cataloging-in-Publication Data

Korea's great Buddhist-Confucian debate : the treatises of Chong Tojon (Sambong) and Hamho Tukt'ong (Kihwa) / translated and with an introduction by A. Charles Muller.
 pages   cm—(Korean classics library: philosophy and religion)
 Includes bibliographical references and index.
 ISBN 978-0-8248-5380-8 (cloth : alk. paper)
 1. Buddhism—Korea—Early works to 1800.   2. Confucianism—Korea—Early works to 1800.
3. Religious disputations—Korea—Early works to 1800.   I. Muller, A. Charles, translator, writer of introduction.   II. Chong, To-jon, 1342–1398. Simgiri p'yon. English.   III. Chong, To-jon, 1342–1398. Pulssi chappyon. English.   IV. Kihwa, 1376–1433. Hyonjongnon. English.   V. Series: Korean classics library. Philosophy and religion.
 BQ656.K68 2015
 294.3'359512—dc23

2015003841

This work was supported by the English Translation of 100 Korean Classics program through the Ministry of Education of the Republic of Korea and the Korean Studies Promotion Service of the Academy of Korean Studies (AKS-2010-AAA-2101).

University of Hawai'i Press books are printed on acid-free paper and meet the guidelines for permanence and durability of the Council on Library Resources.

Design and composition by Wanda China
Printed by Maple Press

Contents

Acknowledgments

The contents of this book reflect the culmination of a project that extends back more than twenty years, when I encountered the debate between the Confucian statesman Chŏng Tojŏn (1342–1398) and the eminent Korean Sŏn monk Kihwa (1376–1433) in the course of my studies of Kihwa's works. An outline of the arguments and treatises treated in this book formed a chapter in my dissertation. Since that time I have returned to this topic on numerous occasions to write papers, each time digging a bit further into the history, background, and philosophical contents of this debate, which has in turn led me somewhat deeper into the study of (Neo-)Confucianism than most of my colleagues in the field of Buddhist Studies. Thus, I have been gradually developing an understanding of the texts in this volume, along with their background, over the course of a couple of decades, and am absolutely delighted to have the opportunity to bring that work to fruition in a first-rate publication series such as that of the Korean Classics Library series. And I am honored to be able to have my work edited by Patricia Crosby of the University of Hawai'i Press, in what is likely one of her final works in her official capacity of East Asia editor for the Press, due to her well-deserved retirement at the end of 2014.

For the invitation to contribute a monograph for this series, I am extremely grateful to Robert Buswell, who never ceases to amaze me in his immense capacity as a scholar, colleague, editor, and overall manager of large publication projects. It is always a pleasure to work with him, since one can always have complete confidence that things will get done, and get done right. I would also like to offer my thanks to Jennifer Jung-Kim and the rest of the editorial staff of the series, who have been capable, efficient, and a delight to work with.

Finally, I cannot but offer my deepest expression of gratitude to my long time mentor at SUNY Stony Brook, Sung Bae Park. It is Sung Bae who most deeply stimulated my interested in East Asian religions — and not only the study of Buddhism for which he is best known, but as well for his deep appreciation and understanding of Confucianism and Daoism, an appreciation and understanding that I hope has, at least in some measure, been imparted to me. It is this influence that has led me to also become a student of the "three teachings" of Confucianism, Daoism, and Buddhism, and has also stimulated me to try to integrate some of the better principles from all these traditions into my own character.

Translator's Introduction

Initial Meeting

The history of the relationship between Confucianism and Buddhism in East Asia is long and complex, extending from the time of the earliest meeting of the two thought systems down to the present, when, although no longer interacting as distinct traditions in any significant way, their traces still impart a discernible combined influence on East Asian culture. Buddhism entered the Middle Kingdom during the first century CE along with missionaries from India and Central Asia, whose texts and teachings were as exotic to the Chinese as were their languages, clothing, and customs. The speed and extent of the spread of Buddhism in East Asia were somewhat remarkable considering that it was not a religion transmitted by military conquest or other forms of coercion. An important element of its success was the apprehension of Buddhism by Chinese rulers as a religion of a powerful foreign god capable of ensuring good fortune. Thus, for the greater part of the first several centuries of its importation and assimilation, a significant factor in the spread of Buddhism was the support it received in the form of imperial patronage.

From a religious perspective, a major attraction of the new religion was its ability to articulate a profound, yet precise and systematic, explanation of where people come from before birth and where they go after death—matters that previous indigenous forms of Chinese religion had addressed only vaguely. Most important was the teaching of reincarnation: endless rebirth propelled in a flawless manner by the impetus of one's activities, or karma. While teachings bearing a close similarity to the doctrine of karma can be extrapolated from pre-Buddhist Chinese philosophical works (as Kihwa argues in his treatise translated in this volume), nowhere in the indigenous tradition was the matter of the afterlife addressed in the kind of explicit detail as in the Buddhist scriptures. Nor did indigenous Chinese religion explain the principle of cause and effect in anything but the vaguest terms. Buddhism, on the other hand, spoke with certainty of the possibility of the cessation of suffering, the attainment of a state of pristine, pure awareness. Buddhist missionaries, furthermore, laid out a clear and logical path toward achieving this state.

From the outset of their meeting in China, the two thought systems of Confucianism and Buddhism existed, along with Daoism, in a competitive yet mutually defining and influencing relationship. Buddhism as it came into China could not but be shaped by the vernacular into which it had to be translated. But the translation of Buddhist ideas into Chinese thought was more than the mere transition from Indic grammar into a Chinese logographic idiom. For although the early Chinese indigenous philosophical-religious tradition may have lacked Buddhism's logical rigor—the millennium-long heritage born out of the matrix of Indian philosophy—China nevertheless had its own profound and deeply embedded intuitions about how the human mind was constituted and the relation of this mind to the cosmos. The assimilation of Buddhism was thus made more problematic by the fact that it had to be accepted into a religious worldview that, while possessing important affinities, had its own well-established approach to interpreting and describing human behavior.

Debate between Competing Religious and Philosophical Systems

Before we delve into the philosophical and historical background of the encounter between Confucianism and Buddhism, I would briefly call attention to the rarity of the event. History is filled with examples of competition and strife between religious and philosophical traditions, confrontations that have all too often ended badly for the losers. Political fortunes are usually also involved, as is the case here, since Buddhists were the clear losers in the political power struggle that took place in early Chosŏn-period Korea. But there was also nonetheless a *debate* that transpired for several decades, taking place on a fairly equal platform where ideas were exchanged through a shared language. This kind of philosophical debate between two distinct religions traditions does not often occur.

One other exception to this pattern can be seen in ancient India, where Buddhism, Jainism, Sāṃkhya, Vedānta, and other competing systems directly debated each other over several centuries. For meaningful exchange to occur, the parties had to agree on a basic set of rules and had to be functioning within a reasonably similar worldview. Indeed, ancient Indians established a set of rules, known as *pramāṇa*, that clearly delineated what constituted a valid proposition, a valid example, a valid reason, and ultimately a valid argument. They also shared the view of a cyclically functioning, infinite universe as well as a belief in intrinsic purity and ad-ventitious affliction and in laws of cause and effect.

The same conditions for a shared set of principles and worldview had to prevail for meaningful debate to take place between Confucians (and in some cases Daoists) and Buddhists in East Asia. The ensuing introduction is my effort to identify the principles that allowed this debate to occur, and I will argue that the chief facilitating principle was the participants' shar-ing of a deeply embedded paradigm known as *ti-yong* 體用 (K. *ch'e-yong*), rendered into English here as "essence-function." We will return to this philosophical structure later, after providing some basic background on the circumstances, participants, and texts of this debate.

Affinities

INDIGENOUS CHINESE THOUGHT

The remarkable success of Buddhism not only in China but throughout East Asia suggests some basic philosophical resonance between the im-ported Indian system and indigenous traditions. Most important is that the mainstream philosophical traditions of both Confucianism and Dao-ism held a positive and idealistic understanding of the human mind. The human mind was seen to be essentially good. This elemental goodness was known in the *Analects* and other basic Confucian works as the qual-ity of *in* (Ch. *ren* 仁), referring to the most fundamental character of the human mind as being morally good. *In* is generally rendered in English as "humaneness" (my own preferred rendering), "benevolence," "kind-ness," and the like. After developing through the earlier Zhou classics and the *Analects,* the term later received more precise definition in the *Mencius* as an inborn human tendency to be concerned for the welfare of others. The human mind's intrinsic goodness is enumerated by Mencius as the first of the four basic good potentialities (K. *sadan;* Ch. *siduan* 四端). It was understood that *in* is what makes humans "humane," setting them apart from other animals.

In the *Analects* humaneness is seen as being the single thread that binds together all other forms of goodness manifested in the human mind, such as sincerity (K. *sŏng,* Ch. *cheng* 誠),[1] wisdom (K. *chi,* Ch. *zhi* 智), trust(-worthiness) (K. *sin,* Ch. *xin* 信), justice (K. *ŭi,* Ch. *yi* 義),[2] filial piety (K. *hyo,* Ch. *xiao* 孝), and so forth. In the *Analects,* humaneness is seen to be not only weightier in terms of importance compared to these other virtues but also to be their "essence" or "root."[3]

Minor variations in interpretation notwithstanding, the notion of humaneness is central to all Confucian philosophy up until the premodern period. Contained within the nexus of this idea of the human mind's essential wholesomeness is the closely related intuition that one's inborn potentiality for humaneness could be enhanced through the practice of certain patterns of behavior. These were the performance of humane activities in human relationships—by giving things their proper due (justice), by showing loving care and respect for one's parents (filial piety), acting according to customary social rules concerning deference and authority between junior and senior, husband and wife, siblings, co-workers, and so forth—"propriety" (K. *ye,* Ch. *li* 禮), discernment between right and wrong (wisdom), and being trustworthy, along with other forms of positive cognitive and ethical activity. In short, the human mind was seen to be fundamentally oriented around a positive ground. Evil was viewed as a condition of imbalance and disharmony that could and should be corrected by aligning one's activities with the values associated with humaneness.

While articulated within a different family of concepts, an analogous underlying paradigm can be gleaned from the influential Daoist texts of China's classical period, most notably the *Daode jing* and the *Zhuangzi.* While mocking the value-laden Confucian categories of humaneness, justice, propriety, and so forth, the authors of these texts nonetheless envisioned a human mind that, if given the opportunity to return to its most natural condition, would be peaceful, harmonious, and sparkling with the wisdom that was its original endowment. The Daoist philosophical classics emphasized that true virtue was to be found in places and ways not usually recognized by the worldly. These philosophical Daoist works therefore placed little stock in visible worldly achievements; they also recommended a program that would lead to sagehood, although its characteristic approach tended more toward "untraining," in contrast to the Confucian mode of training.[4] Regardless of the active or passive character of the approach, its overall accessibility or subtlety, the predominating tendency in the Chinese approach to personal improvement was to see the human mind as a something intrinsically tending in a positive moral and cognitive direction, something with the potentiality of great enhancement, even perfection.[5]

BUDDHISM

During the first few centuries after the importation of Buddhism into China, the Chinese were overwhelmed by both the wide variation in sectarian approaches and the basic profundity of Indian Buddhist doctrine.

The early translation of Buddhist texts was facilitated by preexisting notions in Chinese philosophy that showed affinities with important Buddhist categories. Over time, methods of translation would be informed by improved mastery of Buddhist doctrine, along with improved linguistic skills on both the Indic and Chinese sides. In terms of philosophical understandings of Buddhism, Daoist ideas would long continue their interaction with those of Buddhism, especially regarding such notions as non-appropriating action (K. *muwi*, Ch. *wu-wei* 無爲), an idea understood as being equivalent to the Buddhist concept of "unconditionality" (Skt. *asaṃskṛta*). Similarly, the Daoist notion of "as-it-is-ness" (K. *chayŏn*, Ch. *ziran* 自然) was understood by Chinese translators as being close to the Buddhist "thusness" (*tathatā*); the Way (*dao* 道) was used to translate the Buddhist *bodhi*, or *mārga*, and so forth. While the first few centuries of assimilation witnessed a significantly broad and even attempt to understand the various incoming traditions, certain types of doctrines and adaptations of doctrines would exercise the greatest influence on what was to become East Asian Buddhism.

In the end, the Buddhist doctrines that would be the most successful in East Asia were those that modeled most closely the makeup of the human mind as seen in the early Confucian and Daoist traditions mentioned above, wherein the human mind was understood to be, at its most basic level, pure, luminous, and knowing, that is, free of evil tendencies. A number of texts in the translated corpus had led to the development of a notion of buddhahood—known as *tathāgatagarbha*, or Buddha Nature—inherent in all sentient beings. This notion of innate buddhahood was first introduced in earlier texts such as the *Nirvana Sutra* and *Lotus Sutra*, with the concept being subsequently developed and clarified in such works as the *Śrīmālā-sūtra*, *Ratnagotravibhāga*, and *Buddha Nature Treatise* (Ch. *Foxing lun*), reaching its apex of elucidation in the *Awakening of Mahāyāna Faith*,[6] a treatise composed by a master (or masters) well studied in the Indian Yogâcāra analyses of the operation of human consciousness. The author of the *Awakening of Mahāyāna Faith* was thus able to take long-held Chinese intuitions regarding the mind and express them through the more precise Yogâcāra terminology of layers of consciousness, perfuming of habit energies, and seed-like formations. Most important, the author of the *Awakening of Mahāyāna Faith* saw the One Mind as being simultaneously possessed of two aspects: a pure, good, originary aspect and a mundane, defiled aspect. The text's author describes the relationship between these two in terms of the logic of essence and function (which we will shortly explore at length), and subsequent East Asian commentators on the *Awakening of Mahāyāna*

Faith adopted this same logic as a fundamental hermeneutic approach. It is especially important to clarify this point because when the Neo-Confucian critics (whom we will encounter below) attack something called "Buddhism," they refer to this distinctively "East Asian-ized" form of Buddhism rather than Indian Buddhism, about which they seemed to know very little.

The final codification of the distinct existence of an original purity of the mind came in the form of the *Vajrasamādhi-sūtra* (Ch. *Jingang sanmei jing;* K. *Kŭmgang sammae kyŏng*),[7] a text that took the evolution of the notion of original, pristine enlightenment to its climax in terms of the articulation of an undefiled *amala* consciousness, a distinctive mode of human consciousness that utterly transcended all worldly taints and deceptions and that served as both the soteric basis for and ultimate object of the kind of attitude toward Buddhist practice that would develop in East Asian forms of Buddhism typified by Chan/Sŏn/Zen. This general doctrinal trend, which was most directly and tersely disclosed in the *Awakening of Mahāyāna Faith* and *Vajrasamādhi-sūtra*, is seen in a number of Mahāyāna scriptures that became popular in East Asia; the *Awakening of Faith* would shortly be followed by the *Sutra of Perfect Enlightenment* (Ch. *Yuanjue jing*), even more obviously an East Asian composition, and the *Platform Sutra* (Ch. *Liuzu tanjing*), the first "scripture" to be acknowledged as an East Asian work.

These texts composed in East Asia held important traits in common, the most important of which was a Buddhist view of human consciousness that had been contoured to indigenous Chinese understandings of the human mind as being something intrinsically pure, and that, although existing in a defiled, obscured state, could be perfected through training. The "humaneness" articulated by Confucius and Mencius was transmuted to the "originally enlightened mind" spoken of in these texts, and the structural paradigm for this transmutation, whether stated overtly or not, was that of essence and function, with the original pure mind being essence (K. *ch'e*, Ch. *ti* 體) and good, enlightened, pure behavior being function (K., Ch. *yong* 用). This is the most basic and pervasive philosophical component of what is referred to as the "sinification" of Buddhism, a process that occurred over a period of several centuries, culminating during the early Tang and finding its greatest expression of the fundamental enlightened character of the mind in the *Sutra of Perfect Enlightenment, *Vajrasamādhi-sūtra,* and *Platform Sutra.* We will return to a detailed discussion of the meaning and role of essence-function in East Asian thought at the end of this introduction.

Confucianism and Daoism in the Period of Buddhist Preeminence

Over the several centuries during which Buddhism carried out its amazing spread throughout East Asia, the Confucian tradition maintained its place as the framework for basic education and as the purveyor of the civil service examination system. Thus the ministers, bureaucrats, teachers, and those connected in any way to governance of the realm automatically had a Confucian education. But this tradition could do little to compete philosophically, or as a state religion, with the dominance Buddhists had achieved in the religious fabric of society, a dominance that reached its peak in the early-to-mid Tang. During this period there were few new developments in Confucian philosophy, as the same classics were simply learned by rote for the purpose of passing civil service examinations. Except for occasional rumblings and purges, more often than not motivated by jealousy over the political and economic influence of Buddhists, Confucians did not actively oppose Buddhism, remaining largely unable to compete in the philosophical arena.

Most of this period's major religious and philosophical developments apart from Buddhism's were in the area of Daoism, in the works of the Neo-Daoists, Daoist alchemists, and the Daoist-influenced literati, all of whom were stimulated by Buddhist ideas. At the same time, Daoist views influenced the evolving tendencies of East Asian Buddhism, to the extent that sometimes the texts of the two traditions were almost indistinguishable from each other.[8] Thus, philosophically speaking, the first several centuries of the growth of Buddhism in China can be seen as a period of philosophical stagnation for Confucianism. Nonetheless, Confucianism maintained its intimate position within the educational system and government bureaucracy even as real philosophical/religious creativity occurred in the Buddhist-Daoist matrix. It was a period during which most major literary figures and political persons of Confucian orientation showed neither the means nor inclination to express any telling philosophical opposition to the Buddhist tradition.

The philosophical discourse that took place between the traditions can be regarded to be as much symbiotic as it was confrontational, at least during the earlier centuries when doctrinal Buddhist schools were moving toward their final formations. Overt ideological argumentation from the Confucian side began to appear from about the time that Buddhist schools such as Huayan and Tiantai reached a level of maturity and Chan began its emergence as an energetic Buddhist movement. The origin of this opposition is usually pinpointed in the essays of the Tang scholar

Han Yu 韓愈 (768–824).[9] Han was an elite bureaucrat, as well as a literary figure of considerable stature, who was troubled by the growing influence of Buddhism in the imperial court, a development he believed was leading the rulership to a blindness endangering the security and well-being of the realm. He felt strongly enough about the excesses of Buddhism that he dared to memorialize the throne with a vehemence he knew full well would lead him to trouble.

Han Yu's two best-known critical essays on Buddhism are the *Origin of the Way* (*Yuandao* 原道)[10] and *Memorial on the Buddha's Bone* (*Jianying fogu* 諫迎佛骨).[11] In these essays he lambasted Buddhism as a foreign religion that, he said, was leading the emperor to spend inordinate amounts of time at monasteries and that involved great time, expense, and resources for activities such as the ceremonial circulation of the Buddha's relics (Skt. *śarīra*) around the capital. These arguments pointing out the visible excesses of the Buddhist clergy and the rulers involved with the clerics were mostly emotional in character. However, although Han did not attempt to seriously engage Buddhism for its philosophical shortcomings, his writings raised enough hackles to get him exiled and moreover served as the point of departure for the anti-Buddhist arguments presented by later scholars.[12]

As the Tang drew to an end and the Song began, however, the philosophical matrix of China was sufficiently steeped in Buddhist and Daoist philosophy that many important concepts were taken for granted as being standard philosophical categories (i.e., not necessarily seen as either Buddhist or Daoist in origin). This led to the birth of a new, drastically revamped form of Confucianism called "Song learning" (Ch. *songxue* 宋學), known in the West as Neo-Confucianism.[13] Chinese thought had long had the chance to assimilate Daoist notions of the *dao*, alchemical transformation, Buddhist karma, dependent origination, Huayan principle (K. *yi*, Ch. *li* 理) and phenomena (K. *sa*, Ch. *shi* 事), and Chan meditation. But the gradual waning in late Tang and early Song of doctrinal Buddhism as a state institution and the corruption and stagnation of much of the doctrinal Buddhist tradition itself that coincided with the emergent predominance of Chan had left a bit of a creative intellectual vacuum. The influence of the great doctrinal systems of Chinese Yogâcāra, Tiantai, and Huayan had faded. In their place in the Buddhist intellectual realm was the flowering of schools of Song Chan, known even then for the worst extremes of iconoclasm, antinomianism, and escapism, in terms both of behavior and in what was contained in their popular texts. As de Bary points out (citing Yanagida), there were numerous texts containing passages that provided targets for Neo-Confucian accusations of nihilism.[14]

On the other hand, it seems that there were relatively few Buddhist scholars of the time sufficiently capable and motivated to point out that many of the lines cited by their critics—namely Zhu Xi 朱熹 (1130–1200) and the Cheng brothers—had been skillfully selected out from discussions that, taken in their entirety, were not at all nihilistic. The extent of the validity of these anti-Chan criticisms is an issue central to the two essays we will study below, but these trouble spots in the Chan Way were already being pointed out by their philosophical opponents during the late Song.

Regardless of the tendentious character of the criticisms of Chan made by the leading figures of this reenergized Confucian movement, it is no secret that there was a strong strain of anti-intellectualism in the literature of the Chan tradition, and the question of whether this lack of intellectual response was a result of internal trends notwithstanding, there is no doubt that the overall attitude within Chan toward academic study was different from that of the doctrinal schools.[15] This attitude demonstrated by the members of the Chan schools may well have contributed to an intellectual vacuum that would be filled by the New Confucians.

Sources of Neo-Confucian Doctrine

Although the classics that were the object of study for the Neo-Confucians were essentially the same as they had been for their Confucian predecessors (the Four Books,[16] the Five Classics,[17] and so forth), they were re-analyzed under the lens of a new hermeneutic that was the result of several centuries of Buddhist and indigenous Chinese cross-fertilization. Emerging from this cross-fertilization was a new iteration of the classic essence-function approach in the form of the categories of principle (Ch. *li* 理) and material force (Ch. *qi* 氣), both derived from the notions of principle and phenomena popular in the Huayan and Tiantai schools.[18] The Neo-Confucians brought this new metaphysics, which also included a heavy reliance on the *Yijing* and yin-yang cosmology, to re-articulate the relationship of humans to humans and humans to the universe, along with a much more precisely articulated path of cultivation relying heavily on the *Mencius*.

The most important early figures in this movement were the Neo-Confucian founders Zhang Zai 張載 (1020–1077) and Zhou Dunyi 周敦頤 (1017–1073),[19] whose combined works established the bases of this new metaphysics while creating schema for a new way to understand humans and their world. What is noteworthy about their writings, however, is the degree to which they were energized by anti-Buddhist polemic. Though these two initiated the polemic, it is not especially vehement in their works. Zhou, after all, was known to have been a Chan practitioner of sorts.

It is in the writings of the Cheng brothers (Cheng Hao 程顥, 1032–1085; and Cheng Yi 程頤, 1033–1107) that the distinctive Neo-Confucian philosophy reaches maturity, as the philosophical elaboration of the categories of *li* and *qi* within the framework of commentary on the classical texts takes a sophisticated form.[20] It was Cheng Hao who developed the *li-qi* cosmological view and who, in rereading classical passages such as *Analects* 12:1,[21] declared that "the humane man forms a single body with the world." Even more so than the works of the earlier generations of Neo-Confucians, the criticism of Buddhism becomes an integral part—and at times the central aspect—of the Cheng brothers' discourse. Interestingly, the brother who exhibited the more mystical, or "Channish," tendencies in his writings, Cheng Hao, is the one who composed the most damaging critiques of the Chan tradition. The Cheng brothers criticized Chan Buddhism for its antinomian, escapist tendencies and its doctrine of emptiness, which they construed as nihilism.[22] The arguments composed by the Chengs and their mentors were digested, explicated, and organized in the writings of Zhu Xi, who would come to be regarded as the grand systematizer of the Neo-Confucian tradition, the single individual most responsible for the reinstatement of Confucianism as the predominant ideology of the Chinese imperial government until the opening of the modern era. Zhu Xi formalized and firmly embedded the *li-qi* paradigm at the center of the new Confucian doctrine, using it as a primary hermeneutic tool (together with its analog, *ti-yong*) to explicate the Four Books that he selected to form the core of Confucian education. The notion of *li* henceforth becomes the linchpin of Confucian thought, and the precise nature of this underlying principle to the psycho-physical "stuff" of the universe (material force, *qi*) would become the subject of debate and discussion for centuries in China, Korea, and Japan. As we will see, it plays a central role in the treatises by Chŏng Tojŏn that we will read below.

It is important to reiterate that when Zhu and the Chengs talked about Buddhism, they were talking about the form that was in vogue during their lifetimes: Song-dynasty Chan, the same tradition that was in the process of compiling *gong-an* collections, teaching strike-and-shout Linji methodologies, and so forth. Popular Buddhist writings at that time contained very little in the way of explanation of Indian-style notions of dependent origination, emptiness, or the two levels of truth. The popular scriptures of the day were mostly East Asian apocrypha (such as the *Sutra of Perfect Enlightenment* and the **Śūraṃgama-sūtra*) and works overtly composed within the Chan tradition (such as the *Platform Sutra*) that taught a "suddenistic" approach to the attainment of enlightenment, giving short shrift to scholarly study.

While the Chan schools were drawing continuous harsh criticism from their Confucian contemporaries, I have found very little in the literature that would represent a sustained effort at written self-defense from the Chan side. More than two centuries earlier, Zongmi 宗密 (780–841) had composed a response of sorts in his *Inquiry into the Origin of Humanity* (discussed in some detail below). And in the eleventh century the Chan monk Qisong 契嵩 (1007–1072) wrote extensively in defense of Buddhism against Neo-Confucian criticisms.[23] But both Zongmi's and Qisong's treatises were composed long before the development of the sophisticated metaphysics of Zai, Zhou, and the Cheng brothers, systematized by Zhu Xi, and thus they responded mainly to the relatively unsophisticated arguments of Han Yu. Aside from the Koryŏ-Chosŏn monk Kihwa (whose works we will read below), I have not found any sustained commensurate response from within the Chan/Sŏn tradition to the fully developed Neo-Confucian position—and this holds true down to modern times and even among modern scholars. On the other hand, in the several volumes on Neo-Confucianism published by deBary and colleagues, we find repeated examples of the Neo-Confucian polemic, without any balanced critical assessment that might take seriously the Buddhist perspective.

Why the lack of commensurate Buddhist response? This is a question that requires further attention. One possible explanation is that, knowing the general character of Chan with its self-proclaimed dissociation from discursive argumentation, such a debate was outside the purview of what a Chan teacher was supposed to be doing. It could also be that the Buddhists were sufficiently confident of the status of their religion that they believed that such diatribes were never going to have a concrete effect in terms of government-authorized restrictions. It may also have been that the vibrant energy of the Neo-Confucian movement, coupled with the bright young minds being attracted to it, was simply too much for the Chan leaders to contend with.

Neo-Confucianism in Korea

The geographical proximity of Korea to China, along with the concomitant extensive and continuous exchange of commodities and ideas, allowed Koreans to participate in the Chinese philosophical world at a relatively early point. Korean thinkers were even able to make significant contributions to the greater East Asian religious discourse, as many of them traveled to the Tang and Song centers of learning and made their own mark. Koreans learned well Chinese ways of thinking, and, bringing Chinese ideas back their homeland, made their own enhancements and sometimes took off in their own creative directions.

During the two centuries after Zhu Xi, a confrontational situation between Neo-Confucianism and Buddhism developed in the Koryŏ (918–1392), although in a somewhat different context than that seen in Song China. The most important difference between the two scenarios was the markedly greater degree to which the Korean Buddhist establishment was embedded in the state power structure as compared with the situation in the Song. In the case of Korea, there was a decadent, stumbling government in place, supported by and supporting a religious organization plagued by scandal and corruption. The Buddhist *saṃgha* owned vast tracts of tax-free territory, traded in slaves and other commodities, and was influential at all levels of government. There were too many monks ordained for the wrong reasons and corruption was rampant. Thus, the ideological fervor with which Neo-Confucianism arose in Korea had a special dimension, with the venom of their rhetoric fueled not only by the earlier philosophical arguments of the Cheng brothers and Zhu but also by the extent of the observable degeneracy of the Buddhist establishment. Thus, in Korea the mostly philosophical arguments against Buddhism that had originated with the Cheng brothers became the ideology of a rising movement of resistance on the part of influential members of the intelligentsia determined to overthrow a decaying Koryŏ dynasty — along with the rotting Buddhist monastic system with which it was deeply entangled. Thus, the anti-Buddhist polemical dimension of the Neo-Confucianism that developed in Korea took on a focus, a vehemence, indeed an exclusivism[24] not previously seen in China.

It was the Neo-Confucian stream of the Cheng-Zhu school that was accepted as orthodoxy in Korea, becoming established as a government ideology and as the environment for philosophical inquiry to an extent not seen in China. The exclusive influence of the Cheng-Zhu school in Korea stands in some contrast to the situation in China, where the Neo-Confucian field later was influenced by the "school of mind" of Wang Yangming 王陽明 (1472–1529).[25] In Korea, as in China, the central thrust of the Neo-Confucian argument came in the form of anti-Buddhist discourse. In Korea, however, the anti-Buddhist tenor would be magnified due to political and social issues that had not existed in China. Whereas Neo-Confucianism in China struggled against Buddhism and did succeed in wresting a sizable portion of its following back from the literati class, the tradition also fragmented into branches, some of which (such as the

Wang Yangming school) often showed more similarities to Chan than to the Confucian doctrine espoused by Zhu Xi.

While there were anti-Buddhist memorials presented in Korea as early as 982, serious concentrated attacks on Buddhism did not begin until the mid-fourteenth century. The initial major charges, presented by individuals such as Yi Saek 李穡 (1328–1396), were that excessive patronage was deleterious to the well-being of the state. The attacks on Buddhism by Cho In'ok 趙仁沃 (?–1396) and Chŏng Mongju 鄭夢周 (1337–1392) were also made on political and economic rather than philosophical and religious grounds. After this period, the anti-Buddhist polemic took a turn toward the philosophical in the writings of such prominent Neo-Confucian figures as Kang Hoebaek 姜淮伯 (1357–1402) and Chŏng Ch'ong 鄭摠 (1358–1397), both active in the late fourteenth century.[26] Toward the end of the fourteenth century the political and economic problems of the Koryŏ court intensified, and with the Buddhists firmly embedded in a weakened political structure, Neo-Confucian activists rallied to the side of the rebel general Yi Sŏnggye 李成桂 (1335–1408). Yi, having toppled the Koryŏ government in a sudden coup d'état and establishing the Chosŏn dynasty in 1392, was automatically endowed with a cabinet composed of Neo-Confucian advisors. With the coup, the Buddhists were thrust out of their position of political power. They would for the most part gradually be relegated to an existence in their mountain monasteries, prohibited from setting foot in the cities. The final polemical push for a Buddhist purge came during 1370–1398, led by the essays of Chŏng Tojŏn 鄭道傳 (pen name Sambong 三峰; 1342–1398), Yi's main political strategist, who would play a major role in the development of the political structure of the new Chosŏn dynasty.[27] Chŏng wrote three major philosophical essays critical of Buddhism. In the first, *Simmun chŏndap* 心問天答 (The Mind Asks, Heaven Answers; 1375), he presents a critique of the Buddhist doctrine of karma, offering instead a Neo-Confucian interpretation of the interaction of principle and material force. The second, *Simgiri p'yŏn* 心氣理篇 (On the Mind, Material Force, and Principle; 1394), presents the argument that Buddhists confuse material force with the mind, Daoists confuse material force with the *dao*, and both confusions are engendered by a lack of awareness of the role of principle (*yi*) in guiding all things. He also argues that the Confucian definitions and usages of the three terms of "mind," "material force," and "principle" are clear and consistent, and those of Buddhism are vague and inconsistent. Third is *Pulssi chappyŏn* 佛氏雜辨 (Array of Critiques of Buddhism; 1398), in which can be found his final and most sustained anti-Buddhist polemic. Here he carries out an extensive refutation of Buddhist doctrines and practices, including the content of the prior two essays along with summaries of virtually all the arguments of his Neo-Confucian predecessors going all the way back to Han Yu.

In these anti-Buddhist treatises Chŏng focused on comparisons of Buddhist and Confucian positions on issues of doctrine and practice. His intention was to show that Buddhist doctrine was deeply and intrinsically flawed. He believed that the Buddhist establishment had to be disciplined at the present moment and that the government should curtail and, if possible, put a permanent end to the activities of this dangerous belief system. His critique is thorough and systematic, covering every major aspect of the Buddhist doctrine that was being presently taught. Given the composition of Korean Buddhism at the time, the primary object of his criticism was the Sŏn school, which the Neo-Confucians had long perceived as having strong tendencies toward otherworldliness and denial of the importance of human relationships, of respect for the state, and even of Buddhism's own principle of cause and effect.

The influence of Chŏng's Chinese predecessors—primarily the Cheng brothers, via Zhu Xi—is omnipresent in his writings. The majority of his arguments and examples are drawn from the Cheng brothers, through the commentaries of Zhu. Because of this obvious reliance on the Chengs and Zhu, when I first began to read Chŏng's essays I for the most part agreed in my evaluation of his level of originality with mainstream Korean intellectual historians who regard him as more of an ideologue than a philosopher. But while his qualifications as an "original thinker" might be questioned, none of Chŏng's worthy predecessors composed such a well-organized, complete, comprehensive, and systematic attack on Buddhism as can be found in the *Simgiri p'yŏn* and the *Pulssi chappyŏn*. In his arguments against Buddhism, he demonstrates a solid grasp of its representative doctrines. His clever rhetorical strategy shows that he knows where and how to subtly adapt citations from Buddhist sutras and sayings such that they will serve the purposes of his argument. He clearly understands the mainstream doctrinal and practical issues of Koryŏ Son; he is familiar with the works of Chinul 知訥 (1158–1210) and Zongmi; and he has an undoubted mastery of the representative texts and tropes of Daoism. In short, Chŏng is no second-tier hack. He is, rather, a first-rate scholar, a clever rhetorician, and a skillful writer, all qualities that explain why his works have been preserved, commented upon, and studied into modern times.

We will return to examine the contents of the *Simgiri p'yŏn* and the *Pulssi chappyŏn*, but first let us review what was happening in terms of the Buddhist response.

Buddhist Responses and the Influence of Zongmi

We have noted above that despite the intensity of the critiques made against Chan Buddhism by the Song Neo-Confucian leaders, there was little in terms of sustained and reasoned written response from the Chan community from the time that the criticism began to take hold during the Song. The most significant early response came from Zongmi at the very outset of the Confucian anti-Buddhist polemic, in the mid-Tang. Those who know the history of Korean Buddhism will recognize Zongmi as one of the Chinese scholar-monks who most directly influenced the later character of the Korean Sŏn tradition. In the history of the development of Korean Sŏn, issues related to the reconciliation of various approaches to practice came to play a central role, one of the most significant of which was the relationship between meditation practice and scriptural study. Zongmi, who would have the unusual distinction of being recognized as a "patriarch" of both the Chan and Huayan traditions, advocated the complementarity of the approaches of meditative practice and scriptural study. His statements on this and related matters, such as explanations of the notion of intrinsic enlightenment and discussions of the relationship between sudden and gradual in practice and enlightenment, were followed and repeated by the most influential of the Korean Sŏn formulators, including Chinul, Kihwa, and Hyujŏng 休靜 (1520–1604). And as it turns out, the texts that most interested these later Korean Sŏn masters — the *Sutra of Perfect Enlightenment, Awakening of Mahāyāna Faith, Diamond Sutra,* and *Huayan jing* — were also the subject of Zongmi's most extensive commentarial efforts.

One of the works for which Zongmi is most noted in Chinese intellectual history is his *Inquiry into the Origin of Humanity* (*Yuanren lun* 原人論).[28] Composed around 830, this treatise was written for a broad audience. Typical of the writings of Chinese doctrinal scholars of the sixth to eighth centuries, it is a hermeneutically oriented text that classifies the teachings of Buddhism into five levels. Such classifications had been carried out before Zongmi by such people as his Huayan predecessor Fazang, de facto Tiantai founder Zhiyi, and many others.[29]

While the *Inquiry* is primarily a textbook that utilizes the classification scheme as a pedagogical methodology for the purpose of understanding Buddhism, the opening passages take a clear polemical shot at Confucianism, obviously intended as a response to the essays of Han Yu. Zongmi criticizes indigenous Chinese philosophy for failing to articulate the basic laws of cause and effect. Thus, he debunks the Chinese classical view of spontaneous production, the lack of a rationale accounting for the differences in individual endowments of vital force, and the unexplained unfairness seen in the operation of the "mandate of heaven" (Ch. *tianming* 天命). According to Zongmi, careful thought reveals all of these as logically untenable, incapable of matching even the most elementary of the Buddhist teachings, that of the law of karmic retribution. There is, nonetheless, an ecumenical character to the *Inquiry*, since, although Confucianism and Daoism are judged as inferior to Buddhism, they are nonetheless accorded a certain amount of value, with Confucius and Laozi being regarded as bona fide sages along with Śākyamuni. As Gregory notes:

> Although it should be no surprise that Tsung-mi [Zongmi] regards Buddhism as a higher level of teaching than either Confucianism or Daoism, what is especially noteworthy is that his attitude toward the two teachings is sympathetic and inclusive. Even though his designation of them as exclusively provisional places them in a category inferior to the Buddhist teachings, it also — and far more significantly — places them within the same realm of discourse. Its concrete forms of expression may differ, but the truth realized by the three sages is universal. (*Inquiry into the Origin of Humanity*, 81)

Given that Han Yu's tracts and Zongmi's *Inquiry* were written in the early part of the ninth century, almost five centuries before the exchange between Chŏng and Kihwa, it is noteworthy the extent to which the content of the works of the earlier Chinese writers finds its way into the treatises of the two Korean receivers of their respective traditions. Chŏng, for instance, will continue to invoke Han's criticism of Buddhism as a "foreign" religion. Kihwa for his part will open his own treatise with a correlation borrowed from Zongmi (and repeated by Qisong) matching the five constant virtues of Confucianism with the five basic Buddhist precepts — a correlation first made as far back as the *Diwei boli jing* 提謂波利經 (Sutra of Trapuṣa and Bhallika).[30] While the *Inquiry* stands out as the major precedent for Kihwa's work, there are nonetheless significant differences in content and structure based largely on the circumstances in which they were written. The *Inquiry* is first and foremost a treatise on doctrinal taxonomy that takes up the critique of Confucianism only in its opening sections. Zongmi's Buddhist tradition at the time, even if marred by the rants of the likes of Han Yu, certainly did not have its back against the wall. Buddhists in the early Chosŏn on the other hand were on the ropes, as it were, and so Kihwa's treatise is in its entirety a defense of the Buddhist tradition, with issues of doctrinal classification long since forgotten. There are also significant personal stylistic differences. But before addressing these, we need to introduce Kihwa himself.

Kihwa

Kihwa 己和 (original name Hamhŏ Tŭkt'ong 涵虚得通; 1376–1433) was born just sixteen years before the Koryŏ-Chosŏn dynastic transition. The son of a diplomat, he was educated with his upper-class peers at the recently established Sŏngyun'gwan 成均館 Confucian academy.[31] In the course of his studies at this institution, Kihwa is said to have attained to a remarkable level of proficiency in Chinese philosophy and literature. His biographer goes to unusual lengths to convey the extent to which Kihwa's professors esteemed him.

> Entering the academy as a youth, he was able to memorize more than a thousand phrases daily. As time passed, he deeply penetrated the universality of the single thread, clarifying the meanings of the classics and expounding their content. His reputation was unmatched. Grasping the subtlety of the transmitted teachings, he disclosed all their profundities in his explanations. His sonorous voice and graceful beauty were like flowers laid upon silk brocade—even such a metaphor falls short of description. People said that he would become the minister truly capable of transmitting the heavenly mandate, extending upward to the ruler and bringing blessings down to the people. In his grasp of the correct principles of society he had no need to be ashamed even if he were to appear before the likes of Zhou and Shao.[32]

Kihwa is said to have abandoned his Confucian studies in favor of Buddhism at the age of twenty-one, after the tragic death of a close friend.[33] Acknowledging the obvious hyperbole characteristic of hagiographical sketches written by disciples of eminent Buddhist teachers, we might want to take note of what is contained in this passage. First, there is not, in the entire corpus of Korean Buddhist hagiographies, an appraisal of scholarly (Confucian) acumen comparable in scope to this; and second, the strong assessment of Kihwa's early abilities described in the passage is corroborated by what is known of his later Buddhist career, in which he displayed a strong interest and outstanding ability in literary/philosophical/exegetical pursuits. His unusual erudition is also evident in his later works, where there are an unusual number of citations from the Five Classics, Four Books, and Daoist classics such as the *Daode jing* and *Zhuangzi*.

After turning to the Buddhist path, Kihwa entered into a short period of wandering and study. He subsequently became a disciple of the national preceptor Muhak 無學 (1327–1405), a master of the Imje Sŏn (Ch. Linji Chan 臨濟禪) *gong-an* 公案 (J. *kōan*) tradition. Kihwa spent the rest of his days immersed in meditation, travel, teaching, and an extensive literary pursuit that included commentarial work, essay writing, and poetry. Despite the diminished influence of Buddhism in early Chosŏn Korea, toward the end of his career he served as preceptor to the royal family. He thereafter retired once again to the mountain monasteries, where he taught and wrote until his passing in 1433. During his life Kihwa wrote several important and influential treatises and commentaries on Buddhist works that established him as one of the leading exegetes in the Korean Buddhist tradition.[34]

Positioned as he was as the leading representative of the Buddhist *saṃgha* at a time when it was coming under great pressure from the new Neo-Confucian-dominated government, Kihwa no doubt felt obliged to offer a response to the Neo-Confucian charges. Respond he did, in the form of a philosophical treatise that has become a landmark in Korean intellectual history: the *Hyŏnjŏng non* 顯正論 (Clarification of Orthodoxy). In the *Hyŏnjŏng non* Kihwa attempted to answer the full range of criticisms made by the Neo-Confucians that had been organized and articulated in Chŏng Tojŏn's *Simgiri p'yŏn* and *Pulssi chappyŏn*. As we will see below, it seems clear that the *Hyŏnjŏng non* was written specifically to refute the arguments of these two essays, and thus the titling of the present work as Korea's "great debate."[35]

As mentioned above, the circumstances of Kihwa's composition of this treatise in defense of Buddhism against Confucian-based criticisms have a direct precedent in those surrounding Zongmi's *Inquiry*. Zongmi and Kihwa had much in common, both being Chan/Sŏn–Huayan/Hwaŏm scholars of considerable classical Chinese philosophical background and both solid respecters of many aspects of Confucian and Daoist learning. The two men shared a broad vision that all three masters—Confucius, Laozi, and Śākyamuni—were genuine sages, but their way of evaluating the two non-Buddhist traditions differs somewhat.

While treating similar topics from similar perspectives, the two treatises differ in their basic line of argumentation. Zongmi's work, reflecting its author's interest in doctrinal classification, is primarily an attempt to show how Confucianism and Daoism are related to Buddhism as expedient, but nonetheless heterodox (K. *oegyo* 外教) teachings. His tone toward Confucianism and Daoism is conciliatory, but he will clearly distinguish the two from Buddhism as being even less sophisticated than the teachings of "men and gods," that is, the basic teaching of karmic retribution for moral and immoral actions. Kihwa's argument, on the other hand, relies primarily on an understanding of essence-function and interpenetration that operates equally in Confucianism, Daoism, and Buddhism but that he claims has been brought to different levels of actualization by the practitioners of each of the three teachings. Kihwa perceives the three teachings as various ways to access a singular reality. Despite his conversion to Buddhism, he never really rejected his earlier Confucian and Daoist learning. Accordingly, in his Buddhist apologetic writings he shows no intention to discredit fundamental Confucian principles; nonetheless, he argues that the Confucians had often missed the deeper implications of their own texts.

Kihwa's treatment of the relationship between the three traditions as being fundamentally in agreement is a typical Buddhist response that became common in the Tang and Song in China, as well as in Chosŏn Korea, where Korean monks regularly invoked the phrase *samgyo hab'il* 三教合一 to characterize the relationship among the three traditions. Like Kihwa, later Korean Buddhists such as Hyujŏng would take this conciliatory stance while nonetheless declaring Buddhism to be more profound. One might see this as an example of broad-minded Buddhist thinking. And once again, because the educational system basically consisted of mastering the Confucian canon, these Buddhist monks had learned the Confucian classics in a decidedly positive environment. Nonetheless, throughout the Chosŏn, Buddhists were basically on the defensive, so there was also probably a pragmatic dimension to their conciliatory attitude.

The Texts: Content Analysis

SIMGIRI P'YŎN (ON MIND, MATERIAL FORCE, AND PRINCIPLE)

Compared to the *Pulssi chappyŏn*, which can be seen as Chŏng's magnum opus, the *Simgiri p'yŏn* is a relatively short work. The latter text focused directly on what Chŏng takes to be the metaphysical weaknesses in the Buddhist and Daoist systems, an assertion he works through via the framework of the three important metaphysical categories of mind (K. *sim* 心), material force (K. *ki* 氣), and principle (K. *yi* 理).

In Chŏng's view, Confucians alone have properly recognized principle for what it is, being the most fundamental value, both metaphysically and ethically, and therefore deserving priority within any philosophical or meditative system. The Buddhists and Daoists, on the other hand, miss the fundamental importance of principle and mistakenly base their systems on either the mere cultivation of the mind (Buddhists) or the mere nourishment of material force (Daoists). In arguing these points, Chŏng composes his essay in three main sections.

1. The first section is a polemical summary of the Buddhist teachings, describing them as focused on the cultivation of the mind. This exclusive focus on mental cultivation leads Buddhists to become escapists, who are out of touch with the everyday world, who avoid basic responsibilities in society, and who lack a value system. Their definition of mind is nebulous, and their mental cultivation is based on material force rather than principle. He cites passages from various popular Buddhist texts to make his point, but not in a way that would be accepted by a representative of the Buddhist tradition.

2. The next section is Chŏng's polemical summary of the Daoist teachings in which he describes them as focused on the cultivation of material force—hence the Daoists' obsession with health, longevity, and so forth. Again, as in his critique of Buddhism, Chŏng skillfully selects representative Daoist passages from the *Daode jing* and the *Zhuangzi* that are intended to prove this obsession with material force, which implies that Daoists are wholly immersed in the physical (形而下) world, having no access to the metaphysical elaborations of Confucianism. It is a fascinating argument but, again, one with which a good Daoist would take serious issue. Especially objectionable would be Chŏng's assertion that when the Daoists talk about "that which precedes heaven and earth" they are referring to material force; a Daoist would certainly maintain that the *dao* is a notion that far transcends that of material force.

3. The third section critiques the teachings of Buddhism and Daoism as characterized in the prior two sections from a typical Neo-Confucian position that centers on the importance of recognizing principle as a guiding and organizing force in ordering the natural and human worlds. The paramount importance of individual actualization of the cardinal Confucian value of justice (*ŭi*) is stressed in great detail to make the case that a person who understands justice cannot avoid the responsibilities encountered in societal interactions. This section amounts to a superb and succinct articulation of the central Neo-Confucian doctrine.

In the case of both the *Simgiri p'yŏn* and the *Pulssi chappyŏn*, it would probably be safe to estimate that 80 to 90 percent of Chŏng's prose is based on the works of the Cheng brothers and Zhu Xi.[36]

PULSSI CHAPPYŎN

Chŏng begins in the first two chapters of his treatise with a critique of the Indian notions of karma and transmigration, arguing against these "foreign" Indian paradigms and advocating instead for Chinese cosmological schema such as were developed in connection with the *Yijing* and its commentaries: yin-yang, the five phases (K. *ogyo,* Ch. *wuxing* 五行), *hun/hon* 魂 and *po/paek* 魄 souls, and the like. From a present-day perspective, these chapters do not necessarily establish a metaphysical high ground for Confucianism because Chŏng's proof rests on dubious assertions such as the non-increase or decrease of the total number of beings in the world at a given time, positions that were never really articulated as such in the foundational Confucian works. He does make a good point, however, in bringing to mind the fact that when it comes to practical matters, such as the healing of disease, virtually all East Asians of the time, Buddhists included, relied on Chinese yin-yang cosmology in the form of traditional medicinal practices. The traditional Chinese medicine practiced in the present day is still based on these principles.

It is in the third through fifth chapters that he most directly employs the Cheng-Zhu philosophical arguments, using them to attack Buddhism at one of its traditional weak points: the contradictory character of the discourse on the nature and the mind as found in *tathāgatagarbha*-influenced texts such as the *Awakening of Mahāyāna Faith* and *Sutra of Perfect Enlightenment,* texts based on logic similar to that found in the *Simgiri p'yŏn.* He provides textual examples from the *Śūraṃgama-sūtra* and from the writings of Chinul that show inconsistencies among the various accounts and definitions of the relation between the mind and nature (K. *sŏng* 性). Chŏng reveals these inconsistencies in a series of citations showing that, in one place in the sutra, nature is equivalent to mind; in another place nature is an aspect of the mind; yet again it is a principle contained in the mind; and in yet another place a function of the mind. Referring to the disparities and circular reasoning that he finds in the Buddhist descriptions of the nature, he says, "[The Buddhist explanations regarding the notion of "nature" are] all based on nebulous supposition rather than explicit facts. The teachings of the Buddhists have lots of wordplay but lack a definitive doctrine, and through this, their actual intentions can be understood" (*SBC* 1.78b).

The Confucian teachings are, by contrast, consistent from beginning to end. They clearly distinguish between the mind and its nature, between principle and external events. They allow for clear value and evaluation, with uniformity throughout. Consistency is paramount for Neo-Confucians, as the Chengs, and especially Zhu Xi, placed great importance on working out all matters of inconsistency within their system.[37]

A similar theme carries into the fourth chapter, where Chŏng criticizes Buddhists, in this case especially Chan Buddhists, for conflating the notion of the nature with that of mundane function, citing the likes of Layman Pang, who said, "Hauling water and carrying firewood are nothing but marvelous function" (SBC 1.78d). Chŏng here relies directly on Zhu Xi, who said, "If you take functional activity to be [the same as] the nature, then are not people's irresponsible actions such as taking a sword to murder someone and transgressing the Way [also] the nature?" (SBC 1.79b). This line of argumentation is carried into chapter six, where the focus is directly on the relationship between the mind and its external, functional manifestations. To clarify the Confucian position (which he takes to be rationally and metaphysically consistent), Chŏng cites the Mencian four potentialities (K. *sadan* 四端) that are innate to humans, along with their four concomitant manifest functions of humaneness, propriety, justice, and wisdom. The Buddhists, by contrast, espouse doctrines that dissociate the innate capacities of the mind from the manifestations of human activity. This chapter contains the passage that constitutes the crux of Chŏng's argument. He says:

> It is like the saying "essence and function spring from the same source; the manifest and the subtle have no gap between them."[38] The Buddhist method of study addresses the mind, but does not address its manifestations. This can be seen in the Buddhist's saying things like "The bodhisattva Mañjuśrī wanders through the taverns, but these activities are not his mind."[39] Excuses like this for sloppy behavior abound [in the Buddhist teachings]. Is this not a separation of the mind from its activities? Chengzi said, "The study of the Buddhists includes reverence to correct the internal, but does not include justice to straighten the external."[40] Therefore those who are stuck in these [incorrect views] wither away. (SBC 1.79c–d)

Chŏng's critique runs through several more chapters, addressing issues such as the Buddhists' abandonment of societal obligations, perverted application of the notion of Buddhist compassion (Skt. *maitrī*), criticism of the idea of two levels of reality, the practice of begging, and most of all, the perceived escapist and nihilistic views of Chan. But all can be summarized with Chŏng's understanding of the components of the Buddhist doctrine, which are disconnected from each other, contradictory, conveniently used for abdicating responsibility, and failing to provide a viable system of values. Confucianism, by contrast, is completely aligned through essence and function, principle and material force; is cohesive and without contradictions; and teaches a concrete system of values, articulating a clear relationship between inner and outer.

HYŎNJŎNG NON

To set the tone for his argument, Kihwa goes to some lengths to clarify the Buddhist position on the nature of the mind and the relevance of and gradations of methods of practices, basically summarizing the view of mind that is expressed in the foundational East Asian Buddhist scriptures such as the *Awakening of Mahāyāna Faith* and the *Sutra of Perfect Enlightenment*. That is that the mind is originally pure, but when it moves into activity, it has the potential to be distorted. Kihwa opens the *Hyŏnjŏng non* by saying:

> Although its essence neither exists nor not-exists, it permeates existence and non-existence. Though it originally lacks past and present, it permeates past and present: this is the Way. Existence and non-existence are based in nature and sentiency. Past and present are based in birth-and-death. The nature originally lacks sentiency, but when you are confused about the nature, you give rise to sentiency; with the production of sentiency, wisdom is blocked—thoughts transform, and the essence is differentiated. It is through this that the myriad forms take shape and birth-and-death begins. (*HPC* 7.217a)

In this way, Kihwa begins by grounding his argument in an essence-function view of the mind and its activities. The mind is originally pure, but as it engages in situations, it can become entangled and enmeshed. As Zongmi had well clarified more than five centuries earlier, for the purpose of recovering the original mind, Buddhism has a wide spectrum of practices, which range from the most expedient and superficial to the most profound. In outlining the teachings starting from the most profound and extending to the most superficial, he ends up with the teaching of the law of cause and effect. As was stated in Zongmi's *Inquiry*, this teaching, no matter how superficial, is one level above the typical application of the Confucian teaching. But Kihwa later shifts his position and shows how the true Confucian teaching, when applied with the right understanding, can also extend to profound levels. This Kihwa does to an extent not seen in Zongmi's *Inquiry*.

The *Hyŏnjŏng non* is also markedly conciliatory in tone compared to the *Pulssi chappyŏn*. As someone who retains great respect for the Confucian teachings, Kihwa has no intention of entirely discrediting that tradition. Rather, like Zongmi, Qisong, and other Buddhist apologists before him, his aim is to point out the underlying unity of the three teachings and to reveal them as varying expressions of a mysterious unifying principle. What Kihwa will say is not that the Confucian teachings are wrong, but that they serve an important purpose. Unfortunately, however, they have been incorrectly understood and practiced by even the most important figures of their own tradition.

Kihwa defends Buddhism against the charges that its practices—practices such as the abandonment of family relationships—are antisocial by showing how they are actually helpful rather than harmful to society when practiced correctly. He makes excesses indulged in by *saṃgha* members answerable by individuals rather than attributable to tradition as a whole. On the other hand, Chŏng criticizes the Buddhist doctrines of karma and causation by means of logical argumentation, showing that the law of cause and effect cannot but be universally valid; he defends criticisms of the doctrine of rebirth with anecdotes of people who have memories of past lives.

The core of Kihwa's argument lies in what he takes as the common denominator of all three traditions of Confucianism, Daoism, and Buddhism: a doctrine of humaneness (using the Confucian notion of *ren*) based on the Cheng-Zhu truism that the myriad living beings of the universe are deeply interlinked with one another. While the notion of the mutual containment of the myriad things is ostensibly Buddhist (Huayan) in origin, it ended up being one of the central tenets of the most influential of the Song Neo-Confucian founders, including Zhou Dunyi and the Cheng brothers and especially Cheng Hao, who declared that "the myriad things and I form a single body."[41] With this being the characteristic and seminal Neo-Confucian development of the Confucian-Mencian humaneness, Kihwa finds inconsistencies between what Confucians say and what they do and makes this point the central issue of his treatise.

Buddhism and (Neo-)Confucianism share in the view that it is fundamentally wrong to harm others. Since others are intimately connected with oneself, harming others is the same as harming oneself. The doctrine of *ahiṃsā* (non-injury) is at the core of the Buddhist practice of moral discipline; *ahiṃsā* is observed completely in all Buddhist practices. Confucians, on the other hand, take humaneness as the most fundamental element of their path of cultivation. Confucius himself continually referred to humaneness as the source of all forms of goodness. Mencius made it clear that humaneness was innate to all people, explaining its function through a variety of metaphors, the best known being that of the stranger who automatically rushes to prevent a toddler from falling into a well (*Mencius* 2A:6).

Kihwa says, however, that the Confucian corpus is riddled with inconsistencies on this matter. For example, although Cheng Hao has told us that humaneness means that we form a single body with the myriad things, Confucius himself only went halfway in his practice of single-bodiedness, as he still enjoyed the sports of hunting and fishing.[42] For Mencius, the taking of the life of an animal was not problematic for the humane man as long as he didn't hear the animal's screams in its death throes.[43] And, in general, the Confucian tradition endorsed the practices of ritual sacrifice. Kihwa says:

> [Since animals share, with people] the sense of aversion to being killed, how do they differ from human beings? With the sound of ripping flesh and the cutting of the knife, they are in utter fright as they approach their death. Their eyes are wild and they cry out in agony. How could they not harbor bitterness and resentment? And yet people are able to turn a deaf ear. In this way human beings and the creatures of the world affect each other without awareness and bring retribution to each other each other without pause. How could a humane person, observing such suffering, continue to act as if nothing is wrong? (*HPC* 7.220a–b)

As Kihwa goes on to tell us, it was precisely the difference on this point that turned him toward Buddhism during the time when he was weighing the two systems in the balance.

> One time, during the period when I still had not yet entered the Buddhist order, a monk named Haewŏl (海月) was reading the *Analects* to me. He reached the passage [*Analects* 6:28] that says:
>
> > [Zi Gong asked,] "Suppose there were a ruler who benefited the people far and wide and was capable of bringing salvation to the multitude; what would you think of him? Might he be called humane"? The Master said, "Why only humane? He would undoubtedly be a sage. Even Yao and Shun would have had to work hard to achieve this."
>
> He commented, "The humane man forms a single body with heaven and earth and the myriad things." With this, he put the scroll aside and asked me, "Was Mencius a humane man?" "Yes," I replied. "Are 'fowl, pigs, dogs, and swine' to be counted among the 'myriad things?'" "Yes," I replied. [Haewŏl continued, citing Cheng Hao,] "The humane man forms a single body with heaven and earth and the myriad things."

If this statement is to be taken as a true expression of the principle, how are we supposed to see Mencius as being humane? If "fowl, pigs, dogs, and swine" are to be counted among the "myriad things" then how could Mencius say "If, in the raising of fowl, pigs, dogs, and swine, their breeding times are not missed, then people in their seventies can eat meat" [*Mencius* 1A:3]. I was completely stymied by this question, and could not answer. I pondered over all of the classical transmissions and could not come up with a single text that could support a principle condoning the taking of life. I inquired widely among the brightest thinkers of the day, but not one of them could offer an explanation that could resolve my perplexity.

This doubt remained buried within my mind for a long time without being resolved. Then, while traveling around Samgak-san in 1396, I arrived at Sŭnggasa (僧伽寺), where I had the chance to chat throughout the night with an old Sŏn monk. The monk said, "In Buddhism there are ten grave precepts, the first of which is to not take life." Upon hearing this utterance, my mind was suddenly overturned, and I recognized for myself that this was indeed the behavior of the truly humane man. I was thereupon able to deeply embody the teachings of the Way of humaneness. From this time forth, I was never again to be confused regarding the differences between Confucianism and Buddhism. I subsequently composed a verse, which went:

> Up till now, knowing only the teachings of the classics and histories
> And the criticisms of the Chengs and Zhu,
> I was unable to recognize whether the Buddha was wrong or right.
> But after reflecting deep in my mind for long years,
> Knowing the truth for the first time, I reject [Confucianism]
> And take refuge in [the Buddhadharma]. (*HPC* 7.220a3–18)

The charge, then, that Kihwa levels against the Confucians is strikingly similar to that which Chŏng wants to apply to the Buddhists; both want to show the other side to be guilty of inconsistency. The main difference, however, is that Chŏng wants to point out inconsistencies within the Buddhist doctrine itself, where Kihwa centers his argument on showing inconsistencies between Confucian doctrine and practice: that is, Confucians say one thing but do another. Kihwa's final pronouncement of his treatise, however, is the conclusion that the three teachings should be understood as three types of expression of the same reality. Here he no doubt had in mind the concluding chapter of the *Pulssi chappyŏn*. There, Chŏng gives a final summation of all the ways that the Buddhist teaching is vacuous and nihilistic and thus inferior to Confucianism, which is substantial and consistent. Chŏng says:

> Prior Confucian scholars have [already] shown that the Confucian and Buddhist paths differ with every single phrase and every single situation. Here I will elaborate based on these. We say voidness, and they also say voidness. We say quiescence, and they also say quiescence. However, our voidness is void yet existent. Their voidness is void and non-existent. Our quiescence is quiescent yet aware; their quiescence is quiescent and nihilating. We speak of knowledge and action; they speak of awakening and cultivation. Yet our knowledge is to know that the principle of the myriad things is replete in our own minds. Their awakening awakens to the fact that the mind is originally empty, lacking nothing. Our action is to return to the principle of the myriad things and act according to it, without error. Their cultivation is to sever connection with the myriad things and regard them as unconnected to one's mind. (*SBC* 1.84a)

Kihwa, in obvious reference to Chŏng's summation, concludes his own argument by focusing on these same two concepts of voidness and quiescence. However, he contends here—in a section that provides the most solid evidence that he was responding directly to Chŏng when he wrote the piece—in contrast to Chŏng that the connotations of these terms are basically the same throughout all three traditions and that the three are fundamentally equally valid approaches to the same reality.

> The answer is this. Laozi said, "No doing and no not-doing; with something to do yet not-doing."[44] The Buddha said, "Quiescent yet eternally luminous; luminous yet eternally quiescent."[45] Confucius said, "The Changes have neither thought nor activity, still and unmoving they respond and penetrate the world."[46] Now this "stillness," which has never failed to "respond," is the same thing as the "quiescence" that is "eternally luminous." The "responding and penetrating," which has never not been "still," is exactly the same as the "luminosity that is eternally quiescent." "No doing and no not-doing" is none other than "still, yet eternally responding." "Eternally doing yet with nothing to be done" is none other than "responding, yet eternally still." If you can grasp this, then the words of the three teachers fit together like the pieces of the same tally—as if they had all come out of the same mouth! If you would like actually to demonstrate the high and low among these teachings, exposing their sameness and difference in function, then you must first

completely wash the pollution from your mind and completely clarify
your eye of wisdom. Then you can study all of the texts contained in the
Buddhist, Confucian, and Daoist canons. Compare them in your daily
activities, at the times of birth and death, fortune and misfortune. Without needing words, you will spontaneously nod in assent. How strong
do I need to make my argument to get you to listen? (*HPC* 7.225b)

At least after the time of the transmission of Buddhism out of India,
philosophical exchanges of this type, and of this level of sophistication,
between Buddhists and the thinkers of competing religious traditions are
extremely rare. We intellectual historians can only wish for our own selfish edification that Chŏng had lived long enough to enter into rejoinder
with Kihwa here. In any case, a comparative study of these two works is
invaluable, not only for understanding the intellectual climate of fifteenth-
century Korea but also for understanding the fundamental character of
pre-modern East Asian thought as a whole.

Aftermath

Modern scholarship in both Korea and the West has long moved beyond
the misperception that Buddhism in the Chosŏn period was entirely suppressed. We now know that political leaders as well as ordinary people
openly engaged in Buddhist practice during that time.[47] The Confucian
arguments having been nearly exhausted in the *Pulssi chappyŏn,* no major polemical publications appeared from the Confucian side afterward.
Buddhists, on the other hand, fully adopted Kihwa's "essential unity of
the three teachings" approach. The most important representative work
of this type is Hyujŏng's *Samga Kwigam* (三家龜鑑),[48] which takes the three
teachings as together forming a large system of spiritual cultivation. Buddhism is taken as a more "essential" teaching, Confucianism as a more
"functional" teaching, with Daoism occupying the place in between. Generally speaking, this view of the three teachings prevails down to the present day in Korean Buddhism.

East Asian Philosophical Underpinnings: Essence-Function and Interpenetration

The three texts introduced above together represent a pivotal moment in
Korean intellectual history, and thus their titles and authors are quite of-

ten known to modern-day Korean intellectuals from many areas in the humanities, not only specialists in philosophy and religion. But the importance of these texts extends beyond Korea and even East Asia to world philosophy and religion in the sense that they constitute a rational, sustained, and substantive debate among members of different religious or philosophical systems. This kind of inter-tradition debate does not happen all that often. Such interactions are more often typified by outright fighting, even war, or are superficial attempts at restrained co-existence.

The difficulty with interreligious debate is that it necessarily takes place under certain conditions. One is physical proximity, the fact that the traditions are forced to compete for adherents within the same society. This forces them to deal with each other, whether or not in an amiable manner. But more important for such debate to occur is the requirement of a shared worldview, a shared vocabulary, and some sharing of basic values. One of the best examples of a situation that meets this requirement is ancient India, where Buddhists, Jainas, Sāṃkhyas, Vedantists, and members of other Indian philosophical traditions engaged with each other in public debate. That they were able to do so is due to the fact that their worldviews held in common a number of important principles: belief in the eternal return of the soul, belief in the liberation of the human being through the practice of a path (*mārga*), and adherence to a proper set of beliefs (*darśana*). These ancient Indian traditions were even able to agree on some ground rules of debate (*pramāṇa*). In similar fashion, Confucians and Buddhists—as well as Daoists—shared some important principles. Perhaps because I view the debate from the vantage point of an outsider, I discern in this discourse a clear sharing of the principle of *ti-yong,* or essence-function.

What is Essence-Function?

Essence-function is a characteristic traditional East Asian way of interpreting the world, society, events, phenomena, and the human being. It understands that all things have two contrasting yet wholly contiguous and mutually containing aspects: (1) an underlying, deeper, more fundamental, hidden aspect called in Chinese *ti* (K. *ch'e* 體), usually translated into English as "essence" or "substance"; and (2) a visibly manifest, surface aspect called *yong* (K. *yong* 用), translated into English as "function," "activity," or "manifestation." This pair has many analogs in East Asian thought, one of the earliest and most readily recognizable being the "roots and branches" (Ch. *benmo* 本末) paradigm taught in the *Great Learning* (Ch. *Daxue* 大學), epitomized in the saying, "Things have their roots and branches, affairs have their end and beginning. When you know what comes first and what comes last, then you are near the Way." It can also be seen in the Confucian pairing of "nature" (Ch. *xing* 性) and "emotions" (Ch. *qing* 情) foregrounded in the opening passage of the *Doctrine of the Mean* as well as in the relationship between "humaneness" and "propriety" (Ch. *li* 禮) taught in the *Analects*.[49]

In the *Daode jing*, analogous pairs abound that express the dynamic relation of inner-outer or fundamental-superficial. Among the most prominent are the notions of the Way and its power, or charisma (Ch. *de* 德), as well as the "white" (Ch. *bai* 白) and the "black" (Ch. *hei* 黑),[50] the uncarved block (Ch. *pu* 樸),[51] and the implements carved from it (Ch. *qi* 器). Later on, when Buddhism becomes thoroughly sinified, the same paradigm finds expression in a general manner in the pairs of nature (Ch. *xing* 性) and aspects (Ch. *xiang* 相), and specifically in Huayan Buddhism in principle (Ch. *li* 理) and phenomena (Ch. *shi* 事).[52]

This paradigm is applied as an interpretive tool to articulate a wide range of situations in human behavior and society at large, but its most common application is seen when classical East Asian philosophers attempted to describe the complex relationship of the fundamental essence of the human mind (always seen as good, pure, and wise) as juxtaposed with people's manifest behavior and appearance (which fall somewhere on the spectrum of good versus bad, wise versus foolish, but by and large not very good). As explained above, the most widely understood view regarding the psychology of the human being developed within the classical East Asian tradition is that despite all of the obvious evil and suffering in the world, the human mind (interpreted as the person's "essence") is, at its most fundamental level, good and pure. But whether or not this goodness actually ends up being reflected in a person's day-to-day activities, and if so, to what extent, can depend on a wide variety of factors, most important of which is the degree of one's own effort/attention, but is also contingent on factors such as the quality (or "orthodoxy") of the religious, philosophical, or moral instruction with which one has been inculcated.

The translation of the sinitic concept of *ti-yong* into English as "essence-function" is one that is in continual need of clarification, especially in regard to the first part of the term, *ti*. The ideograph *ti* originally denotes the physical body as an assemblage of its parts. In the philosophical context, however, the first articulation of which is traditionally attributed to Wang Bi 王弼 (226–249),[53] it refers to the deeper, more fundamental, more internal, more important, or invisible aspects of something: any kind of being, organization, phenomenon, concept, event, and so on. Its usage in the major East Asian thought systems is mainly centered in the realm of human affairs or human psychology, with *ti* referring to the human mind, especially the deeper, more hidden dimension of the human mind, the mind as it is before entering into the realm of activity. In terms of the objective universe, *ti* is used to express the deeper, more fundamental or invisible aspect of things, the "principles" of things as opposed to their more outwardly manifest, phenomenal aspects.

The translation of *ti* with the English word "essence" became problematic in recent decades in the context of the essence-reviling discourse of postmodernism. And, indeed, the English term "essence" in its technical philosophical applications usually has strong dualistic connotations. Nonetheless, in rendering *ti* into English, it is hard to get around such options as "essence," and "substance," since simply translating the term literally as "body" does not promise to be very helpful. *Ti*, moreover, certainly does indicate a kind of interiority or depth that is indicated by the English word essence. But in its East Asian matrix, *ti* is bereft of any association with dualistic Platonic/Christian metaphysical baggage. There is no connotation of a nature that is in any way otherworldly, transcendent, unchanging, or eternal; it is not a fixed ontological or metaphysical "basis." It is neither a "logos" nor an "idea" of a higher order and distinct from the manifest world. It does not refer to a reified hierarchical signified-signifier relationship nor to an eternal *ātman*-like soul or brahmanistic substrate.

To get at *ti* through its translation as "essence," the English term is better understood according to its everyday applications rather than through specialized Western metaphysical connotations. We can then work with the definition of "the most important, crucial element."[54] A good metaphor is also provided by the concept of "a concentrated substance which keeps the flavor, etc. of that from which it is extracted"[55] or "an extract that has the fundamental properties of a substance in concentrated form,"[56] in the sense that *ti* has strong connotations of density or thickness (Ch. *hou* 厚, *nong* 濃, etc.). *Ti* is paired with the term *yong*, which has the basic meanings of "usage," "activity," "function," or "means." In its special usage as part of a pair with *ti*, *yong* can reflect a range of these meanings depending on the context but also carries such connotations as "apparent," "manifest," and "external."

One ready indication that the basic connotations of the essence-function set have been missed is when a scholar refers to it as a "dichotomy" or "polarity," or understands *ti* to be a "substrate." Strictly speaking (according to any reliable dictionary), the definitions of "dichotomy" and "polarity" both indicate an intrinsic separation and/or opposition not implied in the application of *ti-yong*. The point of the usage of *ti-yong* is not to indicate separation but rather to indicate intrinsic unity, a pervasive interpenetration between two things or two aspects, which might, from a less insightful point of view, be seen as distinctly separated or of unclear relationship. The metaphor of perfume is a good starting point for understanding the non-dualistic character of the essence-function structure, as the concentrated nature, the "essence" of the perfume is always wholly unified with the most distant permeation of its aroma. The emphasis of *ti-yong* is first and foremost on the continuity that exists between internal and external aspects rather than on difference or opposition, and it is instructive to note that the instances in which there seems to be difference, conflict, or contradiction between essence and function are precisely the societal or psychological conditions of disharmony, dis-ease, deception, and so forth, which are criticized by the adept teachers of the tradition. We will see this sort of application of the concept surface repeatedly in both of the treatises translated below when our Buddhist and Confucian protagonists each accuse the other's tradition of being "disconnected," that is, expressing a break between essence and function.

The interpretation of *ti-yong* as a "polarizing" metaphysical formula is also undermined by the fact that objects, beings, or situations described by the formula are never reifiable in either a *ti* or *yong* position, as what is taken to be *ti* (more internal, of greater priority) in one situation might be regarded as *yong* (more external, of lesser priority) in another. For example, the first chapter of the *Great Learning* has a famous passage addressed to a ruler in the process of bringing peace to his kingdom. The passage consists of a list of priorities in the form of matters of greater and lesser importance. In this list, each of the elements in this case (roots) can be seen to be the "essence" of the matters (branches) that are subsequent, and as the function of the matter that is antecedent.[57]

MACROCOSM AND MICROCOSM

Macrocosm

Despite the range of permutations in expression of the concept of essence-function, we may characterize its usage as two general (but greatly overlapping) paradigms. The first is that which is seen in the macrocosmic view, typified by the role of "essence" as Way (Ch. *dao*), or organizing principle of the universe, and "function" as the phenomenal activity of the Way. A general view of "Way" is evident in all forms of Zhou-period thought. Although there are significant variations among these, they agree to a certain extent on the understanding of the Way as a forming/informing principle of the behavior of human beings and/or nature. Most obvious in this usage is the Way of the *Daode jing,* to which one may become gradually attuned by means of various processes of shedding of cultural conditioning. As one becomes attuned to the Way, s/he, as in the disfigured characters of the *Zhuangzi,* becomes filled with charismatic power (Ch. *te* 德) whereby one's thoughts and actions become harmonious and natural (Ch. *ziran* 自然). Although the descriptions of the processes of attainment show significant differences, it is the case in both Confucianism and Daoism that the sage-king who is sensitive to the Way will be eminently capable of rulership. If he pays due attention to *ti* (his own mind or the fundamental needs of his people), *yong* (harmony throughout the realm) will be the natural outgrowth. After the influx of Buddhism, East Asian religious thinkers, far from being inclined to let go of this paradigmatic symbol, utilized the term Way extensively in their re-articulation of Buddhism to the point where it came to be equivalent to the concept of enlightenment.

As Mahāyāna Buddhism became fully absorbed into the Chinese cultural sphere, its most basic soteriological principle, emptiness (Ch., K. *gong* 空; Skt. *śūnyatā*), was reinterpreted as the East Asian Buddhist "essence," with form (Ch. *se* 色; Skt. *rūpa*) as its manifest function. At a superficial level, of course, the connotations of *śūnyatā* and essence would seem to be about as far apart as can be, but from a Buddhist perspective, one might well argue that it is precisely the apprehension of this paradox that constitutes the Buddhist insight and thus the famous dictum from the *Heart Sutra* that "form is emptiness, emptiness is form." On the other hand, an "essentialization" of the experience of insight into emptiness — that is, "enlightenment" — is problematic in a number of ways. Yet despite these problems, which have been well identified for us by thinkers associated with modern Japanese Critical Buddhism, I would argue that there were always an ample number of Buddhist teachers in various East Asian schools who understood the problems engendered by the inclination of our cognitive processes toward reification and who thus continually worked at overturning and reinventing the teaching to offer new ways of escaping the traps of language. Thus, the Huayan category of *li* (principle) refers precisely to a non-reified and dynamic insight into the underlying (empty) character of things, while *shi* (events, phenomena) refers to the manifest appearance of that same emptiness, which is form.

As Buddhism attained preeminence in the East Asian intellectual arena, Confucian and Daoist thinkers were compelled to compete with the foreign religion in the realm of philosophical discourse, and hence the Neo-Confucianism that developed after this time displayed a greatly enhanced level of philosophical sophistication as compared to its Warring States period beginnings, as it was now clearly imbued with Daoist and Huayan influences. But the reinvented Neo-Confucian metaphysics-like description of human beings and their world was more distinctly than ever framed by the *ti-yong* construction, as evidenced by the fact that the explication of the categories of principle and material force formed the basis of the entire discourse of the orthodox Cheng-Zhu school. The founding Neo-Confucians, most importantly the Cheng brothers and Zhu Xi, borrowed heavily from this Huayan paradigm in constructing their new categories. The Neo-Confucian articulation of these categories was done overtly and in great detail through *ti-yong* language, and the same is true of the later debates regarding the relationship of these two categories of *li* and *qi* to the human mind, most famous of which was the encounter that took place in Korea between T'oegye 退溪 (Yi Hwang 李滉; 1501–1570) and Yulgok 栗谷 (1536–1584).[58]

As Neo-Confucianism rose in stature and promulgated its new sophisticated metaphysical system, Buddhists were in turn forced to respond, and it was through this stimulus that exponents of "the unity of the three teachings" (Ch. *sanjiao heyi* 三教合一) began to come to the fore. Among the "three-teachings" thinkers, those whose writings had the most widespread influence in their respective spheres of activity were Zongmi of the Tang and Kihwa of the Koryŏ-Chosŏn. Both men were highly evaluated for their mastery of traditional Confucian studies before they turned to Buddhism, and both retained a deep respect for much of the content of their classical learning. They were both naturally soaked in the essence-function approach, and thus it is not surprising to find that *ti-yong* was the hermeneutical principle by which they articulated a unified view of Confucianism, Daoism, and Buddhism. Yet these three-teachings thinkers also differed in their ways of comparing the three, and these differences can in turn be interpreted according to the particular understanding of essence and function that dominated their personal thought systems.

Microcosm

By far the predominating usage of essence and function is that related to the traditional East Asian concept of the human being, which has its roots in antiquity and is described formally in the Zhou texts.[59] In this view, all human beings by nature are inherently good, and it is the goodness of their true nature that is the foundation of the mind. While sharing an essential goodness, human beings differ from each other at the level of function. Function in this case could refer to the person's physical appearance, facial expressions, speech, and actions, as well as his or her thoughts.

This formulation is thus quite different from a simple mind-body or spirit-matter dichotomy. With occasional exceptions, the prevailing view of the major thought traditions of Confucianism and Daoism was that the human being was inherently perfect, highly mutable, and capable of consummating such perfection through following a certain course of action (or in Daoism, non-action).

In this relationship, the goodness or perfectibility of all human beings shows a strong "inner-to-outer" (or *ti* penetrating *yong*) tendency. But there is also a vitally important outer-to-inner (or *yong* penetrating *ti*) tendency simultaneously at work, as the originally pure *ti* is brought to its fullest manifestation through proper *yong*. It is because of this fundamental conception of essence-function in personal transformation that there is in East Asian "study-as-practice" language such a strong development of rich and diverse metaphors in the category of "polishing," "training," "smelting," "purification," "accordance," "harmonization" (of, or with the essence), and the like.

Daoist classics such as the *Daode jing* and *Zhuangzi* also clearly imply the human capacity for sagehood, but with its accomplishment occurring through a decidedly more "hands-off" and observational approach and with a greater emphasis on recognizing and harmonizing with *ti* rather than external training of and through *yong*. The *Daode jing* alludes to the human mind in its pure nature variously as the "uncarved block" (Ch. *pu* 樸), which ends up becoming chopped up into "utensils" (Ch. *qi* 器), and the "newborn babe" (Ch. *chizi* 赤子), originally soft and pliant but becoming in old age or through non-harmonious activities rigid and lifeless. The process of reaching sagehood is a "return" (Ch. *gui* 歸, *fan* 反) to this pristine state. Instead of attempting to embody Confucian norms such as humaneness, justice, filial piety, or trustworthiness, one is advised to free oneself from these worldly constructions.[60]

The newly formulated doctrine espoused by the Neo-Confucians was compounded of various strains of essence-function thought derived from *Yijing*, early Daoist, Confucian, and Buddhist sources, and the *ti-yong* structure of the human being. The latter was brought into play in such forms as the Neo-Confucian "mind of *dao*" (Ch. *daoxin* 道心), which reflected the pure essence of humanity to be sought through Neo-Confucian practices such as "reverence" (Ch. *jing* 敬), and "the human mind (Ch. *renxin* 人心)" which is prone to errors of selfishness and bias.[61] Most instructive in Neo-Confucianism is the degree to which the debates internal to the tradition are variations in interpretation of Confucian doctrine that lean in either the *ti* or *yong* direction. This is the case in the debate between the Cheng-Zhu orthodoxy and the Lu-Yang-ming "school of mind," as well as that which occurred in the Korean "four-seven" debate between the schools of T'oegye and Yulgok.

Overlap

In actual practice, the distinction between the above "macrocosmic" and "microcosmic" aspects of the essence-function framework can only be nominally designated, as the apprehension of the universal *dao* was, in all time periods and traditions, fully contingent upon its apprehension and/or consummation at the personal level; that is, it is precisely in the mediating dimension of integral practice that the macro- and microcosmic were directly connected to each other.

Such a view of intrinsic unity between universal and particular can be seen as closely related to the tendency of sinitic philosophical discourse to be fully connected with real human behavior, as the phenomena of the universe as a whole were always seen to be connected to, acting upon, and receiving influence from the actions of individual persons. Thus, starting from earlier forms of Confucianism and Daoism and reaching up to the flowering of Chinese Chan, mere theoretical understanding was never accepted as sufficient when it came to such matters as the apprehension of the Way. And here I would argue that it was precisely the integrated, non-dualistic understanding of essence-function that prevented self-transformation, or religious practice, from being divorced from activity in the "real" secular world.[62] This means that mystic absorption into the infinite was almost always considered inferior to the "marvelous function"[63] of the true sage, who was deeply in touch with and greatly valued his *ti* but who superbly manifested that *ti* in his function within the world of everyday phenomena. Numerous early Confucian texts reflect this tendency, but it is probably most succinctly summed up in the adage from chapter 28 of the *Daode jing*, which says "know the white [知之白, "everyday world," "manifest world," *yong*] but cleave to the black [守之黑, "the essence," "the *dao*," *ti*]."[64] Down through time in the three traditions, it was this balanced approach to religious practice that would command the greatest respect. It becomes particularly manifest in the Chinese Chan school (as well as in Korean Sŏn and Japanese Zen), where, despite the intrinsic mystical tendencies of the meditational schools, great value comes to be placed on the "marvelous function" of the virtuosic master.

INTERPENETRATION

The notion of essence-function cannot be appreciated or understood in anything close to its thick and pervasive role in East Asian thought without also taking into consideration its necessary counterpart, that of intrinsic inner connection, or interpenetration (*tong-da*), as it eventually comes to be articulated in Huayan Buddhism.

The concept of interpenetration, indicated in Chinese by such terms as *tong-da* (K. *t'ongdal* 通達) and *yuanrong* (K. *wŏnyung* 圓融), is normally associated with the Chinese Huayan school of Buddhist thought. It represents a Chinese transformation of the Indian Buddhist concepts of *pratītya-samutpāda* and *śūnyatā*, stimulated by the Indra's Net discourse found in the *Avataṃsaka-sūtra*. While certainly beholden to these Indian Buddhist constructs, the origins of Chinese intuitions of interpenetration can be seen in the earliest Zhou writings. In other words, one must have some sort of understanding of *transparency* and *permeability* that is highly reminiscent of Buddhist notions of emptiness and interpenetration if one is to thoroughly and correctly grasp the implications of the essence-function worldview operative in these early times.

Despite some differences in language and approach, I believe that Robert Sharf, in devoting a long chapter — tellingly entitled "Chinese Buddhism and the Cosmology of Sympathetic Resonance"[65] — saw something similar in what he identifies as a pan-East Asian phenomenon threading through the three teachings. Sharf takes the organismic model of Chinese thought as understood by scholars such as Joseph Needham and Frederick Mote and shows how this model can be related to an intrinsic Chinese sensitivity toward the mutual resonance between things belonging to the same categories. He then extends the paradigm to show its influence in the development of the Buddhist theory of "response body." As if to express our understanding of the necessity of a sense of something like an organismic wholeness, interpenetration, or sympathetic resonance to be implicit in the function of the essence-function paradigm, Sharf writes:

> The organismic view entails the notion that localized phenomena affect the state of the whole, and the state of the whole is reflected in local phenomena. This holistic model was much more than an abstract metaphysical hypothesis; it could be observed, tested, and applied in the fields of politics, divination, and the arts. (*Coming to Terms with Chinese Buddhism*, 79)

An understanding of penetration of inner by outer and vice versa is necessary for the apprehension of one of the more basic aspects of essence-function usage, that of the mind of the human being and its apparent manifestations. In order for essence-function to work as it does, it is necessary to see the human being as a continuum from inner to outer rather than as a mind-body dichotomy. There are also numerous textual passages in the *Yijing, Analects, Daode jing, Zhuangzi,* and so on that, to be fully appreciated, require a worldview in which the thoughts and actions of an individual penetrate, and carry influence throughout the entire world, in a way that can only be compared to that seen in Huayan metaphysics. One notable example is passage 12:1 from the *Analects,* which reads:

> Yan Yuan asked about the meaning of humaneness. The Master said, "To completely overcome selfishness and keep to propriety is humaneness. If for a full day you can overcome selfishness and keep to propriety, everyone in the world will return to humaneness. Does humaneness come from oneself, or from others?"

This passage has always created problems for translators and commentators. Modern English translators either alter the grammar or interpolate the word "king" to make sense of the notion that the power of the mind of a single individual can bring peace to the world.[66] The implication of these translations is, in other words, that since we all know that Confucius could not possibly have believed that a single person has the power to influence the whole world, he obviously must have intended us to understand that only one in a position of political power can do so. But in trying to work through this passage, we might take another tack. For instance, do we really know what it means to "completely overcome our selfishness" for a "full day" and be perfectly guided by proper action? Might it not be that we actually do not know the level of spiritual influence that actualization of one's inner perfection may bring about? One might also conjecture that even in the case of a ruler, political power in itself might not suffice to manifest the goodness of the people.

The concept of interpenetration is indicated by the Chinese binome *tong-da* but is also commonly signified by the ideographs *tong* and *da* by themselves. The basic meaning of *tong* 通, which has changed surprisingly little over three millennia of East Asian literary history, is to "go through" or "pass through." It especially carries the connotations of passing, going through a path, or moving along a course that is already opened and that merely needs to be traversed. The ideograph *da* 達 is close in meaning and is often combined with *tong* in Buddhist texts, but it has an interesting and important etymological difference, as it originally signifies piercing through a barrier or breaking open a passageway where there was none before. Thus, when the two are combined as a binome, a complementary connotation is created that indicates both passing through that which is already open and piercing through that which has heretofore been closed.

Tong and *da* are ancient concepts to which strong philosophical overtones were added in early Confucian thought, notably in such texts as the *Analects, Yijing,* and the *Liji.* Especially relevant among these implications is the function of the mind of the sage, which is able to penetrate without limit in time and space. The sage's mind is capable of "penetrating to" (i.e., "understanding") the principles of things. Other shades of meaning include to "unify" or "be the same" in the sense of the dissolution of a barrier. Both *tong* and *da* can mean to "apprehend," "understand," "grasp," "permeate," "fill," or "influence."[67] They were used adjectivally and adverbially to the same effects. The nuance of "penetration" (even if not always specifically indicated by the words *tong* and *da*) is ubiquitous in the texts that reflect the early East Asian intuitively transparent worldview. It is a basic underpinning of both the *Great Learning* and the *Doctrine of the Mean,* in both of which the inner and outer aspects of the person are understood to penetrate each other such that the quality of the person's inner mind is always discernible in his outer appearance.

The classical pre-Buddhist intuitions of *tong* were rationalized and codified as they were employed to facilitate Chinese expressions of Buddhism. The conceptual bases of *tong* in East Asian Buddhism could now be explained through the notions of emptiness and dependent arising, since it is due to the lack of self-nature that phenomena can mutually contain, reflect, and comprise—or interpenetrate—each other. The Sanskrit term for the supernatural powers of the Buddha or great bodhisattva (*abhijñā,* literally "superknowledges")—specifically those that pertain to the power of the minds of the adepts to transcend limitations of time, space, and materiality—was also translated into Chinese as *tong,* indicating that the mind of the Buddha penetrates to all places.[68]

The most important development of the meaning of *tong* came with the emergence of Huayan philosophy, where the metaphysics of interpenetration–non-obstruction became the hallmark of the school. The key usage of *tong* is in the discourse of the third and fourth "reality realms," or *dharmadhātu*s (Ch. *fajie* 法界), suggested by the early Huayan patriarchs. These are the realms of *li-shi wu-ai* 理事無礙 (non-obstruction between principle and phenomena) and *shi-shi wu-ai* 事事無礙, (non-obstruction between phenomena and phenomena; perfect interpenetration of phenomena). In the third realm, the conceptually differentiated spheres of principle and phenomena (emptiness and form 空色) are shown to be mutually containing. Since they are mutually containing, it follows that individual phenomena also contain each other without obstruction.

Study as Practice

The most important implications of both essence-function and interpenetration can only be fully apprehended when seen as descriptions of developments in actual practice rather than as abstract metaphysical categories. The concept of "study as practice" reflects an aspect of the East Asian religious/philosophical attitude that encourages study as manifested in actual practice. Conversely, it refers to the character of "religious practice" in Confucianism, Daoism, and East Asian Buddhism, which in most cases is deeply informed by textual study.[69] One of the foremost aspects of this kind of integral practice is the intimate relationship of notions of personal transformation with the classical Confucian/Daoist/East Asian Buddhist concept of "learning" or "study" (Ch. *xue* 學). In this approach to study—evident in almost every branch of Confucianism, Daoism, and East Asian Buddhism—one's level of scholarly attainment is recognized to be greatly contingent upon the degree to which one has "embodied" (Ch. *dide* 體得) the object of study, has demonstrated a change in behavior. In other words, the classical East Asian conception of scholarship was intimately connected with what is distinguished in modernity as "practice." Confucius said:

> When the noble man eats he does not try to stuff himself; at rest he does not seek perfect comfort; he is diligent in his work and careful in speech. He avails himself to people of the Way and thereby corrects himself. This is the kind of person of whom you can say "he loves learning." (*Analects* 1:14)

Looked at another way, the sharp distinction that modern scholarship makes between study and practice did not exist in East Asian classical thinking.

The primary objects of inquiry in the East Asian classical philosophical texts of the three teachings were the human mind and human behavior. Accordingly, the most seminal of the Confucian, Buddhist, and Daoist texts were written to encourage reflection on the nature of the mind and one's actions in order to reveal their purity and dross such that the purity could be enhanced and the dross eliminated. Moreover, in the sense that these texts, whether the *Analects, Mencius, Daode jing, Zhuangzi, Awakening of Faith,* or *Diamond Sutra,* were considered to reflect the minds of the sages, they were understood to be agents of transformation in and of themselves. By earnestly studying the text, one could embody its message such that the text's underlying theme would permeate one's behavior. In most East Asian philosophical streams, such embodiment of a text was a fundamental stage in the process of self-transformation.[70] While this process was normally initiated by memorization of the text, memorization itself was not the final aim but rather an important first step, a preliminary qualification allowing for the deeper investigation into the text and the apprehension of its principles. In this sort of "scholarship," the criterion of achievement was not one's command of a breadth of knowledge of facts about a certain area but rather the degree to which one has assimilated the teachings of the sages into one's behavior. It is for this reason that the "scholar of broad learning" (Ch. *duowen* 多聞) was, in all three East Asian classical traditions, considered to be of a lower level than one who could actually demonstrate the insight and actions indicative of self-transformation.

Concomitant with this understanding of "study" as the process of attaining a unity with its object is the basic premise that such study includes a training and refinement of the person's character. This refinement, when assiduously carried out, contains the possibility of attainment of human perfection, since "perfection" (defined variously in different traditions) was considered to be an innate endowment of all persons.[71]

A final connotation of this concept of study-as-practice to be noted is the high degree to which the process of personal transformation was related to how well one's function harmonized with the realities of the mundane world. Examples of such evaluations abound in the classics of all three traditions but especially so in the *Mencius*. For example, in *Mencius* 2A:2 Gongsun Chou asks Mencius, "What do you mean when you say 'I understand language'?" Mencius answers:

> When I hear deceptive speech, I know what it is covering up. When I hear licentious speech, I know its pitfalls. When I hear crooked speech, I know where it departs from the truth. When I hear evasive speech, I know its emptiness. Once born in a person's mind, these words harm the government. Spreading through the government, they damage all sorts of affairs. When a future sage appears, he will attest to my words.

Or, again, *Mencius* 7A:2:

> Mencius said, "There is nothing that does not have a destiny, so follow your own and accept it as it is. If you do this, when you understand what destiny is, you will not stand under the wall of a high cliff. To fully traverse one's course and then die—this is correct destiny. To die in handcuffs and chains is not correct destiny."

This tendency toward sacred-secular integration was a core component of the major streams of Confucianism and Daoism. It also made a significant impact on East Asian Buddhism, where, despite its origins in a highly mystical Indian tradition that placed significant importance on world renunciation, a noticeable amount of stress (most notably in the Chan/Sŏn/ Zen movement) came to be placed on one's ability to act without hindrance in response to phenomenal situations.

Notes on the Source Texts

For Kihwa's *Hyŏnjŏng non,* I used the edition contained in volume 7 of *Hanguk Pulgyo Chŏnsŏ* (*HPC*). In order to make the best use of the available digital reference tools, I digitized this text, using scan/OCR. Since that time, the EBTI project at Dongguk University has produced a digitized version, now available on the Web at http://ebti.dongguk.ac.kr/. For the *Pulssi chappyŏn,* I worked from two versions: (1) the text from the *Sambong chip* (Seoul: Minjok munhwa chujin hoe, 1977) vol. 1, 75–85, and (2) that contained in volume 1 of *Sambong chip* (Seoul: Kyŏng'in munhwasa, 1987). The *Sambong chip* being a woodblock reproduction not fit for OCR in the 1990s, when I was preparing the translation, I typed the whole text. For the *Simgiri p'yŏn* I used the Kyŏng'in munhwasa 1987 version (pp. 465–470) but was able to put most of the text together through Web searches and thus used the printed version only for final proofing. I have created critically edited versions of these texts, which are available in the appendix to this work.

Translations

On Mind, Material Force, and Principle (*Simgiri p'yŏn*)

by Chŏng Tojŏn (Sambong)

Contents

1. [The Buddhists'] Conflation of the Mind with Material Force

[Chŏng will first summarize the main characteristics of the Buddhist teachings, typical of Song-period Chan, which is also roughly characteristic of the Sŏn Buddhism of the Koryŏ. The original text is arranged with sections separated by single lines that indicate the topic to be discussed. Quite often they are references to passages from classical works, but rarely actual citations. They are also too long to be taken as titles or section headings in the usual sense. I have rendered these in boldface type at the beginning of each section. — Trans.]

This section focuses on the Buddhist teaching of the cultivation of the mind. Since it does not discuss the teachings of Laozi, in this section we use a lot of Buddhist technical terminology. Now, "mind" combines principle and material force and is regarded as the locus of the spiritual luminosity of the individual — Zhuzi's so-called spiritual subtlety without darkness.[1] It includes myriad principles and responds to ten thousand circumstances. Since the foolish regard it as mere space, therefore [we point out that] it includes myriad principles. Since it is entirely numinous, it responds to ten thousand circumstances. If it did not include myriad principles, then its transparency[2] would be nothing more than blankness and vacancy. Its numinousness would be a gushing outflow of confusion, and nothing more. Even though we say it responds to myriad circumstances, if it confuses right and wrong, how could it serve as the residence of divine numinousness? Therefore we call it "mind" and do not call it "principle." Hence, you know that it has this abode, but you do not know that it has this master.

All things that have characteristics are nothing but various types mixed in a totality. It is only the self that is most numinous, standing independently within their midst.

"All things that have characteristics" is a term from the *Diamond Sutra*.³ "Mixed into a totality" is the appearance of multiplicity. "Self" is the mind's own self. "Numinousness" is the so-called rarefied numinousness. These two phrases are the same great numinousness expressed in Huineng's "There is one thing..."⁴ Above, it supports the heavens and below, it supports the earth. This is the meaning reflected in Gautama's "above and below heaven I alone am honored."⁵

These are the mind's own words. It means that the sounds and shapes that exist everywhere fill out the space between heaven and earth. There is a great variety of things, but only the self is perfectly numinous. It stands out distinctly and independently among the totality of all types of miscellaneous things.

The self-essence is quiescent, like the emptiness of a mirror. Following conditions it does not change — it responds without limit.

The essence of the mind is quiescent and without marks, yet its numinous intelligence is not dulled.⁶ It is like the original emptiness of the nature of a mirror, which when reflecting does not fail to display anything. Now, "following conditions" means that the numinousness of the mind is like the reflective quality of a mirror; "it does not change" refers to mind's quiescence and the mirror's emptiness. Because of this, it responds to a myriad changes inexhaustibly. This is none other than the *Diamond Sutra's* saying, "They should give rise to the aspiration while not abiding in anything."⁷ Now, although externally there are visible effects of this response, within, all is silent without the movement of even a single thought. This is the cardinal teaching of the Buddhists.

From this the four gross elements and things are temporarily formed.⁸ Having eyes, one desires form; having ears, one desires sound; good and evil are also phantoms, produced from the images of conditions. They assail the self and steal from the self, and the self has not a moment's peace.

"This" (關) refers to material force.[9] The "four gross elements" is also a Buddhist technical term referring to earth, water, fire, and wind. The *Sutra of Perfect Enlightenment* says, "My present body is a conglomeration of the four gross elements."[10] It also says, "The conditioning images of the six objects form the nature of the mind."[11]

This merely follows on the theme from the above section that says that the essence of the mind is originally quiescent. However, based on the material force of these four gross elements it seems to congeal, by bringing about the formation of a body with characteristics. In this, there are eyes and the desire to see beautiful forms, ears and the desire to hear pleasing sounds, as well as nose, tongue, skin, and the thinking mind, each of which has its own object of desire. When these objects are agreeable, they are regarded as good; when they are disagreeable, they are regarded as bad. From this, all illusions are generated; it is not reality. From this, one clambers about in the reflections of external objects, being continually reborn. All of these [illusions] are attacking and stealing from the quiescent essence of the self. In disarray and confusion, the self cannot gain a moment's rest.[12]

"Severing characteristics, free from essence; without thoughts, forgetting about discriminations. Luminous but quiescent; silent but fully alert."[13] In this case, even if I want to act, how can I clarify the clouds in my vision?

The *Diamond Sutra* says, "All existent characteristics are deceptions."[14] Huineng said, "Neither good nor bad is deliberated in any way whatsoever."[15] These are later distinguished into the four approaches of no-thought, abandoning discriminations, stopping falsehood, and according with the [Buddha] nature. This is called the exercise of cultivating the mind.[16] "Characteristics" means visible form. "Essence" means principle as essence. All characteristics are non-characteristics;[17] they are to be cut off and abandoned. What is essence is non-essence; it is to be ignored and discarded. If the self is always quiescent, without the movement of a single thought, and you always abandon the discrimination of arising and ceasing, then deceptive objects are already eliminated and true emptiness naturally appears. Even though I experience illumination, the essence is always perfectly still. Even if I am silent, within, I am naturally alert. Now, if one is luminous and still, then there will be no distracting thoughts. If one is silent but alert, then there will be no lingering in dullness. If you are able to be like this, then in the case of the material force of the four gross elements and the desire for the objects in the six sense fields, even if you want to leap into the crevice to avoid the ravine, there will still be agitation to the self. Why should one becloud oneself so as to constrict the clarity of the original essence of the self? This section's articulation of the essentials of [Buddhist] mental cultivation is short, but covers the point fully.

2. The Material Force Conflated with the Mind [The Daoist Teachings]

This section focuses on the Daoist methods of nourishing the material force. Since this part doesn't deal with Buddhism, a lot of Daoist technical terminology is used. As for "material force," heaven produces the myriad things through the transformation of yin and yang and the five phases,[18] and sentient beings obtain it to live. Yet material force belongs to the physical realm. Only after there is a metaphysical principle (K. *yi* 理) can there be material force.[19] To speak of material force and not speak of principle is to know the branches of being while not knowing its roots.[20]

I abide since great antiquity, dark and mysterious; just as I am, self-so, unobtainable, yet named.[21]

The word "I" is material force referring to itself. "Great antiquity" means the distant past. Laozi says, "There is something that is completed from disorder, which is born before heaven and earth."[22] He also says, "How deep! How dark! In it there is an essence; the essence is so real — therein is belief."[23] He also says, "Heaven follows the Way; the Way follows the way things are."[24] He also says, "I don't know its name, so I style it as the Way."[25] All of Laozi's words are referring to material force; hence this section takes material force to be essential by saying that it abides prior to heaven and earth and the myriad things.[26] Vague and obscure, it is real as it is. Unobtainable, yet it is named.

At the inception of the myriad things, with whose support are they born? The self congeals and the self gathers, becoming form and becoming essence. If the self did not exist, how could the mind be "independently numinous"?

Zhuangzi said, "The birth of people is [through] the gathering of material force."[27] Here again material force is taken as the source by asking what thing it is in the beginning of the production of the myriad things that supports their creation. Is it not material force that supports their coming into being?[28] If one thinks that it is only after material force mysteriously combines and congeals that the self takes form and vitality is produced, then if material force does not congeal, to what shall the mind, even though it is perfectly numinous, attach itself?

Aah, this possession of knowledge is the sprout of all calamities. [The Way] can't be reached by thought or arrived at through deliberation. Calculating gain and assessing loss, fearing dishonor and yearning for glory; in the icy cold and burning heat, one busily rushes about morning and night. One's vitality is shaken daily, and one's spirit has no respite.

"Aah!" (嗟) is a sigh of lamentation. "Its" (闕) refers to the mind. This section shows the cases where the mind impairs material force. [Our ostensive Daoist] laments and says that the mind's possession of intelligence is the sprout from which all calamities arise. It can't be reached by thought or attained by deliberation, [by] calculating profit and wanting to attain it or assessing loss and wanting to avoid it. Fearing dishonor, afraid of failure; hoping for glory, and unexpected success. Fear is like the cold of ice; anger is like the heat of fire. Thousands of loose ends to deal with, all tugging at one's mind. Morning and night, we hustle about without respite, agitating our spirits every day; gradually consumed, we have not a moment's peace.

I do not act blindly, but with calm internal mental focus; I am like a withered tree, like ashes without fire. Without deliberation, without expectation-driven activity (*wu-wei*). Completely embodying the Way. Now, even if my knowledge bores deeply,[29] how can it harm my inborn nature?

This is called the work of nourishing the material force. Zhuangzi said, "Can you really make the body like a withered tree and the mind like dead ashes?"[30] He also said: "When you are without thought and without deliberation, you know the Way for the first time."[31] Laozi said, "The Way is always not-doing, yet there is nothing it does not do."[32] This section bases its terminology on these.

Carrying on the above section's discussion of the mind's desire for profit: Even though there is a chaotic struggle, material force obtains its sustenance and acts in a deluded manner. By regulating the external, one is also able to attain internal stability and focus. It is like a dried-up tree that does not again bloom with spring flowers. It is like the deadness of ashes, which never again blaze up into flames. The mind has no concerns for deliberation and the body has no business to handle. If one embodies the marvels of the obscure perfection of the Way, then even if the mind's intelligence is said to bore holes, how can it bring harm to my original natural state? Thus, the "Way" being referred to here is actually material force. The eight words "no deliberation, no doing, fully embodying the Way" (無慮無爲體道之全) indeed serve to best summarize the essential teachings of the Daoists.[33]

3. Principle Clarifying Mind and Material Force [the Confucian Teachings]

This section focuses on articulating the correctness of the Confucian justice and principle. By clarifying the notions of the Daoists and Buddhists, we can know their errors. "Principle" (K. *yi*) is the inherent virtue of the mind and that through which material force is produced.

Aah, this sublime principle! It exists prior to heaven and earth. Material force is produced based on me; the mind also gets its character from me.

"Aah" (於) is an expression of praise. "Sublimity" (穆) is the apex of purity. This principle is pure and is the apex of goodness, originally having no confusion. Therefore, in praising its excellence [our interlocutor] says "aah, sublime!" "Me" is principle referring to itself. When referring to the mind and material force, [our interlocutor] directly said "me" and "I," while here it points to the ideograph *yi* (理) in order to praise its excellence. Subsequently, the naming as "me" is done in order to see principle as the Way that is shared in common, which is respected without opposition. It is not the self that is characterized by the Daoists and Buddhists in order to protect the extremes of their own views.[34]

It's being said here that principle is the origin of the mind and material force means that only after there is principle is there material force. And only after there is material force does the lightness and purity of yang rise up to become heaven, and does the heaviness and turbidity of yin settle down and become earth. The four seasons circulate around these and the myriad things are born out of these. Human beings within this space all obtain the principle of heaven and earth; they all obtain the material force of heaven and earth and are taken as the most precious among the myriad things while participating in heaven and earth. When the principle of heaven and earth dwells within people it is called "nature" and when the material force of heaven and earth dwells within people it is called "form." In the case of mind, it also shares in obtaining principle and material force while becoming the master of an individual body. Therefore, principle exists prior to heaven and earth while material force is born from it. To the extent that the mind accords with it, it is regarded as virtuous.

Having mind but no self, one is driven by profit and loss; having material force but no self is [nothing more than] a body of blood and flesh. In a state of commotion, one ends up in the same lot as the birds and the beasts; how rare are those who differ from them!

"Commotion" is a state of unawareness. "Rare" means "few." Zhuzi said, "In the commotion of awareness and motion, humans and animals are the same. In terms of the clarity of humaneness, justice, propriety, and wisdom,[35] humans and animals are different."[36]

This means that the way people differ from the birds and beasts is in terms of their possession of a sense of justice and principle. If humans lack a sense of justice and principle then their awareness is limited to nothing more than the personal matters of carnal desire and profit and loss. Their movements are nothing more than those of the noisy crowd. Even though you are called a human being, after all how far are you from the birds and the beasts? This is the way the Confucians preserve their mind and nourish their material force; they necessarily take justice and principle to be of primary importance. In the case of the study of Buddhism and Daoism, it is purity and quiescence that are revered. They must also desire to reject and get rid of even the greatness of their ethical principles and the elegance of their ritual music. In terms of their hearts being desireless, are they perhaps not also being chased by profit and loss? No matter what, they do not know to emphasize the justice of the heavenly principle in order to control selfish human desires. Hence their daily function can be characterized as falling blindly each time into profit and loss.

Furthermore, there is nothing that humans desire more than life and nothing that they hate more than death. Now, if we examine the teachings of these two schools on this topic, the Buddhists want to avoid death and birth. This is fear of death. The Daoists definitely seek to extend their life. This is greed for life. If this is not gain and loss, what is it? Furthermore, within this there is no governance by a sense of justice and principle, and therefore the Buddhists and Daoists are vacant, with no attainment, and dim, without awareness. Nothing exists but a mere bodily husk, which is absolutely nothing more than blood and flesh. And even though these four patterns of behavior can be seen in the people in general, within these two schools they are truly a sickness. The reader should examine carefully.

Seeing a crawling infant, the feeling of sympathy is generated. This is why the Confucians aren't afraid of giving rise to thought.

Mencius said, "Now, anyone who suddenly sees an infant about to fall into a well will naturally have a feeling of concern and sympathy."[37] He also said, "The sense of concern for others is the starting point of humaneness."[38] This saying that the sense of concern for others is originally an intrinsic part of our minds is used to clarify the Buddhists' error of thoughtlessness and lack of feelings. Now, it is by virtue of their attainment of the mind of heaven and earth and living creatures that people can be born into this world. The so-called fully developed humaneness is the principle with which our minds are truly endowed. Therefore when we see an infant about to crawl into a well, this feeling of sympathy naturally wells up and can't be suppressed. When one develops this mind by enlarging it then humaneness can never be used up, and all those within the four seas can nurture each other. The Confucians are therefore not worried about giving rise to thought. Acting in accord with the heavenly principle and discovering it as it is, how can they be like the Buddhists and fear the arousal of thoughts and feelings, doing nothing but forcing themselves to revert to extinction?

When you are ready to die, then die; justice is more important than your body. Because of this, the noble man sacrifices himself to fully perfect his humaneness.

The *Analects* says, "A determined scholar who is bent on humaneness would not seek to save his life by damaging that humaneness; there are even cases where he will sacrifice himself in order to perfect his humaneness."[39] This description of the matter of valuing justice and taking life lightly are used to clarify the error of the Daoistic nourishing of material force and greed for life. Only after the noble man sees and attains the true principle is it acceptable for him to die. His body cannot endure even one more day comfortably in life. Are death and life regarded as important? Or are justice and principle regarded as important? Therefore, the Confucian should save his ruler and parents from calamity; there is even the case where he abandons his body and his life in order to accomplish this. This is not like the Daoists just going along with things and training themselves so as to steal a little more life.

The sages are a thousand years distant; studying deception is called confusion. Material force is taken as the Way (the Daoist approach); the mind is taken as one's doctrine (the Buddhist approach).

"Confusion" is disorder. This means that the reason heterodox teachings bring about a raging fire is because the age of the sages is already long past. Yet Daoist studies do not clarify this confusion. Hence the Daoists don't know that material force originates in principle and so take material force as the Way. The Buddhists don't know that principle is endowed in the mind and hence take the mind as their doctrine. These two teachings take these two things (material force and mind) to be the peerless, most excellent marvels, but they don't know what exists beyond the realm of form. In the end they refer to the physical world when they speak; they lapse into superficialities or go totally off the map without ever knowing it for themselves.

To have longevity without justice—this is something that tortoises and snakes can do. Sitting in blankness, the body is like earth and wood.

"Blankness" is dullness. The first two phrases criticize the Daoists and the two phrases following criticize the Buddhists. Thus, in the prior passage the point that is expressed is that of the existence of mind without self and the existence of material force without self. Yet while the prior section generally speaks about their presence in people in general, in this section it is stated specifically in reference to the two teachings.

When I preserve this mind, it is clear and transparent; when I nourish this material force, it flourishes and produces.

Mencius said, "I am good at nourishing my vast, flowing material force" [*Mencius* 2A:2]. These words express the efficaciousness of the mutual nourishment of inner and outer in the Sagely Learning. If one preserves one's mind by justice and principle and nourishes it, then it will not be clouded by the desire for things; one's entire essence will be transparent and one's great function will not differ. If in accumulating justice one nourishes one's material force, filling it out and developing it, then the greatest and firmest material force will overflow and be naturally produced, thoroughly filling out the space between heaven and earth. The roots and branches supply each other, inner and outer nourish each other. This is the study of the Confucians, which can be regarded as accurate. It is not like the extreme teachings of the two other schools.

The ancient sages had a maxim: In the Way, there are not two venerables. Mind? Material force? I respectfully accept these words.

Hu cites the *Liji*'s "In the heaven there are not two suns, in the country there are not two rulers..."[40] to show that the Way does not have two destinations. Therefore the Daoist arts are supposed to make one "return to the One." That which is articulated in the above lines is all originally in the maxims passed down from the sages and worthies and not my own private ideas. One's veneration in the practice of the Way cannot be directed toward two things. It is not something that the mind and material force can be compared to. Therefore, here at the conclusion I especially cite the mind and material force in order to warn about [prioritizing] them. My intentions in raising these up and showing them are of the utmost sincerity.

An Array of Critiques of Buddhism (*Pulssi chappyŏn*)

by Chŏng Tojŏn (Sambong)

Contents

1. Critique of the Buddhist Doctrine of Transmigration

The unending production and reproduction of human beings, along with the transformations of heaven and earth, operate continually without break. Originally the supreme polarity[1] has motion and stillness, which generates yin and yang. Yin and yang undergo changes and recombination, and the five phases are contained within this. The reality of the non-polar and supreme polarity and the germinative essence of the five phases of yin-yang mysteriously combine and congeal, and humans and creatures are [thereby] produced and reproduced. That which is born fades away, while that which is not yet born comes forth and endures without a moment's interruption.[2] The Buddha says that when people die their spirit is not annihilated; they subsequently take on [new] form. The theory of transmigration starts with this.

The *Yijing* says, "[The sage] traces things to their beginning and follows them to their end; therefore he understands birth and death. [The union of] essence and material force gives form to things, and the wandering of the soul produces the change [of their constitution]."[3] An earlier scholar explained it by saying that even though the changes of heaven and earth are produced again and again without cease, what is gathered must [eventually] be scattered, and where there is birth, there must be death. If you are able to trace back to the origin and know the birth-taking that is gathering, then you will also necessarily know that subsequently there must be scattering and death. If you are able to know the way of taking birth, then you gain [understanding of] the natural course of the changes in material force. Since there are from the start no spirits hanging about in the great void, you can know that in the death [of beings] their material force is scattered and there is no subsequent taking on of form. How could there be such a thing as abiding in a state of limbo?[4]

Again [the commentator] says, "[The union of] germinative essence and material force becomes creatures, and the wandering soul is changing [in its constitution]," [which means that] the material forces of heaven-and-earth and yin-yang combine and directly bring forth human beings and creatures. Having completed this, the material force of the spiritual soul (K. *hon* 魂) returns to heaven and the bodily soul (K. *paek* 魄) returns to earth.[5] Here the transformation is completed. As for the germinative essence and the material force becoming beings, this means that the germinative essence and material force combine to produce beings. The germinative essence is the bodily soul and the material force is the spiritual soul. [When the classics say] "the wandering of the soul produces the change [of its constitution]," "transformation" here means that the spiritual and bodily souls separate from each other. It is a transformation of wandering away and dispersal. This "transformation" is not the kind of recurring transformation [taught in Buddhism]. Once this kind of transformation occurs, that which is solid decomposes and that which exists disappears never to return as a living being. The space between heaven and earth is like an oven: Even though there are living things, they are all completely burnt away without a trace. How can you possibly say that that which has been dispersed is again joined and that which has passed away can return?

We can also test this concept in the case of our own bodies in the moment of a single inhalation and exhalation. When air goes out we call it "one breath." But that which goes out in one exhalation is not what is taken in with the next inhalation. In this way then, the respiration of people is continually produced without end. The principle of the departing of that which goes forth and the continuation of that which comes in can be seen in this. We can also confirm this in other living things in the world. In the vegetation, a single material force penetrates from the roots through the trunk, the branches, the leaves, flowers, and fruits. During the spring and summer this material force peaks in its activity and flowers and leaves grow thickly. Reaching fall and winter, the material force contracts and the flowers and leaves fall away. When the spring and summer of the next year arrive, [the foliage] again grows thickly. But it is not the case that the fallen leaves return to their roots, back to their origin to be reborn.[6]

When we draw water from a well each morning to boil for cooking and drinking, it is eventually boiled away. When we wash our clothes and put them out to dry in the sun, the water disappears completely without a trace. The water in the well is drawn out continuously, but it never runs out. Yet it is not the case that the water returns to its original place and is reborn.[7] There is also the case of the various grains that we farm. In the spring we plant ten bushels and in the fall we gather one hundred bushels. We can keep going like this, multiplying the yield until we reach one hundred thousand [bushels]. So these grains are also produced again and again.

Now, if we look at it from the point of view of the Buddhist theory of transmigration, all animate creatures come and go in fixed numbers, with never any increase or decrease [in the total]. But if this is the case, then the creation of living beings by heaven and earth is not like the profitable work of the farmer. Also, these animate creatures do not become human beings. This being the case, then the total number of all of the birds, fish, and insects is also fixed. That means that if one increases in number, the other must decrease; or if one decreases in number, the other must increase. It should not be the case that all simultaneously increase or that all simultaneously decrease.[8]

From the present point of view [however], during times of prosperity the population of human beings increases, and at the same time the population of the birds, beasts, sea creatures, and insects also increases. During a period of decline, the population of human beings decreases, as does the population of the birds, beasts, sea creatures, and insects. This is because human beings and the myriad things are all born from the material force of heaven and earth. Therefore, when the material force is waxing, [the number of all things] increases simultaneously. When the material force is on the wane, [the number of all things] decreases simultaneously. I have had it with the Buddhist's teaching of transmigration, which is nothing but a hideous deception to the people of the world! If we deeply fathom all the transformations of heaven and earth and clearly examine the production of human and creatures, then we cannot but understand it as I have explained here. For those who share my views, let's reflect on this together.

2. Critique of the Buddhist Notion of Karma

Some say "Your criticism of the Buddhist notion of transmigration is extreme. You claim that human beings and the [myriad] creatures are born through the reception of the material forces of yin-yang and the five phases." Well, among people there are the inequalities of wise and foolish, capable and incapable, poor and rich, noble and low class, long- and short-lived. In the case of the animals, there are those that are captured, raised as livestock, and made to suffer in labor without remittance until their death. There are some that are inevitably caught by the fisherman's and fowler's nets, the angler's hook, or the hunter's arrow. [There are] the large and small, strong and weak, eat or eaten. In heaven's creation of the creatures, each receives its own lot. How can there be such an unequal situation? With this in mind, are not the Buddhist's teachings on the mark [in teaching] that there will be retribution for all the good and evil activities that one does when one is alive? Those good and evil activities that one carries out in this life are called "causes." The rewards that appear at a later date, these are called the "effects."[9] Doesn't this explanation seem reasonable?

[I answer by] saying that I have explained the matter in full in the above discussion on the continuous production of humans and creatures. Once you grasp this point you cannot but be critical of the theory of transmigration. And if the critique of the theory of transmigration [is properly grasped] then the [shortcomings of] the theory of karma are self-evident without any special effort at critique. And yet you still ask this question? I take the prerogative of not repeating my explanation from the beginning again. Now, [in the activity of] yin-yang and the five phases, the twists of fate and the alternations in patterns are uneven and offset. Therefore, in their material force there are differences of free flow and congestion, imbalance and balance, purity and pollution, substantiality and insipidness, high and low, long and short.

And in the production of humans and animals, if the timing is right they obtain balance and penetration, becoming human beings. If they end up with imbalance and congestion, they become animals. The respective nobility and wretchedness of humans and animals is differentiated in this. Furthermore, while existing as a human, those who attain clarity are the wise and the adept. Those who are turbid are the foolish and the inept. Those who are thick [in virtue] attain wealth and those [whose virtue] is insipid end up in poverty. The high are ennobled and the low are miserable. Those endowed with longevity are long-lived and those limited to brevity die young. This discussion is greatly abbreviated, yet the case is the same with the creatures. The *qilin*,[10] the dragon, and the phoenix are spiritual, while tigers, wolves, and snakes are poisonous. The camellia, cassia, bracket fungus, and epidendrum are auspicious,[11] while crows-beak,[12] aconite, and cogongrass bring suffering. Although these all lie in the category of the congested and imbalanced, there are inequalities in relative good and evil. Yet they do not become so by their own intention. The *Changes* says, "The Heavenly Way transforms, determining the constitution of each thing."[13] An earlier scholar said, "This indicates that Heaven's Way is distributed to the myriad things without intention." The same principle can be seen expressed in the minor arts of physicians and fortunetellers. When fortune tellers determine people's ill and good destinies, they must inevitably look back to the basis in the rise and fall of the five phases. For example, some people's destinies are determined by the phase of wood: in the spring they will flourish and in the autumn they will decline. Their appearance tends to be green and tall and their hearts tend to be warm and compassionate. Other people's destinies are determined by the phase of metal: they do well in the autumn and falter in the summer. Their appearance tends to be whitish and square, their minds strong and bright. The same sorts of examples can be drawn from the phases of water and fire; there is no place where they do not have application. Ugliness in appearance and coarseness and dullness of mind are also rooted in imbalances in the endowments drawn from the five phases.

When physicians are diagnosing people's sickness, they also must investigate the root causes of the mutual influences of the five agents. This can be seen in the fact that sicknesses related to cold will be related to the water-based kidneys, and sicknesses of heat will be related to the fire-based heart.[14] The prescriptions given for treatment are adapted to the various natures of warm and cool, cold and hot, prescribing medicine that tastes salty and sour, sweet and bitter, which are in turn categories related to the five agents. In this there are no [remedies] that are not perfectly matched [to the disease and personal constitution]. This is what our Confucian teachers mean when they say that the production of people and creatures occurs based on the attainment of the material forces through yin-yang and the five agents. This is supported by direct testimony that is beyond doubt.

If you follow the explanations of the Buddhists then fortune and misfortune and sickness are unrelated to yin-yang and the five agents. Instead, all are manifested as karmic retribution. [If this is so,] why, when it comes to the divination of fortune/misfortune and the diagnosis of disease, is it that not a single person has abandoned our Confucian yin-yang-five-agents paradigm and adopted the Buddhist theory of karmic results? Their theories are nonsensical and error-laden and not worth being adopted. How can you allow yourself to be deceived by such teachings?!

3. Critique of the Buddhist Theory of Mind and Nature

The mind is the material force that the human being takes from heaven at birth. It is spiritually subtle and undarkened,[15] and takes its position as lord of a single body. [A person's] nature is the *principle* that the human being takes from heaven at birth. It is pure and perfectly good; it is endowed in each individual's mind. The mind is both aware and active, while the nature is neither aware nor active. Therefore it is said that the mind is able to fathom the nature, but the nature is not able to assess the mind. It is also said that the mind encompasses the emotions and the nature. The mind is also said to be the abode of spiritual luminosity, while the nature is the principle with which it is endowed. Observing this, the distinctions between the mind and nature can be understood!

The Buddhists take the mind to be the nature. But if you examine their theory thoroughly, it doesn't add up. They furthermore say that delusion is none other than the mind and that awakening is none other than the nature. They also say that "mind" and "nature" are synonymous, just as are the words *yan* and *mu*.[16] And even the *Śūraṃgama-sūtra* says, "Complete, marvelous, luminous mind; luminous, marvelous, complete nature." (Interlinear Note: This is a reference to the passage in the *Śūraṃgama-sūtra* that says, "You have abandoned the originally marvelous and completely marvelous luminous mind, the jeweled luminous marvelous nature. While admitting awakening, you speak deludedly" [T 945.19.110c24]. In the case of the mind it is from its marvelousness that the luminosity arises. It is completely interfused, and its illumination is complete. Its illumination is like that of a mirror, and therefore it is called the complete, luminous, marvelous mind. In the case of the nature, then it is simultaneously luminous and marvelous. It is silent and profound, like the essence of the mirror. Therefore it is called "jeweled, luminous, marvelous nature.") They are named by discriminating luminosity from completeness.

Pojo [the noted Sŏn master Chinul] said, "Outside of the mind there is no Buddha,"[17] and "outside of the nature there is no Dharma."[18] So a distinction is also being made from the perspective of the terms "Buddha" and "Dharma." This seems simple, but there is something to be gleaned here. Indeed, this is all done based on nebulous supposition rather than on hard facts. The teachings of the Buddhists have lots of word play and lack a set argument, and so their actual [deceptive] intentions can be understood. Our Confucian teachers say, "Exhaust your mind to understand the nature."[19] Here the original mind is used to fathom a profound principle.

The Buddha's teaching says "observe the mind and see the nature,"[20] and "mind is none other than the nature."[21] This means that you use a separate one mind to observe this one mind. But how can a person have two minds? From this we can also readily know the impoverishment of their theories. We can sum it up by saying that using one's mind to observe the mind is like using the mouth to eat the mouth. What kind of nonsense is this to say that we will use the unobserving to observe?!

Moreover, our Confucian teachers say that "within the space of a square inch, [every single thing has its definite principle]"[22] and "the rarefied spirit is undarkened [including within it a multitude of principles responding to myriad circumstances]."[23] The rarefied spirit that is undarkened is the mind; that which contains a multitude of principles, is the nature. Those things that respond to a myriad of circumstances are the feelings (K. *chŏng* 情).[24] Now, since this mind is endowed with a multitude of principles, when all affairs and things impinge upon the mind none are not responded to appropriately. Therefore affairs and things are treated according to their correctness and incorrectness, and affairs and things follow the lead of the self.

This is the learning of our Confucian masters. From inside the body and mind, extending out to [all] affairs and things — from the source, flowing out to the branch streams — all are penetrated by one; like the water that comes down from the fountainhead to flow out to a myriad branch streams, there is no place where it is not water. It is like holding the handle of the Big Dipper, which assesses the worth of all things under heaven. The relative worth of those things is just like the weighing of a *zhu* and *liang* on a scale.[25] This is what is meant by saying that there has never been a moment of interruption.

The Buddhists say that the empty numinous wisdom accords to conditions without changing.[26] (Interlinear Note: The Buddhists take the pure mind's accordance with conditions as its "marks" and its changelessness as its "nature." It is like the single element of true gold, the marks of which change according to its usage in larger and smaller vessels, and so forth. This accordance with conditions is called "marks." The fact that the original gold does not change is called its "nature." The single true and pure mind adapts to good and evil, defilement and purity, and so forth. This accordance is called its "marks." The original changelessness of the mind is called its "nature.") There is no principle contained in it. Therefore, upon impingement by events and things, those who are restricted by them desire to sever and escape from them. Those who can engage with them desire to follow and accord with them.

Now, cutting off and escaping are definitely unacceptable. Following and according are also unacceptable. What [the Buddhists] are saying is: Follow conditions in a state of detachment from the world; just let things be what they are according to their nature. Pay attention to what things develop into and nothing more; do not repeatedly try to correct and manage them. This kind of mind is like the moon in the sky; its adaptation is like the reflection in a thousand rivers. The moon is real and its reflections are false; between the two there has never been any connection. It is like using a starless scale to evaluate the worth of the things under heaven, their lightness and heaviness, their highness and lowness. Things can only be accorded with, and the individual has no means to appropriately evaluate them. Therefore I say: Buddhism is void, while Confucianism is substantial; Buddhism has two realities, while Confucianism has one; Buddhism has gaps, while Confucianism is consistent. This is something that learned people should clarify and discern.

4. Critique of the Buddhists' Conflation of Function and Nature

I submit to you that in the discourse of the Buddhists, functional activity is taken to be nature. For instance, Layman Pang said, "Hauling water and carrying firewood are nothing but marvelous function." (Interlinear Note: This is from the verse of Layman Pang that says, "In daily activities, no discrimination, only oneself merging. Each moment grasping and letting go at each point; one should neither go along nor resist. Supernatural power together with marvelous functioning; hauling water and carrying firewood."[27])

The "nature" [of something] is the principle that one obtains from heaven in order to be born. "Functional activity" is the material force that one obtains from heaven in order to be born.[28] The congealment of the material force brings about substantial form and spiritual pneuma. The acuity of the mind, sharpness of the eyes, grasp of the hands, and speed of foot — all kinds of sensation and movement are [manifestations of] the material force.

Therefore it is said, "Form is already produced; the spirit generates awareness."[29] People already possess the physical body and material force. This means that the principle that is included in body and material force exists in the mind as the nature of humaneness, justice, propriety, and wisdom, as well as the feelings of sympathy and pain for the sufferings of others, shame and disgust, courtesy and respect, and right and wrong.[30] It exists in the brain as correctness, exists in the eyes as precision, and exists in the mouth as restraint. All norms that are regarded as proper behavior and that are not to be taken lightly are principle. Prince Liu Kang said, "What human beings receive within heaven and earth in order to be born is called 'life.' Therefore there are norms of behavior and deportment to give order to life."[31]

The phrase "within heaven and earth" refers to principle. The phrase "norms of [behavior and] deportment" is principle manifesting itself in functional activity. Zhu Xi also said, "If you take functional activity [of something] to be [the same as] its nature, then are not people's irresponsible actions such as taking a sword to murder someone and transgressing the Way [also] the nature?"[32] Now, principle is something metaphysical, while material force is something physical. Is not the Buddhists' taking the highest, sublime, peerless [principle] and reducing it to something physical indeed ridiculous? Learned persons must take our Confucian norms of deportment and compare them with the Buddhist conflation of functional activity and nature. [If in doing so they] experience them in their own mind and body and examine them in external things and events, then they will naturally understand.

5. Critique of the Buddhist Notion of the Mind and Its Functions

The mind is the master residing in a single body. Traces are externalia that appear as the mind is activated in response to events and contact with things. Therefore it is said that when this mind exists, its traces necessarily exist. They cannot be separated into two. Now, the principles of the four potentialities,[33] the five constants,[34] and the myriad events and things are integrated and replete within this mind. When faced with impingement by events and things, this principle does not transform to become identical with them. Yet the principle [contained in] this mind receives and responds to impressions, treating each appropriately, and cannot be confused.

When a person sees a toddler about to stumble into a well, he spontaneously reacts with sympathy.[35] This means that the mind [of human beings] has an altruistic nature. Therefore their seeing of the child, which is manifested externally, directly results in the mind of sympathy and its traces. How could they be two [separate things]? Whether you are talking about [the basic sense of] shame and disgust [for one's own evil activities], the basic sense of courtesy and respect, [the basic sense of] right and wrong, there are none that do not operate like this. Next is the case of the relationships between people. When you see your father you think in a filial way; when you see your children you think with love. So it is with serving your ruler with loyalty, treating your subjects with propriety, and interacting with friends with trust.[36] These are all viable examples. Since their minds possess the natures of humaneness, justice, propriety, and wisdom, they are visible on the outside.

It is like the saying "essence and function spring from the same source; the manifest and the subtle have no gap between them."[37] The Buddhist method of study apprehends the mind but does not apprehend its traces. This can be seen in their saying things like "the bodhisattva Mañjuśrī wanders through the taverns but these external phenomena are not his mind."[38] Excuses like this for sloppy behavior abound [in the Buddhist teachings]. Is this not a separation of the mind from its activities? Chengzi said, "The study of the Buddhists includes reverence to correct the internal but does not include justice to straighten the external."[39] Therefore, those who rigidly stick to their [incorrect views] wither away; those whose minds flow freely end up wandering off the path. This is the teaching of the Buddhists. It contains the means for internal discipline but lacks a sense of justice to straighten the externals. But even in the matter of correcting the internal, they still miss the essential points. Wang Tong was a Confucian, and he also proposed the division of the mind from its activities.[40] Well, he was deceived by the Buddhist teaching and did not know it. Therefore I have dedicated myself to explaining this.

6. Critique of the Buddhists' Obscuration of [Transcendent] Principles and Concrete Entities

"'Way' refers to principle, which is metaphysical. 'Concrete entities' are things and are material."[41] Now, the great fount of the Way issues forth from heaven;[42] there is no thing that does not exist and no time that it is not so. Wherever there are body and mind, there is the Way of body and mind. Close at hand [it is seen in the relationship between] father and son, ruler and minister, husband and wife, elder and younger, and between friends. Further reaching, it is found in heaven and earth and the myriad things. There is no thing that does not possess its own Way. The person who abides in the space between heaven and earth is not able to exist independently of things for a single day. Therefore it is universally the case that each person's treatment of affairs and relationship with things is replete with its own Way as well. It can't be the case that there is variation here. In this way the discipline of we Confucians goes from mind to body to people to things, each one fulfilling its nature with no place not penetrated.

The Way is not mixed with concrete entities, nor is it distinct from concrete entities. The way of the Buddhists is such that even though [they say] there is nothing to be attained, their long development of powers of concentration gives the appearance of having some kind of vantage point. Yet [this perspective] is like peeping at the heavens through a narrow tube. They one-pointedly depart straight upwards, but are not able to [practice their realizations] pervasively throughout the world. That which they perceive cannot but fall into partiality. When you observe their Way, it is not mixed with concrete activity. Thus they take the Way and concrete activity and separate them into two. They say, "Wherever there are marks, all are nothing but voidness. If you observe all marks to be no-marks, then you are seeing the Tathāgata."[43] (Interlinear Note: This passage comes from the *Prajñāpāramitā-sūtra*, which says that before the eyes there are no phenomena. When all that the eyes touch upon becomes like this, and awareness is like this, then you are seeing the Tathāgata.) One is expected to seek to disentangle oneself from all existent things and drop away into oblivion.

[The Buddhists,] seeing their Way as not distinct from concrete entities, end up taking concrete entities to be the Way. Thus they say, "Good and evil [phenomena] are all mind. The myriad phenomena are nothing but consciousness."[44] According with all things, going along with their activity without contrivance, acting wildly and arbitrarily, there is nothing that they do not do. (Interlinear Note: This means that the good mind, upon attaining rebirth, follows all the myriad phenomena, going along without contrivance; the evil mind that attains rebirth acts wildly and arbitrarily, and there is nothing that it will not do. The consciousness that the mind possesses, then, is only good or only evil. Without mind there is no consciousness and without consciousness there is no mind. The mind and consciousness are concomitant; good and evil arise and cease.) This is what Cheng Hao meant when he said "those who are rigid become like dry wood, and those who are unrestrained end up being arbitrary and reckless."[45] When [the Buddhists] talk about their Way, they are referring to the mind. But they end up falling back down into the physical realm of concrete things without even being aware of it. How regrettable!

7. Critique of the Buddhists' Abandonment of the Basic Human Relationships

The teacher Ming Dao[46] said, "Outside of the Way there are no things; outside of things there is no Way. Thus within heaven and earth, there is nowhere without the Way. It is found in the relations between father and son, and the way of father and son lies in intimacy. It is found in the relationship between ruler and minister, and the way of ruler and minister lies in respect for authority. It is the same with the relationship between husband and wife, elder and younger, and among friends: [in these relationships] there is no activity that is not the Way. That is why 'it is not possible to be separated from [the Way] for a moment.'[47] This being the case, to abandon human relationships and do away with the four elements (Interlinear Note: The four elements here are feeling, perception, impulse, and consciousness.) are to deviate far from the Way."[48] He also said, "They say that there is no place where it does not operate. Yet in reality they are outside norms of morality."[49] Is not the analysis of our teacher thorough indeed!

8. Critique of the Buddhist Notion of Compassion

"Heaven and earth take living beings as their mind";[50] human beings take this mind of the living beings of heaven and earth in order to obtain birth. "Therefore all people are endowed with the mind that cannot stand and watch the suffering of others."[51] This is what is known as humaneness. Even though the Buddha was a foreigner, he was still a human being. So how could he alone lack this mind? What we Confucians call the feeling of sympathy for the suffering of others the Buddhists call "compassion." Both are functions of humaneness. Even though these two expressions are basically the same, vast differences can be seen in the way that they are actually carried out.

My family members and I share the same material force. Other people and I are of the same species. Other living beings and I share in being alive. Therefore, in the manifest expression of the mind of humaneness, one starts with one's family, then extends to other people, and then to other beings.[52] It is like water filling up one hole and then going to a second and third hole. The source of humaneness is deep and its extent is far-reaching. Including all the creatures in heaven and earth, there is not one that does not exist within our heartfelt love. Therefore [Mencius] said, "[The noble man] loves his parents intimately and is humane to people. He is humane to people and cares about creatures."[53] This is the Confucian Way. Therefore it is unitary, it is substantial, and it is coherent.

The Buddhists are different. In their treatment of other living beings, whether the beings are fierce animals like leopards and tigers or insignificant bugs like mosquitoes and flies, [Buddhists] shamelessly desire to feed them with their own bodies.[54] In their treatment of people, if a man from Yue[55] is hungry, they are concerned about giving their food to him. If a man from Qin is cold, they want to donate their clothing to him. And this offering of clothing is a "donation."[56] But in the case of someone extremely close, like one's father or son or someone to whom great respect is due, such as the prince or minister, they unfailingly seek to sever the relationship and run away.[57] What is the meaning of this!?

Moreover, that people learn to act with care and discretion is by virtue of their having fathers and mothers, wives and children. [Human relationships] cause them to learn proper values. The Buddhists regard human relationships as nominal combinations. [When] the son does not treat his father as a father and the minister does not treat his prince as a prince, humaneness and justice go to ruin. People regard their most intimate family members like passersby on the street, and they treat the most venerable person like a mere child. The original basis has already been lost. Therefore, if they try to reach out to other people and beings, it is like a tree without roots, a river without a source, which easily dries up. In the end there is success neither in bringing benefit to people nor in giving aid to living beings, and the sword is drawn to kill the snake.[58] They haven't the slightest feeling for them.

[The Buddhists'] teaching about the hells is extreme in its cruelty and shows them to be people of little feeling. Where is "compassion" to be seen in this? Nonetheless, in the end the spirituality of this mind cannot be completely darkened. Therefore, even though one may be in the most extreme state of blindness [regarding the principle of human relationships], with just one meeting with one's father and mother the heart of filial love spontaneously springs forth. [The Buddhists] even trace back to the roots and seek [the basis of love] and then say, "Since the karmic impressions created over many lifetimes are not yet eliminated, the root of love still remains. One clings to delusion and does not awaken."[59] Is this not extreme!? This is what is meant when we say that the teaching of the Buddhists lacks justice and principle and therefore does not really qualify to be called a genuine teaching.

9. Critique of the Buddhist Notions of the Real and the Nominal

The Buddhists regard the nature of the mind to be real and enduring and take heaven and earth and the myriad things to be nominal combinations. They say, "Good sons, all sentient beings' various illusions are born from the perfectly enlightened marvelous mind of the Tathāgata, just like the sky-flowers come to exist in the sky....just like a second moon."[60] (Interlinear Note: This passage comes from the *Sutra of Perfect Enlightenment*, where it is explained how the karmic consciousness of sentient beings is not aware of the mysterious mind of the Tathāgata's perfect enlightenment that resides within their own bodies. If one uses wisdom to illuminate the matter, then the unreality of the existent world is comparable to [illusory] flowers seen in the sky, and the false marks of sentient beings are like seeing a second moon. The mysterious mind is represented by the original moon, and the second moon is only a reflection.)

[The Buddhists] also say, "Space arises in the midst of great enlightenment, like the ocean producing a single bubble [of foam]. A myriad of contaminated lands all arise based on space." "Space arising from the midst of great enlightenment is like the ocean producing a single bubble; a myriad of defiled lands are born from the sky."[61] (Interlinear Note: This passage comes from the *Śūraṃgama-sūtra*, which explains that within the ocean of great enlightenment, which is originally completely separated from emptiness and existence, stimulation from the winds of delusion mistakenly produce air bubbles. [The bubbles are a metaphor for] all living beings. Once the winds of delusion have stilled then the air bubbles also disappear. All the existent things that depend upon this delusion, if sought for cannot be found, and emptiness and enlightenment merge perfectly, returning to their original mystery.) The words of the Buddhists contain much that is harmful. In this way they nullify human mores without the slightest reservation. This is a sickness at the very foundations, which cannot go untreated.

Now, prior to the existence of heaven and earth and the myriad things, there is at the very beginning the supreme polarity, and the principle of heaven and earth and the myriad things, already fully integrated in their midst. Therefore it is said that "the supreme polarity gives birth to the two primary forces; the two primary forces give rise to the four forms."[62] A thousand transformations and a myriad changes all manifest following this. It is like when a river has a source that pours water into the ten thousand branch streams. It is like a tree that has roots whose branches and leaves grow thickly.[63]

This is not something that comes to be through the power of human intelligence; nor can it be halted by human intelligence. Yet it is certainly hard to teach to beginning students, and therefore we explain it through phenomena so that people can readily see [for themselves]. For the thousands of years from the death of the Buddha to the present, heaven's amorphous form has existed above. Once heaven is clearly apparent, then the earth spreads out limitlessly below. If the earth is obediently accorded with, then humans and creatures are born in the space [between heaven and earth]. If these are vividly distinguished, then the sun and moon, cold and heat come and go. If these are well ordered then the heavenly bodies of extremely great size revolve in their systematic orbits; the sun, moon, stars, and other bodies move this way and that and at varying rates of speed. Yet even in a stormy twilight, none of this lies outside the purview of the eight-foot turntable and several-inch crossbar.[64]

The years pass and pile up in the millions yet are divided equally into the twenty-four [two-week] periods. The shortfall and excess adjustments on the calendar accumulate, reaching the subtlety of a hair's breadth. Yet none fall outside of the two [mathematical] methods of multiplication and division. When Mencius said, "Heaven is so high; the stars are so distant. If we investigate their works, through the solstices of a thousand years, we can sit and attain them,"[65] he was referring to the same sort of principle.

Then who is it that is causing these things to be this way? There has to be a true principle that is acting as the director [of these events]. That which is temporary can only last for a short time and cannot endure for millions of generations. An illusion can only work its deception on one individual and cannot be believed by millions of people. Yet the eternal existence of heaven and earth and the endless production of the myriad living beings are said by the Buddhists to be temporary and illusory. What kind of theory is this?! What kind of discipline is the Buddhist's study, in its failure to investigate principles? If we interrogate their theories, there is nothing of substance to be found. How could they be so narrow-minded: that the greatness of heaven and earth and the abundance of the myriad things cannot be contained within [their minds]?

How is it that they can enjoy maintaining a strict lifestyle and yet dislike the pain of fully investigating principles and the exertion of responding to the endless changes of life. Zhangzi [Zhang Zai] said, "Obviously they are not able to fathom [existence] completely, and so they disparage heaven and earth and the sun and moon, regarding them as illusion and falsity."[66] Therefore, when the Buddhists are subjected to criticism, there is definitely some basis for it. They place priority on the obscuration that they perceive and their discourse is therefore unbalanced like this. Aah, what a pity! Why do I carry on with my lengthy arguments [against them]? No matter what I say, the point can never be exhausted. From the standpoint of correct thinking their delusion is pitiable and the decline of our own Way is distressful indeed.

10. Critique of the Buddhist Notion of Hells

An earlier Confucian philosopher criticized the Buddhist notion of hells, saying:

> People in the world who believe the Buddha are deceived. When carrying out funerals, they never fail to make offerings to the Buddha and feed the *saṃgha*. They say this is so that the deceased may have their crimes erased and increase their merit, bringing about rebirth in the heavenly realm and experiencing all types of bliss. If [the offerings] are not made then they will fall into the hells, where they will be bludgeoned, burnt, pounded, and scraped, undergoing all sorts of suffering, pain, and sickness. They are not aware that the bodies of the dead have already decomposed and that their spirits have been scattered in the wind. So even if there is such a thing as bludgeoning, burning, pounding, and scraping, there is no one there to undergo these punishments. More than this, before the Buddhist teachings entered China, there were definitely [accounts of] people dying and being reborn. How is it that out of all of these, there was not a single person who mistakenly entered hell and saw the so-called Ten Kings?[67] The lack of such accounts makes it clear that there is not sufficient ground to believe such a doctrine.[68]

Some say that the Buddhist teaching of hells is prescribed for those of inferior religious capacities; it is created to intimidate them into good behavior.[69]

Master Cheng said, "Fully actualized sincerity pervades heaven and earth; how could there be anyone who is not transformed?"[70] How could an inauthentic teaching transform people?

In the past a monk queried me, saying, "If there were no [teaching of] hell, what could be used to frighten people away from doing evil?" I said, "The liking of goodness and the dislike of evil seen in the noble man is like 'liking an attractive color and disliking a repugnant odor,'[71] — they all arise from within oneself and there is no contrived intent that brings these feelings out. Once one has an evil reputation then his/her mind is filled with shame. If one receives a public caning, why does he or she need the teaching of hell in order not to behave in an evil manner?" The monk was silent.

I am throwing myself wholeheartedly into the writing of this, to make the people of the world question these theories, to know that they should be criticized.

11. Critique of the Buddhist Notions of Calamity and Fortune

The Way of Heaven is to confer good fortune upon the virtuous and bring misfortune to the licentious. The way of humans is to praise the good and punish the evil. Since in the usage of people's minds there is incorrect and correct and in self-behavior there is right and wrong, fortune and misfortune come in accordance with the type of behavior. The *Book of Odes* says that "you cannot seek fortune by devious means."[72] Confucius said, "He who sins against heaven has no one to pray to."[73] How does the noble man deal with misfortune and fortune? He corrects his own mind and nothing more. He cultivates his own self and nothing more. Fortune does not need to be sought in order to be obtained and misfortune does not need to be avoided for one to keep it at a distance. Therefore it is said that "the noble man experiences a lifetime of trouble without a moment of anxiety."[74] If misfortune comes to him from the outside, he goes along with it and that's that. It is like the cold and hot weather that pass before us, which have no direct relation to ourselves.

The Buddhists, on the other hand, do not discuss human incorrectness and correctness or right and wrong. They even say that if you take refuge in the Buddha, misfortune can be avoided and fortune gained. This means that even if one commits the ten great heinous crimes,[75] if one has faith in the Buddha, he can avoid misfortune. And even a scholar who is [firmly planted] in the Way, if he does not take refuge in the Buddha, cannot avoid misfortune. Let's say, for argument's sake, that these theories are not false. They are nonetheless all derived from a selfish mind rather than the impartial Way and thus belong among that which should be suppressed. What's worse is that the Buddha's teaching has flourished down to the present over a period of a few thousand years. Those such as Wu of the Liang[76] and Xian of the Tang who have served the Buddha, praying all the while with all their hearts, have all been unable to escape misfortune. As Han Tuizhi said, those who serve the Buddha become more and more cautious and their years shrink.[77] Do these words not cut directly to the core of the matter?

12. Critique of the Buddhist Practice of Begging for Food

The importance of food for people is truly great! One should not go without food for a day. Indeed, one should not even have to seek for food for a day. Not having food harms essence and life; having to seek food harms correct principles. Among the eight essentials of governing in the *Hongfan*,[78] food and provisions come first. After the five human relationships only food is placed first when valuing the people.[79] When Zi Gong asked [Confucius] about [the essentials of correct] governance, the Master answered by saying, "Be sure there is enough food."[80] This documents the ancient sages' understanding of the ways of people. They should not have to go a day without food.

Hence all [of the sages] have been busy in this way, teaching [the people] the techniques of farming, regulating the economy with taxation. The military and the state should have their necessities; there should be ample provisions for ceremonies and foreign emissaries; there should be sustenance for widowers and widows, the elderly and the young; and there should be no anxiety over poverty or hunger. The sages planned well in advance for the people's [welfare]. Above are the emperor, the princes, and the high officials from the suburbs, who all eat based on their governance of the people. Below are the farmers and merchants, who work for their own sustenance. In the middle are the scholars, who are filial at home and respectful in public; they are able to eat by preserving the Way of the ancient kings and transmitting [this Way] to the students of subsequent generations.

The ancient sages knew that people should not have to be anxious about food for a single day. Therefore, from the top of society to the bottom, each person has his own form of employment such that he can receive heaven's sustenance. This is the full achievement of seeing to the welfare of the people. To not operate within this model is to betray the people. It is for this kind of behavior that kings should be censured and should not be let off the hook. The *Diamond Sutra* says, "Then the World-Honored One at the mealtime donned his robes and took up his bowl. He entered into the city of Śrāvastī (Interlinear Note: Śrāvastī is the name of a city in Persia.) and begged for food in the city."[81] Since Śākyamuni regarded cohabitation between male and female as immoral, he abandoned society and escaped from the work of farming, severing the roots of continuous reproduction.

If one wants, by means of this "way," to take the people lightly, then believing in this way, there will be no one left in the realm. From whom will you beg? There also being no food in the realm, what food will you beg for? Śākyamuni was the son of an Indian king. But, regarding his father's position as inappropriate for himself, he would not assume it and did not govern his people. Regarding the man's plowing and the woman's sewing as inappropriate, he ran away from them. What kind of effort did he make? Without [the relationships of] father and son, ruler and minister, husband and wife, there is no preservation of the ways of the ancient kings.

These people [Buddhists], eating only a grain a day, will all be anxious about food. If you believe in this kind of way, do you really think that you can eat like an earthworm and continue to function? [If you do,] then why beg to eat? Moreover, should eating due to one's own efforts be regarded as inappropriate and eating based on begging be regarded as appropriate? The words of the Buddhists lack both appropriateness and reason. It can be seen the moment you open their books. Therefore I criticize their discourse.

13. Critique of the Sŏn Buddhist Teachings

The early Buddhist teachings did not go beyond the discourse of causes, conditions, and retribution, so as to ensnare foolish people. Even though they took nothingness as their cardinal teaching and abandoned the obligations of society, they still taught that the good obtain fortune while the evil reap misfortune. This resulted in the custom of people choosing goodness over evil, of observance of the rules of morality, and of not falling into dissipation. Therefore, even though the importance of human relationships was disparaged, appropriateness and reason were not completely discarded.

But when Bodhidharma arrived in China, he was aware of the shallowness of his own teachings and that they would not suffice to move eminently intelligent scholars. Thus he proffered slogans such as "no establishment of words and letters," "cutting off the path of language," "directly pointing to the human mind," and "seeing the nature, one accomplishes buddhahood." Once these teachings had been released they proliferated rapidly, and his followers continued to transmit and elaborate on them. Some said, "Goodness is none other than this mind, and you cannot use mind to cultivate mind. Evil is none other than this mind, and you can't use mind to eliminate mind." Alas, the practices of disciplining oneself against doing evil and endeavoring to cultivate one's goodness disappeared.

Others said, "Even lust, anger, and ignorance are divine practices";[82] regulating one's behavior through observance of the precepts, he loses the Way.[83] Regarding themselves as having avoided falling into the pit of entanglements, having released themselves from bondage and cast off the fetters, they arrogantly abandon themselves, ignoring the norms of social order. Wholly absorbed in self-indulgence, they are as fidgety as madmen, never returning to humane principles. The so-called principle of justice is, at this point, utterly lost.

Zhu Wengong [Zhu Xi] lamented of this situation saying, "The Western teachings of dependent origination and karma have excited and awakened a crowd of fools and have now been long disseminated in the world. Climbing the ladder beyond the heavens, they look back and point to the mind's nature; their sayings transcend being and non-being." (Interlinear Note: The Buddhist teachings can be briefly summarized into three. The first is purifying discipline. This is followed by doctrinal study, which is in turn followed by meditation practice. Dependent arising includes twelve aspects. These are: contact, desire, sensation, grasping, being, becoming, old age, death, anxiety, sorrow, suffering, and affliction.[84] The word "karma" has three connotations: those of bodily action, speech, and thought. Referring to the mind's nature is the point of such phrases as "this mind is itself Buddha" and "seeing the nature, one accomplishes buddhahood." "Transcending being and non-being" means that if you say things exist, then [the Buddhists] reply with "form is emptiness." If you say that they don't exist, then the response is "emptiness is form.")

This [kind of thinking] led directly to the spread of confusion and disputation throughout the world. This is called voidness, which does not produce real results. Treading through this bramble path, who indeed will take up the mantle of the three sages? Would it not be extreme for us to burn their books? Our grief over this situation is extreme, and I myself am depressed to the point of screaming again and again!

14. Critique of the Equivalences and Differences between Confucianism and Buddhism[85]

Prior Confucian scholars have compared the Ways of Confucianism and Buddhism by saying that the words are the same but their application differs. Let me elaborate further on this. We say "voidness" and they say "voidness." We say "quiescent" and they say "quiescent." But our voidness is void yet existent; their voidness is void and non-existent. Our quiescence is quiescent yet responsive; their quiescence is quiescent and destructive. We say "knowledge and action," they say "awakening and cultivation." Our knowledge means to know that the principle of the myriad things is replete within our own minds. Their awakening is awakening to the fact that the original mind is empty, lacking anything whatsoever. Our action means to accord with the principle of the myriad things and act [in harmony with] it without going off course. Their cultivation means to sever the connection with the myriad things and regard them as unconnected to the mind.

We say that the mind is replete with myriad principles. They say that the mind produces myriad things. "Replete with myriad principles" means that these kinds of principles are originally contained in the mind. Thus, when the mind is calmed, one becomes completely still, yet this principle is contained in essence. When [the mind] moves into activity, it feels and responds, bringing these principles into their function. The saying, "[the changes] are quiescent and do not move, but if stimulated they penetrate all situations under heaven"[86] refers to this.

The meaning of "produces myriad phenomena" is that the mind originally lacks these phenomena, but when responding to the external world these phenomena are born. When it is quiescent, this mind has no place where it abides; when it moves into activity, it produces [things] according to the objects that it meets. This is what [the Buddhists] refer to as "this mind is born in accordance with non-abiding." (Interlinear Note: This passage is cited from the [*Vajracchedikā-*]*prajñāpāramitā-sūtra*.)[87] "Accordance without abiding" means the realization that there is neither inner nor outer and in the middle there is not a single thing. And thus there is no way for [such things as] good and evil, right and wrong to be mediated within one's mind. "And yet this mind is produced" means that using the non-abiding mind, one responds to the external world and yet is not entangled by things. Mr. Xie explained the passage in the *Analects* that says "not for or against anything" by citing this teaching.[88]

It is also said that "when mind is produced, all phenomena are produced; when mind is extinguished, all phenomena are extinguished." (Interlinear Note: This is cited from the *Awakening of Faith*.)[89] Both of these citations reflect this view. We [Confucians] take principle as being intrinsic. They take phenomena (*dharmas*) to be dependently arisen. How can there be such an actual difference in application despite the similarity in language? Do not our expression "responding to a myriad changes and transformations" and their expression "according with all [phenomena]" seem to be the same?[90]

Let's take a look at the expression "[responding to myriad] changes and transformations." In this case, when affairs and things approach, this mind responds to them, treating each appropriately. One regulates and manages them, using them without failing to take advantage of them appropriately. With children, one should make them be filial, not rebellious. With ministers, one should make them be loyal rather than traitorous. This kind of principle also applies in the treatment of animals. Cattle should be harnessed for use in cultivation rather than simply leaving them to butt heads. Horses should be used for transport and should not be allowed to kick and bite. Tigers and wolves should be penned up in cages, or placed in pits, and should not be allowed to maul people. Thus, each thing should be handled according to its distinctive principle.

If we follow the "accordance with all things" as taught by Śākyamuni, then in the case of children, if they are filial, we just accept them as filial; if they are criminals, we just accept them as criminals. In the case of vassals, if they are loyal, we just accept them as being loyal; if they are rebellious, we just accept them as being rebellious. As for the usage of cattle and horses, if they work in plowing and transport, we use them for plowing and transport, and if they gore, butt, kick, and bite, then we let them gore, butt, kick, and bite. [The Buddhist way is to] acquiesce to the way things are and nothing more.

We [Confucians] can't accept this sort of thing, but the Buddhist teaching is like this. It is natural that we should subject the beasts [to our usage] and not be subject [to their behaviors]. Should the mere weight of a single gram sink us? Are not our and their actual practices different? Thus, the reason that heaven gave birth to human beings is for them to serve as the guide for the myriad creatures. Placed in the role of manager and assistant, how can we be at ease?[91]

This kind of explanation [can be] repeated again and again, and although there are numerous points that can be made, we can sum them up by saying that our [Confucian] manifest mind is at one with the principle while [the Buddhist] manifest mind is something other than the principle. Their manifest mind is empty, lacking principle. Our manifest mind, although empty, is replete with the myriad things. Therefore it is said that our Confucianism follows a unified [principle] while Buddhism has two realities. Confucianism is coherent while Buddhism is incoherent. Yet if the mind is one, how can there be such differences between our and their way of seeing things?

Now, there are differences between the correctness of what people see. Who is the subject of the body made of the four elements? Within the six faculties and their objects, what could be the essence? (Interlinear Note: The four elements of earth, water, fire, and wind combine to make one body. But if they are separated into four elements, then there is originally no subject. Color, sound, odor, taste, touch, and concepts are the objects of the six faculties, which are produced in dependence on each other. But if they are separated into six faculties, then there is originally no essence. It is just like the existence and non-existence of images in a mirror.)[92] "Opening up our eyes to the endless darkness, all day we listen to sound but do not see form." (Interlinear Note: Here we are referring to Huizhao, who says that even in endless darkness, when we open our eyes the light shines in the darkness. It is just like a mirror's reflectivity producing light within darkness.)[93] This is the Buddhist field of experience of the mind.

[We Confucians] explain [the mind] as something that stops and leaves traces. And we say that it cannot repeat its existence. It only resonates sympathetically according to the occasion. The most exceptional people can see its root. (Interlinear Note: From Zhu Xi's poems.) This is the field in which we Confucians experience the mind. Shall we also say that the mind simply has no form but yet has sound? Nevertheless, there is this principle existing in the mind that serves as the basis for all interactive transformations. Scholars should, within their daily activities, experience and fathom this field of the manifestation of the mind. Then the sameness and difference, strong points and weak points of their [position] and our [position] will be naturally apparent.

We can elaborate on this, relying on the teachings of Master Zhu. "Even though the mind is the master of a single body, its essence is a subtle numinousness, which is sufficient to act as an instrument for the principle of all under heaven. Even though this principle is spread out among the myriad creatures, its function is subtle and mysterious. Its truth is not found outside of the human mind."[94] At first, one cannot discuss it in terms of internal and external or refined and coarse. Yet if someone does not understand this mind's numinousness and has no way to preserve it, then it will become dark and fragmented, with no way to fathom the mystery of myriad principles. Without understanding the mystery of myriad principles and with no way to fathom them, one becomes partial and pigheaded and can never exhaust this mind's totality. This is the mutual dependence of principle and impetus. Is this not absolutely necessary?

Therefore, the sages established their teachings to allow people to quietly discern the numinousness of this mind. Thus they abide in a state of dignified mental focus in order to fathom the root of the principle and

allow people to understand the mystery of the existence of myriad principles. And they fathom it in their moments of study and deliberation in
order to fully develop the mind's sharpness. Gross and subtle nourish
each other; movement and stillness nurture each other. While originally
there has never been such a thing as differentiation between internal and
external or refined and coarse, when truth gathers momentum over a period of time, one understands broadly and deeply. And indeed, when one
knows its undifferentiated unity, then how can one say that there is neither inner and outer nor subtle and coarse?

Now, we cannot but regard this as a theoretical system that is shallow
and fragmentary and that desires to conceal shape and hide form. It can
be regarded as a type of doctrine that is obscure, spellbinding, difficult,
and impedimentary, which makes scholars carelessly place the mind outside the realm of text and words. Yet they say that only when the Way is
known like this can it be attained afterward. Hence, modern scholars of
Buddhism are masters of glibness, lewdness, trickiness, and evasiveness
[in speech],[95] desiring to shift [the meanings] around. They skew the true
learning of the ancients of illuminating virtue and renovating the people.[96] This is certainly wrong! We should deliberate repeatedly on Zhu
Xi's words, which are genuine and clear. If scholars would immerse their
minds in these [teachings], they would naturally understand them.

15. On the Entry of the Buddhadharma into China

(Interlinear note: From here down to section 18, titled "Serving the Buddha Assiduously, the Length of Reign Considerably Shortens," I will cite the *Daxue xingyi* by Master
Zhen.[97])

The Han emperor Ming heard that there was a god in the Western regions and that his name was Buddha. He thus dispatched emissaries, who
brought back with them monks and texts. These texts for the most part
contained a doctrine of nothingness. They valued compassion and absti-
nence from killing and understood that when humans die, their spirits do
not perish but subsequently return to take on new form. The good and evil
activities carried out during one's life all result in retribution; hence, they
prized religious training as the means for attaining buddhahood. They
skillfully promulgated their winning words in order to entice gullible
laypeople. Those who dedicated themselves to the [Buddhist] path were
called *śramaṇa*s.[98] From this time, China began to undergo transmission
of the [Buddhist] technology. Their sculptural styles were adopted, and

among the kings, princes, and the aristocracy, Chu Wangying[99] was the first to appreciate [these Buddhist cultural imports].

16. Serve the Buddha and Reap Misfortune

In the ninth month of the first year of Zhong Datong (527), Emperor Wu of the Liang went out to visit Tongtaisi temple,[100] where he sponsored an assembly of equality in the Dharma for the four groups of Buddhist disciples.[101] He took off his imperial garb and donned ecclesiastical robes, practicing the pure great donation. All of the vassals were obliged to donate large sums of money, pray to the three treasures, and make offerings to his highness, while the monks remained silent. All those in the emperor's imperial court as well as his administrators practiced the Buddhist teachings. They underwent long periods of abstention from the consumption of meat and limited themselves to a single meal per day, which consisted of nothing more than cooked vegetables and brown rice. He built many temples from public and private funds.

At that time there were many among the regional rulers and their followers who were arrogant, debauched, and lawless, and the elder [advisors] were oppressed with many duties. Again [the emperor] applied himself to the Buddhist precepts and put a stop to his deep immersion in sin and therefore from morning to night had no enjoyment. When he became aware of rebellious plots, he accepted them with tears [of resignation]. From this point, the regional rulers became increasingly out of control. Some murdered people in the city streets in broad daylight; some mugged people in public at night. Those who were supposed to be punished by exile hid themselves out in their manors, and the police did not dare to pursue them. The emperor knew well of this breakdown of public order, but sunken in tender compassion, he was unable to stop it.

On the third month of the first year of Zhong Datong (546) the emperor [again] went out to Tongtaisi. He ended up staying at the temple to study and lecture on the *Sutra on the Three Kinds of Wisdom*.[102] He disbanded the lecture in the summer, the fourth month. That evening, the pagoda of Tongtaisi was consumed in a fire. The emperor said it was the work of demon spirits and carried out extensive Buddhist services. He explained it in an edict, saying, "When the Way is heightened, demons abound; when goodness is practiced, obstructions are born." Then he worked intensively at the preparation of raw materials, double the amount used the last time, and erected a twelve-story pagoda. When it was nearly finished, some honest [members of the] nobility arose in rebellion and stopped it. They trapped the emperor within the perimeter of the Forbidden City, imprisoning him at Tongtaisi. The emperor's mouth was parched, and he sought honey from the temple monks. But he was not able to get it and in the end died of starvation.

17. Abandoning the Heavenly Way and Chatting about Buddhahood

The Tang emperor Taizong[103] venerated the Buddha from the beginning [of his life] to the end. His ministers Yuan Zai and Wang Jin both also loved Buddhism, with Jin being more extreme. The emperor once asked, "Buddhism teaches karmic retribution. Does it really exist?" Zai answered, saying, "Your royal house has experienced continual blessings. If it were not for propitious karma from previous lives, how could [your successes] have come to this extent? It has been predetermined by your meritorious activities. Even though there are times of minor calamities, they have, in the end, not been able to bring harm. Therefore, [the two usurpers] An [Lushan] and Shi [Siming] were both killed by their sons, dying in the street while still holding regrets.[104] The two invaders[105] ended up backing down without a struggle. These are all things not attainable by human power, so how could one say that there is no such thing as karmic retribution?"[106] From this time, the emperor deeply believed in this doctrine. He continually observed the prohibitions and fed more than one hundred monks. When invaders came, he richly rewarded them with honors, fertile fields, and excellent profits. The emperor returned often to the *saṃgha* and the monastery, where Zai would wait on him, offering ample of conversation regarding Buddhist matters while the day-to-day administration of laws and punishments was left in disarray.

18. Serving the Buddha Assiduously, the Length of Reign Considerably Shortens

In the fourteenth year of Yuanhe (819), Buddhist relics were brought to the capital, [an event] preceded by an imperial proclamation emperor declaring their virtue: "In a temple stupa in Fengxiang,[107] there are the remains of one of the bones from the Buddha's finger. This reliquary is opened up once every thirty years, and its opening brings plentiful harvests and stability to the people. We will open it next year, so please come and pay your respects." From these words, it came to this: The Buddha's bone arrived at the capital, where it was kept in the palace for three days, after which it was circulated around to all the temples. The princes, dukes, elites, and common people paid their respects and made offerings, as if they were afraid of not doing enough.

Han Yu, a vice-attendant from the Ministry of Justice memorialized the emperor, [admonishing him]: Buddhism is just a another barbarian teaching. From the Yellow Emperor down to Yu and Tang, Wen and Wu, all lived long and the people were contented. At that time, there was no such thing as Buddhism. It was at the time of Ming Di of the Han that the Buddhist teachings appeared [in China] for the first time. Following this [within the empires] there was nothing but rebellion and collapse overseen by short-lived rulers. From the time of the Song, Qi, Liang, Chen, and the beginning of the Wei, the Buddha was served with increasing seriousness, as the length of the reigns steadily became shorter. Only Wu of Liang was able to stay on the throne as long as forty-eight years. But even [Wu] went back and forth three times in his abandonment of his life to Buddhist practice. In the end he was trapped by Hou Jing and made to starve to death in the city stronghold. He served the Buddha seeking merit and instead ended in disaster. Observing this we can understand that the Buddha is not worthy of our belief. The Buddha was originally a barbarian whose language was not understood and whose clothes were different from those of the Middle Kingdom. He did not know the dispositions of our princes and ministers, fathers and sons. Suppose that he was still alive and came to pay his respects to the emperor in the capital. The emperor would greet him and have discourse with him, [but] he would not allow him to mislead the people.[108] How much more so now that [the Buddha] has long since passed away? How is it that a dried up bone should be brought into the Forbidden Palace? [If it is truly efficacious,] why not just hand it over to the officials and use it to chase away all of the natural disasters, to permanently sever the root of misfortune?

The emperor was furious and wanted to inflict the most severe of punishments [on Han Yu]. But ministers such as Pei Du[109] and Cui Qun[110] spoke up [on his behalf], saying, "Even though Yu is crazy, [his protestations] come from a mind of sincerity and loyalty. Please keep an open mind and leave room for appeal." Thus, he was demoted to the position of censor of the region of Chao.[111]

19. Critique to Expose Heterodox Teachings

Yao's and Shun's censure of the four villains[112] was because their clever speech and flattering countenances went contrary to [heaven's] mandate and brought harm to their clans. Yu also said, "Why do I fear clever speakers with flattering countenances? Well, clever speech and flattering countenances damage people's minds, go contrary to the mandate, and subvert the clans. The sages avoid activities that bring harm to people and won't accept them [when they are done by others]." Tang's and Wu's attack on Jie and Zhou is because at one moment they would say, "I am in awe of the emperor and would not dare to act incorrectly,"[113] and at another moment they would say, "I do not go along with heaven. Crimes are all the same; heaven imparts and heaven punishes. I do not speak of the things I have not experienced myself."

Confucius said, "To apply oneself to the study of heterodox teachings is harmful."[114] This word "harmful" can be read as meaning that the people come to hold such teachings in awe. Mencius' love of debate, with which he corrected Yang and Mo, was precisely because the ways of Yang and Mo were wrong and the Way of the sages wasn't being followed.[115] Therefore, Mencius took the critique of Yang and Mo to be his personal responsibility. He said that those able to correct Yang and Mo were indeed the disciples of the sages—Mencius' desire to be supported by others here was extremely great indeed. Mo taught universal love and thus thwarted the teachings of humaneness. Yang taught "every man for himself" and thus thwarted the teachings of justice. The harm brought by these teachings extended to the destruction of the role of father and the role of ruler.[116] It is from this that Mencius got his energy to pursue this issue.

In the case of Buddhism, the teachings are lofty and profound and traverse the discourses of essence and life and the path of virtue; thus their [power to] delude people is extremely great, [a level] to which Yang and Mo cannot be compared. Master Zhu said, "The Buddhist teachings draw close to the principle but greatly confuse reality."[117] This means that since I am ignorant and ordinary, I do not realize that my strength is insufficient and thus I take the critique of heterodoxy as my personal responsibility. Not desiring to transmit the mind of the six sages and the one worthy, I fear that the people of the world will be deceived by the Buddhist teachings and plunge together into a pit. The people's path will lead to destruction. Alas! Treacherous ministers and traitorous children are something that should be recognized and censured by everyone. You should not wait for the chief judge. When erroneous teachings overflow as a trick aimed at corrupting people, everyone should recognize and critique them. You should not wait for the sages and worthies. This is what I desire to see from our rulers—but it should be based on their own efforts.

Exposition of Orthodoxy (*Hyŏnjŏng non*)
by Kihwa (Hamhŏ Tŭkt'ong)

Contents[1]

1. Prologue
2. Distinctions in Levels of Teaching
3. The Constant and the Expedient
4. Śākyamuni's Attainment of Freedom from Attachment
5. Societal Obligations
6. Harming Life
7. The Meaning of Humaneness
8. Drinking Alcohol
9. Making Offerings
10. Defense of the Doctrine of Karma and Rebirth
11. Defense of the Buddhist Practice of Cremation
12. Refutation of the Complaint against Buddhism as a Foreign Religion
13. Refutation of the Accusation of Buddhism as a Harbinger of Calamity
14. Refutation of the Accusation of Monks Being Parasites
15. Refutation of the Charge of Decadence in the *Saṃgha*
16. Refutation of the Charges of Nihilism and Antinomianism
17. The Unity of the Three Teachings

1. Prologue

Though its essence neither exists nor not-exists, it permeates existence and non-existence. Though it originally lacks past and present, it permeates past and present. This is the Way. Existence and non-existence are based in nature and feelings.[2] Past and present are based in birth-and-death. The nature originally lacks feelings, but when you are confused in nature you give rise to feelings; with the production of feelings, wisdom is blocked—

thoughts transform and the essence is differentiated. It is through this that the myriad forms take shape and birth-and-death begins.

Feelings exist in the conditions of both defilement and purity, good and evil. Purity and goodness are the means by which sages appear. Defilement and evil are the causes that give rise to means by which we have ordinary [unenlightened] people. Therefore we know that if feelings do not arise, neither ordinary persons nor sages have the occasion to come into being. Even though the bodhisattvas have already become enlightened to their nature, they still have feelings that have not been eliminated. Therefore they are called "enlightened but having feelings."[3] If it is like this with bodhisattvas, how much more so in the case of the practitioners of the remaining two vehicles?[4] And if it is like this with practitioners of the three vehicles, how much more so is it in the case of other kinds of beings such as human beings and gods?[5] The enlightenment of the Buddha, by comparison, is complete, and there is no place where his wisdom does not reach. His purity is thorough, the accumulation of feelings having been completely extinguished. Therefore the term "feelings" (sentiency) cannot be applied to the Buddha. This is why all those outside of this one person—the Buddha—are called "sentient."

Practitioners of the three vehicles and practitioners of the five vehicles[6] each have their own means of counteracting feelings. Humans and gods have their own way of counteracting their impure defilements and those of the three vehicles have theirs for quelling their pure defilements. Once pure and impure defilements are both extinguished, one directly generates the state of great enlightenment. The five precepts[7] are the means that lead to rebirth as a human being. The ten virtues[8] are the means that lead to rebirth as a god. The practice of the four noble truths and [contemplation on the twelvefold] dependent arising result in the realization of the two vehicles. The six perfections[9] are the means for the production of bodhisattvahood. We can, then, summarize the gist of the entire content of the Tripiṭaka as none other than inducing people to abandon sentiency and manifest their original natures.

The feelings that are born from our nature are just like clouds appearing in the vast sky. The removal of feelings and the coming forth of our original nature are just like the dispersion of the clouds and the vast clarity that appears. Among feelings there are both insipid and dense, in the same way that among clouds there are both airy and thick. But even though clouds show the distinction of airy and thick, they are all the same in their function of obscuring heavenly illumination. And although among feelings there are differences between light and heavy, they are the same in their basic function of veiling the luminosity of the true nature.

When the clouds appear, the illumination of the sun and moon is veiled and the earth is darkened. When the clouds disperse, the illumination extends across the great cosmos and the universe appears limitless.

If the Buddha's teaching is compared to this, it is like the clear wind sweeping away the floating clouds. If you desire to gain this kind of limitless view but you don't like the clear wind, then you will indeed be disturbed. If you desire the expansive peace that extends from oneself to others but don't like our [Buddhist] Way, then you will lose the Way. If you teach people to rely on this teaching and practice it, then their minds can be corrected and their persons can be cultivated. You can regulate your family, you can govern the state, and you can bring peace to all the world.[10]

2. Distinctions in Levels of Teaching

Those who are of sharp faculties are able to accomplish the realizations of bodhisattvas, *śrāvaka*s, and *pratyekabuddha*s. Those of weak faculties are [at the least] able to obtain rebirth as gods or as good people. There has never been a case where this kind of transformation occurred and the world was not well governed. Why? If someone doesn't like to experience the painful results of evil actions, then he or she should cease all evil activities. Even if one does not succeed in curtailing all evil activities, one's effort will certainly suffice to remove a single evil. When one evil action is removed, it will result in the elimination of a single punishment. When one punishment is removed in the family, then myriad punishments will disappear within the state. If someone enjoys fortuitous karma, then that person should endeavor to cultivate all kinds of virtuous behavior. Even if the person does not succeed in fully cultivating all kinds of virtuous behavior, this effort will suffice for the creation of a single virtuous behavior. In practicing one virtuous behavior, this person will experience a single instance of good fortune. If one instance of good fortune arises in each family, myriad instances of good fortune will appear throughout the land.

The five precepts and the ten virtuous forms of behavior are the most shallow among the Buddhist teachings [and were] originally designed for those of the weakest of faculties.[11] Nonetheless, if one succeeds in practicing them, it is sufficient to bring about sincerity in oneself and benefit to those around oneself. How much more so in the case of contemplation on the four noble truths and dependent arising? And how much more so again in the practice of the six perfections? The Confucians regard the five eternal principles to be the pivot of the Way. The moral precepts of

Buddhism are none other than the five eternal principles of Confucianism: [the Buddhist precept of] not-killing is the same as humaneness; not stealing is the same as justice; not engaging in sexual excesses is the same as propriety; not drinking alcohol is the same as wisdom; and not speaking falsely is the same as trustworthiness.[12]

However, the way that the Confucian scholars teach people is not through the example of virtuous action but through laws and punishments. Therefore it is said, "If you lead them by laws and regulate them by punishments, the people will avoid these and be without shame. If you lead them by virtuous action and regulate them with propriety, the people will have a sense of shame and reflect on themselves."[13] Only sages are capable of leadership by virtuous action and regulation by propriety, hence the saying "Accomplishing silently, not speaking yet being trusted constitutes virtuous action."[14] In the case of leading by laws and regulating by punishments, one cannot avoid clarification by reward and punishment, hence the saying "Reward and punishment are the great source of authority for the state."[15]

"Accomplishing silently; not speaking yet being trusted" is strongly characteristic of the Buddhist method of teaching,[16] where it is used in conjunction with the teaching of cause and effect. If you teach people through reward and punishment, then there will invariably be some who will follow you only superficially. If you teach them through the concept of cause and effect, then they will be changed — and changed in their inner minds. Such a situation can be readily observed in this present world. How so? If you encourage them with rewards and discourage them with punishment, then the stopping of evil actions will only be the result of people's fear of authority. Virtuous behavior will only occur as the result of seeking the benefit of rewards. Therefore the change that occurs will only be superficial, not a change in the inner minds of people.

If people want to understand the reasons for success and failure in the present life, teach them regarding the seeds sown in prior lifetimes. If they want to know about the fortune and misfortune to come in the future, teach them regarding present causes. Then those who have enjoyed success will rejoice in the knowledge of the goodness of their seeds and redouble their efforts. Those who have failed will regret their lack of cultivation in prior lives and discipline themselves; and if they seek to invite good fortune in subsequent lives, they will apply themselves unstintingly toward goodness. Wanting to avoid misfortune in subsequent lives, they will grasp the necessity of being careful not to act in an evil way. If people are taught in this way, if they are not influenced, then that will be the end of it. But if they are influenced, they will be influenced in their inner minds, and there will never be a case where someone only goes along superficially.

Even so, how could you possibly cause every single person to change his inner mind? Therefore, those who are not able to change their minds can be guided for the time being through reward and punishment. This will cause their minds to become increasingly joyful and they will sincerely change. Therefore, in addition to the teaching of cause and effect, we may also retain the expedients of reward and punishment. This concept is reflected in the saying "Force those who must be forced; gently lead those who can be gently led,"[17] which is close to the Confucian Way. Seen this way, neither Confucianism nor Buddhism should be rejected.[18]

The Buddha's Way of transforming people is to take his Dharma and confer it on the princes and ministers. If you want to use this Way to lead all the people and play a major role in governing the realm, causing all to tread together on the same path of cultivation of truth, then our Buddha's teaching does not advocate either staying home (remaining a householder) or leaving home [becoming a monk]. All that is required — and nothing more — is to have people not act contrary to the Way. It is not necessary to shave one's head or wear special clothes in order to practice, hence the saying "Unloosening the bonds according to the situation is labeled as *samādhi*."[19] It is also said that "there is no set Dharma that is called Perfect Enlightenment."[20] With the Buddha's mind being like this, why should there be such a limitation in approach?

However, if one lacks self-control, then it is extremely difficult to live in the secular world without becoming polluted, and it is extremely difficult to accomplish the Way as a householder. It is because of this that people are taught to leave the secular world and encouraged to cultivate the practices of detachment. The Confucian saying goes that "the man has his house and the woman has her family"[21] in order to perpetuate the family business and not cut off the ancestral sacrifice; this can be called "filial piety." The Buddhists sever their marriages and abandon the basic societal relationships, wandering long through the mountains and forests, cutting off their posterity. How could this be called filial? [The Classics say,] "At night prepare the bed, in the morning inquire";[22] "be sensitive regarding the expression on their faces and attune yourself to them";[23] and "when going out, let them know, when returning, announce yourself."[24] Now, the Buddhists, without informing their parents, leave the household by their own authority. Once they leave home, they do not return for the rest of their lives. While their parents are alive, they do not offer them sweetmeats, and after they die, they do not provide a substantial funeral. Is this not quite unfilial?

3. The Constant and the Expedient

This can be tested, though, by observing thus: The constant (K. *kyŏng* 經) and the expedient (K. *kwŏn* 權) are the great essentials of the Way. Without the constant there is no way to preserve eternal principles; without expediency, there is no way to adjust to circumstances. When you are able to use the constant to maintain the principles and use the expedient to adapt to circumstances, you can attain to the great completion of this Way, and there will be nothing that you cannot accomplish. But if you don't know how to maintain principles, there will be no way to correct the human mind. And if you do not understand adaptation to circumstances, there will be no way for you to accomplish great tasks.

People receive their lives from their parents. They are able to continue in life by the graces of the ruler and the state. "When inside the home, be filial; when out in society, be loyal";[25] this is certainly the behavior appropriate to citizens and children. Furthermore, the ceremonies of weddings and ancestor worship are certainly the great bonds of human relationships. Without marriage, the connection of the continuity of life would be severed; without sacrifice, the method of honoring one's ancestors would be lost.

Nonetheless, it is not easy for ministers and children to be perfect in their loyalty and filial piety.[26] It is also quite difficult to go through a lifelong marriage and maintain perfect constancy or to always be able to offer sacrifice in a state of perfect mental devotion! One who is able to maintain perfect loyalty and perfect filial piety and at the same time conduct one's livelihood — to be constant in marriage and pure at sacrifice and not waver in the slightest to the end of one's days — will undoubtedly be spoken of highly after one's death, and subsequent to one's death that person will be reborn as a human being. These are the merits of holding to the eternal principles.

4. Śākyamuni's Attainment of Freedom from Attachment

Yet though one does not fail to attain a good reputation, those [who go on to] eliminate attached love and desire are exceedingly few. And although one does not fail to obtain a human rebirth after dying, escaping cyclical existence is difficult indeed. Attached love is the root of transmigration, and desire is the precondition for receiving life.[27] So if someone has not yet escaped the fetters of wife and children, how can he eliminate attached love and desire? And if attached love and desire have not been eliminated, how can he escape from cyclical existence? If you want to escape cyclical existence, you must first sever attached love and desire. If you want to sever attached love and desire, you must first forsake spouse and children. If you want to forsake spouse and children, you must first leave the secular world. If you do not leave the secular world, you cannot forsake spouse and children, sever attached love and desire, or escape cyclical existence. Without the great expedient example of the great sage who offers his compassion, can ordinary unenlightened people be capable of [living in the world and attaining liberation]?

This kind of person is difficult to meet even in a trillion generations and is hard to catch even among a hundred million people. The attraction of attached love is like that between steel and a magnet. If one is deficient in tolerance, it is quite difficult to avoid attached love while living in the secular world. To be able to do as did our founding teacher Śākyamuni—who abode in Tuṣita Heaven with the name Prabhāpāla Bodhisattva[28] and then descended into [this world in] the royal palace with the name Siddhârtha—how could he have been lacking in tolerance?! It would be like "the sun being ashamed of its far-reaching illumination or the upper realm being embarrassed about the disappearance of its conditions."[29]

Even while passing through the clutches of attached love, he was never to be defiled by his entanglement in attached love. He would aspire to become the example for future generations—the rightful heir to the golden wheel. Without any announcement to his father and mother, he slipped away, entering the Himalayas. Showing little regard for his own life, he practiced strict discipline, steadily, without wavering, waiting out the full extinction of all his emotional attachments. Only after the his luminosity had shown in its full brilliance did he return home for audience with his father and ascend to heaven to pay respects to his mother. Through his teachings on the essentials of the Dharma, he brought both of them to liberation. This is an example of the sages' merging with the Way by utilizing expedient methods to adapt to conditions even though they act contrary to eternal societal principles.

5. Societal Obligations

Furthermore, the Buddha had fully achieved the three awarenesses[30] and six superknowledges,[31] the four kinds of wisdom,[32] and eight types of liberation.[33] His virtue would be known to all the world in later generations. Because of this, all in the world in later generations would praise his parents as the parents of a great sage. All of those descendants of his lineage who renounced the world came to be praised as "children of the Buddha." Who can say that this is not great filial piety? Did not Confucius say, "Establishing yourself and practicing the Way, your name is known to later generations. This is the fullest expression of filial piety"?[34] Through this Way he gave guidance to all people in later ages, causing all those of later ages to hear his teaching and experience his transformation. Thus those of both great and small capacity received his Dharma and attained liberation. How could this not be called "great compassion"? Did not Confucius say, "If for a full day you overcome yourself and return to propriety, all under heaven will return to humaneness"?[35]

[The Confucians argue,] saying: Those who are born into this world are obliged to be fully loyal to their ruler, to support their state with utmost sincerity. But the Buddhists do not come for audience with the emperor and do not act in the service of the nobles. Far removed from the concerns of the secular world, they sit and observe its vicissitudes. Can this be called loyalty?

[But I] say: In [Buddhism] it is taught that one who would become a ruler must first receive the precepts, purifying his body and mind. Only after this may he ascend to the jeweled throne. The teachings also call for all monks not to fail to light incense in the morning and light the lamps in the evening, praying for the ruler and the state. Can this not be characterized as loyalty?

Furthermore, while the ruler encourages goodness through the awarding of rank and emolument and discourages evil through the exacting of punishments, our Buddha teaches the people that doing good brings happiness and that doing evil invites disaster. When people hear this, they naturally rein in their evil thoughts and arouse good intentions. Our Buddha's teaching does not encourage [good behavior] through the provisional awarding of rank and emolument nor use authority to enforce penalties. Instead, it leads people to be stimulated toward self-transformation. How could this not be a great help to the ruler and state?

6. Harming Life

[The Confucians argue,] saying: People eat living creatures, and living creatures sustain people. This is certainly the natural course of things. And if those in their seventies are not fed meat, their stomachs will not be filled. Therefore those who take care of the elderly cannot fail to serve them with meat.[36] Also, the methods of hunting for spring, summer, fall, and winter are the means by which the ancient kings helped the people avoid difficulty. These systems, which are established according to the change in seasons, cannot be altered. Furthermore, sacrificial animals have been used as ceremonial objects for making offerings from ancient times to the present. This practice also clearly cannot be abandoned. Now, the parents of Buddhists become aged, but [Buddhists] do not feed them delicacies nor do they serve them meats. They also teach people to abandon the systems established by the ancient kings and the ritual of sacrifice. Is this not excessive?[37]

[But to this, I] say: The doing of violence to heaven's creatures is something in which the sage will have no part. How much less so could one who manifests the Heavenly Way and perfectly accomplished humanity encourage people to kill life in order to nourish life! The *Book of History* says, "Heaven and earth are the parents of all creatures, and of all creatures, man is the most highly endowed with intelligence. Only the most intelligent among men becomes the great sovereign, and the great sovereign becomes the parent of the people."[38] Since heaven and earth are already the mother and father of all things, then those things that are born within heaven and earth are all the children of heaven and earth. So the relationship of heaven and earth to its creatures is just like that between parents and children. Children naturally differ in terms of aptitude, just as human beings and the myriad creatures differ in intelligence. But even if a child is slow-witted, the parents will not turn away from it — in fact, they will love it and treat it with special care. They will even have special concern as to whether or not it is able to attain its proper sustenance. How could they possibly go so far as to inflict harm upon it?

Killing life in order to nourish life is like one's own child killing a sibling in order to nourish itself. If children are killing each other in order to nourish themselves, how are the parents going to feel about this? To have their children killing each other is certainly not the parents' wish. So how could the mutual inflicting of harm between human beings and the other creatures be the will of heaven and earth? Human beings and the myriad things already share in their possession of the material force of heaven and earth. They also share in their possession of the principle of heaven and earth and dwell together in the space of heaven and earth. Sharing as they do in the same material force and the same principle, how could there be a principle that condones the killing of life in order to nourish life? It is like the saying "heaven and earth and I share the same root, the myriad things and I share the same body"[39] — these are the words of the Buddha. "The man of humanity forms one body with heaven and earth and the myriad things"[40] — these are the words of a Confucian. Only when one's actions fully accord with these words can we say that someone has fully achieved the Way of humaneness.

7. The Meaning of Humaneness

The term in the medical texts for numbness in the hands and feet is "non-humaneness."[41] The hands and feet are the extremities of the body. Even if one has only a slight sickness, the material force will not penetrate them. Therefore humaneness implies the interpenetration of heaven and earth and the myriad things into a single body wherein there is no gap whatsoever. If you deeply embody this principle, then there cannot be a justification for inflicting harm on even the most insignificant of creatures. This, indeed, can be called the actualization of the Way of the humane man.

It is like the stories of the goose and the pearl[42] and the monk tied by the grass.[43] This is the kind of person we are referring to here. If one's actualization of humaneness is not like this, then between humans and creatures, material force is obstructed and does not flow; the principle is blocked and does not penetrate. It is like the numbness of the hands and feet. This is why the name in the medical texts for a healthy condition is "humaneness."

The *Book of Odes* says, "One arrow for five boars."[44] The *Analects* says, "When fishing, the master would not use a net; when hunting, he would not shoot at a perched bird."[45] The *Mencius* says, "The noble man keeps his distance from the kitchen, for if he hears the screams of slaughtered beasts, he cannot stand to eat their meat."[46] It also says, "If fine-mesh nets are not used for fishing, there will always be fish and turtles for eating in abundance."[47] These are all examples of an incomplete practice of humaneness. Why don't they live up to the paradigm of forming a single body with the myriad things? The *Doctrine of the Mean* says, "His words reflecting his actions, his actions reflecting his words — how can this noble man not be sincere through and through?"[48] Now, where have we seen this actualized? This is a clear example of the Confucians' skillfully expounding the Way of humaneness but not being thoroughly good. If you think that it is necessary to minimize killing, then why is it necessary to even shoot the arrow at all? If you take pity on birds that are perched, why shoot at them when they are not perched? If you are already keeping your distance from the kitchen, why eat meat at all? If the small are already being subjected to injury, why is it necessary to inflict harm upon the large?

In his Mahāyāna Vinaya, the Buddha placed the precept of not taking life first. Also, the *Yiqiezhi guangming xianren cixin yinyuan bushirou jing* (Sutra on the Omniscient Luminous Sages Who Possess the Causes and Conditions of Compassion in Not Eating Meat) says, "As the Buddha has taught, the eating of meat reflects a deficiency in one's practice of compassion. One will inevitably shorten one's life and undergo numerous sicknesses, becoming lost and submerged in birth-and-death and unable to become a Buddha."[49] Furthermore, Buddhism's recommendation of the use of water filters is based on a concern for taking the life of minute creatures. Once upon a time there were two monks who, intent on seeing the Buddha, traveled through a desert. Being thirsty, they happened upon some water that had bugs in it. One monk said, "We are going to see the Buddha. What harm can there be in drinking?" And so saying, he went ahead and drank. The other monk said, "The Buddha has prohibited the taking of life. If we break the Buddha's prohibitions, even if we see him, what benefit can there be?" He endured his thirst and did not drink. After dying [the second monk] was reborn in the heavenly realm, where he was able to directly see the Buddha and receive his praise. We can call this the genuine words and true actions of the humane man, which accords precisely with the claim of "forming a single body" and "being sincere through and through."

One time, during the period when I had not yet entered the Buddhist order, a monk named Haewŏl (海月) was reading the *Analects* to me. He reached the passage that says:

> [Zi Gong asked:] "Suppose there were a ruler who benefited the people far and wide and was capable of bringing salvation to the multitude, what would you think of him? Might he be called humane?" The Master said, "Why only humane? He would undoubtedly be a sage. Even Yao and Shun would have had to work hard to achieve this."[50]

He commented, "The humane man forms a single body with heaven and earth and the myriad things." With this, he put the scroll aside and asked me, "Was Mencius a humane man?" "Yes," I replied. "Are 'fowl, pigs, dogs, and swine' to be counted among the 'myriad things?'" "Yes," I replied. [Haewŏl continued, citing Cheng Hao,] "The humane man forms a single body with heaven and earth and the myriad things." If this statement is to be taken as a true expression of the principle, how are we supposed to see Mencius as humane? If "fowl, pigs, dogs, and swine" are to be counted among the "myriad things," then how could Mencius say, "If, in the raising of fowl, pigs, dogs, and swine, their breeding times are not missed, then people in their seventies can eat meat."[51] I was completely stymied by this question and could not answer. I pondered over all of the classical transmissions and could not come up with a single text that could support a principle condoning the taking of life. I inquired widely among the brightest thinkers of the day, but not one of them could clarify the matter to resolve my perplexity.

This doubt remained buried within my mind for a long time without being resolved. Then, while traveling around Samgak-san in 1396, I arrived at Seunggasa (僧伽寺), where I had the chance to chat with an old Sŏn monk throughout the night. The monk said, "In Buddhism there are ten grave precepts, the first of which is to not take life." Upon hearing this explanation, my mind was suddenly overturned, and I recognized for myself that this was indeed the behavior of the truly humane man. I was thereupon able to deeply embody the teachings of the Way of humaneness. From that time forth, I was never again confused regarding the differences between Confucianism and Buddhism. I subsequently composed a verse, which went:

Up till now, knowing only the teachings of the classics and histories
And the criticisms of the Chengs and Zhu,
I was unable to recognize whether the Buddha was wrong or right.
But after reflecting deep in my mind for long years,
Knowing the truth for the first time, I reject [Confucianism]
And take refuge in [the Buddhadharma].

The creatures that make nests understand the wind; those that dig holes understand the rain; spiders possess the skill of weaving and dung beetles are adept at rolling things. All creatures are like this, sharing in the same inherent intelligence. Furthermore, sharing in the emotion of loving life and hating to be killed, how do they differ from human beings? Hearing the sound of ripping flesh and the cutting of the knife, they are in utter fright as they approach their death. Their eyes are wild and they cry out in agony. How could they not harbor bitter and resentful sentiments? And yet people are able to turn a deaf ear. In this way human beings and the creatures of the world affect each other without awareness and compensate each other without pause. How could a humane person observe such suffering and continue to act as if nothing was wrong?

The satisfaction of our addictions of taste is compared with the pain we must endure. Pain and pleasure are clear as day, and light and heavy can be measured. When the teaching of cause and effect is forgotten like this, one pursues one's activities with abandon. If one does not ignore cause and effect, then the impending suffering is to be expected. Should we not be careful? Even though the variations of hunting in spring, summer, fall, and winter are customs established by the kings of antiquity, there are also presently places between the mountains and within the islands and seas where the practice of hunting has not reached. Human beings and animals each pursue their own lives, each at home in their own places, living out their naturally ordained years with satisfaction. Observing this, why should it be necessary for these people to depend on hunting to be able to live out their lives well?

The ancient sages taught people to live without corralling and trapping wild beasts.[52] By this we know that killing was not permissible, yet there were cases where killing was carried out. Why was it not permitted as a general rule? In some cases it was found that it was not necessary to adhere to this principle. Still, why should the cases of non-adherence to the principle of not-killing end up becoming the general practice? The *Yijing* says, "The ancients were sharp of sense and keen in intelligence; they utilized supernatural martial power without killing."[53] Now, the sages took the hunting methods of the four seasons and instructed the people how to utilize supernatural martial power to ward of foreign invaders. How could it be that they had killing as their original intention? This is merely a great expedient for all under heaven and nothing more.

If we observe the matter in this way, then the correctness of this "hunting" is exactly equivalent to that of "extending one's hand to save a drowning sister-in-law."[54] Extending one's hand to save one's sister-in-law is just an action that one takes according to the necessity of the moment. How could [the physical contact with women other than one's wife] ever be regarded as a constant principle of human relationships? We can extend the same argument to the matter of the sacrifice of animals. A person lives out his daily life regarding meat as the most prized delicacy. Because of this love of the taste of meat, when he dies [his relatives] think it most appropriate for meat to have a place in the ritual. In this way, beyond the sprinkling of water and the covering with ice, a crime must also be included. Once in the past there was a man who was to kill a lamb in sacrifice for his ancestor, but his ancestor told him in a dream that the killing was forbidden. This was a sign, and if we view it based on this precedent, then we can say that even though the killing of animals makes the sacrifice richer, it is also something that can be done away with.

8. Drinking Alcohol

[The Confucians argue] saying: Alcohol is the lubricant for festive gatherings; it relaxes the blood flow and wards off the effects of the wind and cold. It also is used for sacrificial rituals, drinking games, and to summon the spirits at the sacrifice. We can't do without it. But now the Buddha has forbidden it in his precepts. Isn't this a bit too severe?

[In response to this, I] say: Alcohol is the root cause of dissolution of the spirit and the decay of virtue, bringing deep harm to the Way. Therefore the Vinaya contains over thirty-six items that point out its dangers. The Confucian scholars themselves have clearly noted its faults, saying, "Inside, it dulls the will; outside, it ruins one's dignity."[55] These words well clarify the extreme nature of its dangers. Dulling the will within, it blocks self-cultivation; ruining one's dignity without, it impairs one's ability to teach others. Not only is there no benefit for oneself and others, it invites calamity without limit. Therefore Yi Di's offering of drink resulted in enmity with Yu, and the *arhat*'s drinking resulted in his being scolded by the Buddha.

Given Yu's enmity with Yi Di and the Buddha's scolding of the *arhat*, how could one not see the perils of alcohol? It inevitably leads people to licentiousness and dissolution, including the destruction of self, the ruination of the Way, the usurpation of the state, and the loss of position. One who is preparing to make an offering to the spirits of heaven and earth is expected to first engage in several days of purification [in the form of abstinence]. Only after this may one carry out the one-day ritual. "Purification" entails abstaining from the consumption of pungent foods[56] and alcohol, along with maintaining the attitude of utmost sincerity in order to attain to a pure state. If your sincerity does not attain to utmost purity, then the spirits will not receive your offerings. With the purification of the Buddhist discipline, sincerity endures long without disturbance. Once purified, you remain unpolluted for the rest of your life. So if you compare that to these several days, how can heaven and earth be far away? And once you know this purity is right, how can you just maintain it for several days and stop? Outside of the several days connected to the sacrifice, shall we abandon all restraints? In this we can see a significant difference between Confucianism and Buddhism.

9. Making Offerings

[The Confucians] say: Wealth and possessions are things on which people depend for their livelihood. They are to be used in due measure, to be saved without being wasted so that they can be handed on to their descendants, ensuring the continuity of the family sacrifice, such that [one's descendants] do not fall on hard times. But the Buddhists hide themselves outside the range of society and do not serve the king. Isn't this already enough? But they go even further and deceive people with the doctrine of the making of offerings for karmic reward. Causing these people to exhaust their finances in offerings to the Buddha, they end up hungry, cold, and destitute. Is this not excessive?!

[In response to this, I] say: Wealth and possessions are the instruments of endless craving and the summoning of disaster. The making of offerings is none other than a means of purifying the heart and inducing good fortune. Don't the Confucian scholars say that "when wealth is gathered then the people scatter; when wealth is scattered then the people gather"?[57] The Buddha did not encourage people to make offerings for his own benefit. His only intent was to enable people to destroy their stinginess and craving—to purify the mind-ground and nothing more. The Buddha also admonished his *bhikṣus* regarding the three "not enoughs." These are clothing, food, and sleep, the three things that people can never get enough of. Given that the Buddha admonished his disciples about this, why would he ask people to make donations just to get clothing and food?! [If the simple acquisition of food and clothing were his only aim,] how could the Buddha's teaching have [had the power to] reach down to the present day?

10. Defense of the Doctrine of Karma and Rebirth

As for the theory of karmic reward, how can it be claimed that this teaching is only found in our school? The *Yijing* says, "When you accumulate virtue you will have abundant good fortune; when you accumulate evil you will have abundant calamity."[58] Another example is the teaching given in the *Hongfan* (Great Plan) to the effect that when the people accord with ultimate principles, heaven rewards them with the five blessings.[59] When they do not go along with such principles, then heaven responds by bringing about the six extremes.[60] What is this if not karmic reward? It is already obvious that there is karmic reward while the bodily form is still present. But also after dying—even though the body disappears, the spirit remains. How could it not be the case that we experience good and evil retribution? The Buddha once said, "Even after the passage of a hundred thousand eons, the karma that one has created does not disappear. When the right causes and conditions are encountered, the fruits of each action return to oneself."[61] How could the Buddha be deceiving people?

[The Confucians] say: Human life comes into being through the combination of yin and yang. We receive our material substance from the yin and receive our material force from the yang. One part yin and one part yang are distributed as the *hun* (K. *hon*) and *po* (K. *paek*) souls in the formation of beings. Upon dying, the *hun* soul rises and the *po* soul sinks, completely disappearing.

That by which human beings have intelligence is the mind. This mind is the master of the body that is formed by the combination of the *hun* and *po* souls. At death it separates from the material force: the bodily form becomes non-existent and the spirit ascends to abide in the realm of darkness. Who is there to be the recipient of fortune and calamity? The Buddhists try to encourage people with the concept of a heavenly realm and to scare them with talk of hell. This makes people confused. Heaven is something clear and spacious. It consists of the moon, stars, and other celestial bodies, and nothing more. The earth is made of soil and rock, and those who are supported by it are humans and the myriad beings.[62] To claim that the person who dies does not disappear but continues to exist in heaven or hell, isn't this nonsense?

[I respond to this by] saying: There is no doubt that humans depend upon the forces of yin and yang for their coming-into-existence. It is through the merging of yin and yang that we receive life. It is because of their separation that we die. If humans possess an intrinsic intelligence, then it neither arises nor disappears depending on form. Though it passes through myriad transformations it remains still and independent.

There are two kinds of mind: the "intrinsically real mind" and the "corporeal mind." The corporeal mind is the essence of the *hun* and *po* souls. The intrinsically real mind refers to the real intelligence. The mind under discussion here is the intrinsically real mind and not the corporeal mind.

The mind is the master of the body, and the body is the servant of the mind. The various activities of good and evil are ordered by the mind-lord and carried out by the form-minister. When it comes to the point of receiving the karmic retribution for one's actions, if one is alive, then the lord and minister both receive them. If one is dead, then the form-minister has already passed away and the mind-lord alone receives them. The *Book of Odes* says, "King Wen ascends and descends on the left and right of the lord-on-high."[63] If he is "ascending and descending," how could King Wen not be a spirit abiding in heaven?

Long ago there was a man of ability named Wang Huaizhi.[64] From his youth he did not believe in the Buddhist teachings. One day he died and upon his rebirth said, "In the past I was sure that the bodily form and the spirit both perished together. Now I know for the first time that the Buddha's teaching that the body disappears and the spirit lives on is the truth and not a deception."[65]

There is also the story of Li Yuan of the Song and the monk Yuanze,[66] friends who promised to stay with each other age after age. One day while traveling together, Yuanze, seeing an [elegantly dressed] woman drawing water, said, "This woman is from the Wang family and I will be her child. Twelve years hence, I will meet you outside Tianzhu temple in order to make clear our mutual understanding." When evening arrived Yuanze actually died. After twelve years, Li Yuan, proceeding toward the keeping of his promise, heard that there was a lad leading an ox along the banks of the Gehong River who sang the following song: "On the stone of three lives is an old spirit; appreciating the beauty of nature, it's not necessary to speak. Embarrassed, my intimate friend comes from afar to meet; although this body changes, the nature is everlasting." When they met each other, he said, "Mr. Li—my trusted gentleman!" He again sang, "Before this body and after, events are without limit; we want to speak of previous lifetimes but we fear the heartbreak; I sought throughout the mountains and rivers of Wu and Yue, returning in a light boat, going up to Qutang."[67]

In addition, there are the stories of Yang Hu, who was discovered to be the son of Mr. Li in a former lifetime[68] and the son of the Wang family, who [was reborn as] the grandson of Cai.[69] Having seen this story, I offer a verse for Li-Yang.

Li and Yang are but one person;
The bracelets in his departure and return were not different.

Who would have known that a seven-year-old boy had returned
 five years after dying?

For Wang Cai, I offer this verse.

The boy who was formerly of the Wang family
Is now a grandson of Mr. Cai.

Without having to make a stroke of the brush
The discussion of sameness and difference becomes confused.

Reflecting on these examples, we should be able to realize that the numinous intelligence does not change following the bodily form. Is it not ignorant to say that at death the bodily form together with the spirit both disappear? As far as heaven and hell are concerned, these are not inherently existent places; [rather] they are naturally brought about by people's karmic activity. Confucius once said, "Alas, it has been a long time since I have dreamt of the Duke of Zhou!"[70] Dreams are the wandering of the human spirit, not the agents of the bodily form. Confucius used to dream of the Duke of Zhou because his mind was constantly dwelling in the Way of the Duke of Zhou, and he strove to act accordingly. Since his spirit was naturally attuned to this Way, he had this experience.

All people are like this. Daily, they concentrate their energies on good or evil. In their dreams the good see prosperity while the evil see disgrace. Because of this, the good endeavor with all their energies, following only what is right. The evil become more avaricious, seeking nothing but personal gain. Since the good follow only what is right, they do what is proper in each situation. The evil, seeking nothing but personal gain, act contrary to what is right in each situation. Since the good do what is proper in each situation, people will necessarily regard them as good. Since the evil do what is wrong in each situation, people will necessarily regard them to be evil. Since people regard the good as good, when the time comes for them to be noticed, they will be rewarded with rank and commensurate salary. Since people regard the evil as evil, when the time comes for them to be noticed, their retribution will be punishment. Because of this, the good person continually enhances his goodness and his happiness effervesces. The evil person is tangled in confusion and plots to escape his demise.

Good and evil habits are stored in the mind along with sentiments of joy and displeasure. Thus, in our dreams we see splendor and debasement. When the spirit departs, it does not return but proceeds directly to the next rebirth. This is why the good person experiences the heavenly realm and the evil person experiences hell. Heaven and hell are not created by someone else. When people hear about heaven, they yearn for it and endeavor in the pursuit of goodness. Wanting to avoid hell, they refrain from evil activities. In this way the teaching of heaven and hell serves to transform people. Is this not of great benefit? If this is indeed the case, the good definitely ascend to heaven, while the evil certainly descend to hell. Therefore, if you let people know this, the good endeavor so that they will ascend to the heavenly palace, while the evil restrain themselves so that they do not fall into hell. Why is it necessary to reject the teaching of heaven and hell and to regard it as nonsense?

11. Defense of the Buddhist Practice of Cremation

[The Confucians criticize,] saying: "The sending off of departed souls is a grave matter in the human world."[71] Therefore, one cannot fail to take seriously the matter of preparing a proper funeral for one' parents. The sages taught people the proper order for a lavish funeral to send off one's departed parents in order to demonstrate the gravity of [their feelings]. The matter of having a lavish funeral can be compared to that of a tree and its roots. If its roots are deep, then its branches and leaves spread out luxuriantly in all directions and its fruits are plentiful. If its roots are shallow, then its branches and leaves will be stunted and it will bear no fruit. The relationship of parents to children is like that of a tree to its fruit. The relationship of children to parents is like that of fruit to a tree. Therefore it is said, "The father's transmission through his son is like the transmission of a tree through its fruit." Therefore when it comes to burying the dead, one must select the proper land, make the burial hole deep, make lavish [the funeral] ritual, plant trees in abundance, and store up water. You must deepen the shadow of the tree and nurture your material force. The earth must be fertile and not barren. This will allow your descendants to prosper and the family sacrifice will continue without interruption.

Now, the Buddhists, not reflecting on this principle, have foolishly established the custom of cremation, causing people to lose their posterity, cutting off their descendants. Is this not excessive? Even more, how can the children bear to watch such a sight as the cremation of their parents? In this confusion, the transgressions of people fill all of heaven.

[In response to this, I] say: The human being consists of both bodily form and spirit. The bodily form is comparable to a house, and the spirit is comparable to the master of the house. The fading of the form and the flight of the spirit is just like the collapse of the house and its master's loss of his dwelling. This house was built from earth and wood and decorated by a mixture of dirty things. People regard it as part of themselves, and becoming attached to its interior, they are not aware of how dirty a thing it is. Even though they personally witness its collapse, they are not able to readily forget about it and leave it.

The body takes [the elements of] water and earth for the composition of its form and takes fire and wind to constitute its substance. Within are contained various defilements and a flowing river of impurity, yet people protect these with greater energy than they would protect gold or jewelry. Why should they ever feel any notion of disgust or detachment in regard to the body? When they die the elements of fire and wind are the first to disappear, while the elements of earth and water remain. Since the earthly and watery aspects were precisely that to which they were previously attached and which they protected, [their spirit] is not able to readily forget and appropriately depart without obstruction. Therefore the wise burn away the earth and water elements and point the spirit along its proper course to the next existence. The spirit is no longer obstructed by feelings of attachment and is just like the higher pneuma that ascends to purity.[72]

It is for this reason that our World Honored Buddha, in carefully carrying out his father's funeral, lit the bier himself. The kings of the four heavens carried the casket; the *arhat*s gathered the firewood and carried out the cremation. This enabled his father's spirit to ascend in purity to a heavenly rebirth. In order to bring about the salvation of his mother, Huangbo Yungong opened his heart and implored the Buddha [for her salvation] and then threw the flaming torch onto the bier in the river. In the midst of this blaze, his mother was transformed into a man, and her body was carried on a great beam of light, bringing her up to the heavenly palace. People on both sides of the river all watched with amazement. The river, which had been named Fu River, was renamed by a government official as the Ford of Great Justice.

If we look at it like this, then the custom of cremation is something that allows people to be cleansed of defilement and attain to purity, to purify the spirit and let it return to rise up to heaven. It is a way of lending support in advancing to the next rebirth; it is a great norm that has been transmitted to the world. If you cannot bear to perform a cremation, then go ahead and dig a hole and bury your parents. Can you stand this? Nowadays there are, at the foot of the mountains and in the midst of great plains, numerous ancient graves that have been plowed under by farmers. Skulls are scattered around like the stars; they are baked by the sun and blown in the wind without anyone to look after them. This happens even though, at the beginning, their children did not fail to set up monuments and plant evergreens to decorate the grounds so that they could plan on the prosperity of their descendants and the unbroken continuity of the family sacrifice. So how has it come to this?

However, prior to birth the five aggregates are all empty and the six faculties are pure. And if for one moment thought does not arise, then even though [the spirit] dwells in the world abiding in form, since it is [actually] a visiting spirit whose true existence is outside the physical world, it merges, clear and transparent, with the sky. Deep and unfathomable, it is like the ocean. Since the existence of the body is illusory, the act of cremation is like removing a wart or cleaning off a stain; it is like untying bonds or being released from a pillory; it is like a bird taking flight from a cage, like a horse escaping its stable, free, unbounded, roaming at ease; [it is like] following one's heart's desire, leaving and staying without obstruction. How can one remain stuck in the sentimental attachment to earth and water?!

This person, in the process of disintegration, may be buried underground or may be exposed to the air. You can cut a hole in the rocks and entomb someone or dig a hole and bury them, and they will still end up being burnt away in wildfires or eaten by bugs. There is no limit to what can happen, hence, situations like Bodhidharma's entombment at Xiong'er,[73] the persistence of the corpse of the Sixth Patriarch,[74] Puhua's departure with the tinkling of bells,[75] and Qingliang's offering of his life to the beasts of the forest.[76] These are lofty examples of casting off the world and excellent precedents of forgetting the self, all carried out by men of great ability. If you do not have the ability of these men, then you will not be capable of the selflessness that abandons the bodily form. It is therefore only by passing through the process of cremation that your spirit can be pure and ascend without hindrance. When someone who is traveling dies in another village outside his hometown, if you gather up his bones and burn them, his subsequent good reputation will stand out in the world and the respect that he is due can return to him. His descendants will flourish and his family sacrifice will continue uninterrupted. To say that cremation will prevent one's merits from benefiting one's posterity is nothing but an extreme of selfish worry and mistaken imagination. Don't wait in vain for a report from the divine tortoise while engaged in baseless discussions!

[The Confucians object,] saying: The birth and death of human beings is exactly their beginning and end. Therefore Confucius only spoke about what occurs between birth and death and never discussed what comes before and after.[77] But Buddhists speak of the before and after, putting it together with the time of birth and death, referring to this combination as the "three times." That which comes before life and follows after death is something with which the ears and eyes have never had contact. Who has personally seen these things? Is it not deceptive to confuse people with these ideas?

[In response to this, I] say: The birth and death of human beings is just like the transition of day and night. Since there is transition, there is naturally before and after. When it is daytime, then the night that has passed is before and the coming night is after. When it is nighttime, then the day that has passed is before and the coming day is after. In this way, day and night, when arranged together, naturally constitute the three divisions of time. Since day and night are like this, the same holds true for months and years. Since months and years are like this, the same holds true for birth and death. The beginninglessness of the past and the endlessness of the future can also be known through this. The *Yijing* says, "[The Changes] illuminate the past and interpret the future" and "[Words] clarify the results of loss and gain."[78] How could the words "going and coming" not imply the same thing as "before and after"? To regard the teaching of the three divisions of time as trickery is beyond my comprehension.

12. Refutation of the Complaint against Buddhism as a Foreign Religion

[The Confucians complain, saying:]   The only Way in the world that deserves our veneration is that of the five emperors and three kings, and nothing more. Therefore that which was related by the sagely ancestor Confucius, and has been successively transmitted by numerous worthies, serves as the support for all methods [of governing] and is a standard for statehood that all respect. This Way is to be sought in the Middle Kingdom, and is

not to be sought among the barbarian tribes. The Buddha was a
Western barbarian. How is it that his Way came to permeate the
Middle Kingdom? The story about Ming Di of the Han seeking
the Dharma in the Western regions is vague and unclear.

[In response to this, I] say: He who embodies the Way is the one whom
the people will rely upon. Since the Way was embodied by the
five emperors and three kings, the people relied upon them,
and thus they were the rulers of China. The Buddha's flourishing in India as a king who turned the wheel of the Dharma is
the same sort of thing. The Chinese referring to India as the
West is just the same as the Indians' referring to China as the
East. If we want to find the great center of the world, then it
would be the place where no shadow can be seen at twelve
noon. Since this happens in India and since the Buddha appeared to the world in India, why not regard India as the "great
center" of the world?

"East" and "West" are nothing more than names applied to this or
that place according to the situation. There is no such thing as occupying
the center and determining East and West. If we do not respect the Way
of the Buddha because he is a barbarian, then shall we also not respect the
ways of Shun, who was born among the eastern tribes, and King Wen,
who was born among the western tribes? Can we disparage a person's
Way just on the basis of his being foreign? [It should rather be based on]
the results of his works and the Way that governed his behavior. However, in observing whether one's Way is to be respected or not, it is better
not to be too much attached to external appearances.

Haven't we already said it? He who embodies the Way is the one the
people will rely on. The *Spring and Autumn Annals* takes Xu's attack of Ju
as the act of "barbarians." But when the northern barbarians and the Qi al-
lied themselves with Xing, they were recognized as members of the Middle Kingdom.[79] Xu's being Chinese and yet being labeled a "barbarian"
was because of his lack of a sense of justice. The northern tribes received
the name of Middle Kingdom because they had a sense of justice. Generally speaking, honor and debasement are differentiated by just observing
people's brightness and dimness and by the correctness and incorrectness
of their works. How could you possibly discuss a person's worth based
on where he comes from? It is like trying to know the Way that someone
practices without investigating his works. Hence, even the Way of the five
precepts and ten virtuous actions need feel no shame before the Way of
the five emperors and three kings. How much more so with such teach-

ings as the [four] noble truths, dependent arising, and the six perfections? If it were possible to have the five emperors and three kings encounter these teachings, they would without doubt place their palms together, get down on their knees, and humbly receive the teaching. Was it not appropriate for Ming Di to seek this Dharma?

13. Refutation of the Accusation of Buddhism as a Harbinger of Calamity

[The Confucians argue] saying: Since the time that the Buddhadharma entered China, there has been a degeneration of culture, famine, and a succession of natural disasters. The people have suffered loss in many ways and the periods of pestilence have been extreme. Has not the harm been great?!

[In answer to this, I] say: Yao, Shun, Yu, and Tang have all been regarded by the world as great sages, yet they were unable to avoid the disasters of flooding and drought. Jie, Zhou, You, and Li were known to the world as important men but were unable to avoid becoming isolated. Once the Zhou declined, the people were already in a poor condition. With the arrival of the Jin, the realm descended into great chaos. Confucius is regarded as a great sage, but he was unable to avoid running out of food. Yan Hui was considered to be a near-sage but could not avoid a premature death.[80] Yuan Xian was a great worthy, but he could not avoid poverty in his household.[81] Are these all the fault of the Buddha? The time of the Buddha's flourishing in India coincided precisely with that of the peak of the Zhou. Later on, during the reign of Ming Di,[82] the Dharma flowed into the Eastern lands. But before the time of the Three Dynasties,[83] Buddhism did not exist in China. During the time of Confucius and Yan Hui, the Buddha's name had not even been heard. [It follows] that at that time there should have been no such thing as natural disasters, nor should there have been starvation. So why did Yao experience nine years of flooding and why did Tang experience seven years of drought? How did Confucius and Yan Hui come to be in dire straits, and how did the household of Yuan Xian come into poverty?

Tang Taizong, Wei Zheng, Li Chunfeng, and others worked together with all of their heart and their power to unify the realm and bring all of its people harmony such that good tidings were heard in all lands. Queen Chindŏk of the Silla herself composed the "Song of Peaceful Reign," which she embroidered on silk brocade.[84] This poem, in brief, said:

> Great Tang has produced a great work,
> His glorious empire shines brightly;
> He has stopped war and exercised his authority,
> Making all the kings into men of culture;
> His deep humaneness is equal to that of the sun and moon,
> His handling of the multitudes surpasses that of Yao and Shun…
> From the peaks descend his high ministers;
> The emperor depends upon those who are loyal and good,
> The virtues of the five emperors and three kings are combined
>   in one,
> Illuminating my Tang family sovereign.

In the same way King Taejong Chunchu of Silla worked together with Kim Yusin to combine the three kingdoms into one. Great benefit was [thereby] brought to society.

During those years the harvest was plentiful and commodity prices were cheap. The people were joyful and without anxiety. All regarded this as an enlightened era. If the Buddhadharma really brings about a decline in peace and prosperity, why is it that during precisely this period when the spread of the Buddhist teaching was at its peak, peace and prosperity attained such great heights? The Chan master Zhaozhou Ren lived several hundred seasons; the founding patriarch of Mount Wutai lived for some three hundred years. If the Buddhadharma is something that shortens people's lives, how is it that these Buddhists managed to live to such an advanced age? Ancient and modern, order and disorder, long and short, suffering and pleasure, the waxing and waning according to major junctures in one's life—these all happen directly according to the behavior and activities of people. To look upon things like a decline in peace and prosperity or the inability of people to obtain their livelihood and place the blame on the Buddhadharma is simply ridiculous.

14. Refutation of the Accusation of Monks Being Parasites

[The Confucians complain,] saying: The Buddhists roam about idly
        avoiding the responsibilities of society. Not working for the
        production of either silk or grains, they depend on others for

their food and clothing. Because of this the people suffer, often
being forced into destitution. Is their decadence not great?

[In response to this, I] say: The duty of the monks lies in spreading
the Dharma and bringing benefit to sentient beings. By their
spreading of the Dharma they cause wisdom and life not to be
severed. By bringing benefit to the people, they cause each person to proceed toward goodness. This is the job of the monks.
Who else is capable of performing this task? Therefore, there is
no need for them to be embarrassed about receiving alms from
the people. If a monk proves incapable of [meeting] his responsibilities, it is an individual fault. How could it be the fault of
the Buddha? Mencius said, "Here is a man who is filial at home
and respectful to those he meets in the world. He preserves the
Way of the ancient kings so that it may be picked up by later
scholars. Yet he does not receive his sustenance from you. Why
do you respect the carpenter and the wheelwright and show
disdain for the humane and just man?"[85]

Why does it now suddenly become incorrect for those who preserve
the Way and elevate the consciousnesses of people to receive food and
clothing from those people? Whether one will be wealthy or poor in this
life is based on his karmic predisposition. If one has an abundance of good
seeds from prior lifetimes, then even if he spends money every day, he
will always have extra. But if one lacks good seeds from the prior lifetime,
then even if he saves every day, he will never have enough. There are
people in this world who, upon seeing a buddha, do not show respect,
and seeing monks, vilify them. They never once in their whole lives offer
a single cent for alms. They do not have enough clothes to cover their bodies or enough food to satisfy their stomachs. Have they also come to this
condition because of the *saṃgha*?

15. Refutation of the Charge of Decadence in the *Saṃgha*

[The Confucians complain,] saying: Purification and the reduction of desires, abandoning oneself in pursuit of the Dharma, studying [the
scriptures] widely and memorizing deeply, kindly instructing
those who come after—these are definitely the proper activities of
Buddhists. But the present-day monks do not engage in religious
cultivation; they oppose and defile their teacher's Dharma. When
people question them as to their Way, it is like standing and

facing a wall. They peddle the Tathāgata to garner the necessary
sustenance to preserve themselves. They dwell in regular houses
and act like secular people. They enrich themselves through the
means of regular society and even become ministers in the government. How can the ruler of the state stand for this?

[In answer to this, I] say: The *qilin* and the phoenix do not form flocks.
Exceedingly rare gems are not to be found in the local mar-
ketplaces. Among the three thousand disciples of Confucius,
those who can be called men of truly outstanding intelligence
numbered no more than ten. Among the vast ocean of the
Tathāgata's disciples, those who were categorized as first-rate
also numbered no more than ten. Now, as the time of those
sages passes further and further away and the religious faculties of people grow ever weaker, how can you expect every
single person to be able to possess the morality of Kāśyapa or
the breadth of learning of Ānanda? In the thousand or so years
since the time of Confucius and Yan Hui, the likes of Yan Hui
and Min Ziqian[86] have not been heard of. For a monk to live up
to his name, [only] once he has embodied the five virtues and
cultivated the six kinds of harmony does he deserve to be called
a monk. However, when it comes to the matter of matching the
name with the reality, the problems lie with the individual. In
the forest there is wood that is not fit for use as lumber; in the
fields there are grains that do not bear fruit. Granted, there are
monks who are not capable of acting as repositories and exem-
plars of the Dharma, but one should not be overly alarmed by
these types. Even these fellows, if they formally submit to the
Dharma, will gradually be permeated by habit until it becomes
their nature and will not fail to follow the Way. How can you
castigate their Dharma based on individual failings?

16. Refutation of the Charges of Nihilism and Antinomianism

[The Confucians complain,] saying: If you examine their texts, you will
see that they strive for voidness and revere annihilation. Their
skills far surpass the teachings contained in the *Small Learning*,
and yet it is useless. Their extravagance soars over the *Great
Learning*, and yet there are no tangible results. They cannot be
used as means for the purpose of cultivating oneself and regulating others.

[In response to this, I] say: The texts are the vehicles that carry the Way;
they are the means for dissemination and transformation. In
examining the texts of a tradition, you can know whether its
Way is to be venerated or not. You can know whether its ritual
is to be emulated or not. In [determining whether] its Way can
be venerated and its ritual can be emulated, how can I dis-
card something that I have not practiced. Haven't you heard?
"Under heaven, there are not two Ways. The sages do not have
two minds."[87] The sages, even if separated by the distance of a
thousand *li* or by the time of ten thousand generations, have not
the slightest bit of difference between their minds. Confucius
said, "No willfulness, arbitrariness, stubbornness, or egotism."[88]
The *Yijing* also says, "Keeping his back still, there is no self;
going out to his courtyard, there is no person."[89] Without self
or person, how can there be defilement? The elder Śākyamuni
said, "If, without self and without person, you cultivate all good
dharmas, this is none other than the attainment of *bodhi*."[90] This
is an example of sages being from different ages but being identical in their minds.[91]

As far as the accusations of nihilism are concerned, what text among
the twelve divisions of the Tripiṭaka can you cite that contains the phrases
"vacancy" and "nihilation"? The Mahāyāna precepts say, "Pious obedience is the principle of the ultimate path. 'Piety' is synonymous with
'moral discipline' and also means 'restraint.' "[92] Can you arbitrarily call
this "vacant"? The *Sutra of Perfect Enlightenment* says, "[Your] mind-flow-
er will blossom, illuminating all the worlds in the ten directions."[93] Can
this arbitrarily be called "nihilism"? If you want to determine a teaching's
truth or falsity, you must first examine its texts. If you mindlessly reject
it without examining its texts, you will definitely be the object of derision
among scholars of ability.

Have you not you heard that if you do not exhaustively examine the
texts of the world, you cannot baselessly disparage the past and present?
Confucius said, "Filial piety is the constant of heaven; it is the fairness
of the earth and the correct behavior of the people."[94] How could it not
be the ultimate Way? "Because [the changes] reach out and penetrate the
world."[95] How could this not reflect the meaning of "bright illumination"?
What the Confucians call "illustrious virtue" is none other than what the
Buddha has called the "subtle, pristine, luminous mind." The phrase "still
and unmoving, [the] changes reach out and penetrate the world"[96] has
exactly the same connotation as the Buddhist "quiescent yet luminous."

The phrase "only after there is goodness in oneself may one critique the goodness of others; only after there is no evil in oneself can one correct the evil of others"[97] has the same connotation as our religion's "sever evil and cultivate goodness, then work for the benefit of sentient beings."[98] How are they different?

17. The Unity of the Three Teachings

If the underlying principle of the words is the same, then why should the outward appearances of the teachings differ? Holding stubbornly to one's own opinion while ignoring the positions of others, arbitrarily affirming this and rejecting that, this is the attitude ordinarily seen in people. The man of broad learning and the penetrating scholar follow only what is right. How could they make determinations of right and wrong based on the positions of self and other or this and that? When it comes to the task of motivating people to surrender themselves [to the right Way] without reliance on reward and praise, then among the three teachings, it is Buddhism that works best. It does so because people are affected by the great holiness and compassion of our teacher, the Buddha. "[Emperor] Shun liked to question people and delighted in listening to everyday speech. He would cover over people's bad points and disclose their goodness."[99] "Yu paid homage to the excellent words."[100] If we could have Shun and Yu encounter the Buddha's transformative teaching, would they not praise it? To say that the Buddhist teaching does not work for the cultivation of oneself and the transformation of others is truly ridiculous!

You ask what are the points of sameness and difference and the relative strengths and weaknesses of Daoism, Confucianism, and Buddhism. The answer is this: Laozi said "No doing and no not-doing; with something to do yet not-doing";[101] the Buddha said "Quiescent yet eternally luminous; luminous yet eternally quiescent";[102] Confucius said "The Changes have neither thought nor activity, still and unmoving they respond and penetrate the world."[103] Now, this "stillness" that has never failed to "respond," is the same thing as the "quiescence" that is "eternally luminous." The "responding and penetrating" that has never not been "still" is exactly the same as the "luminosity that is eternally quiescent." "No doing and no not-doing" is none other than "still, yet eternally responding." "Eternally doing yet with nothing to be done" is none other than "responding yet eternally still." If you can grasp this, then the words of the three teachers fit together like the pieces of the same tally — as if they had all come out of the same mouth! If you would like actually to demonstrate the high and low among these teachings, exposing their sameness and difference in function, then you must first completely wash the pollution from your mind and completely clarify your eye of wisdom. Then you can study all of the texts contained in the Buddhist, Confucian, and Daoist canons. Compare them in your daily activities, at the times of birth and death, fortune and misfortune. Without needing words, you will spontaneously nod in assent. How strong do I need to make my argument to get you to listen?[104]

Appendix 1:
Simgiri pyŏn
心氣理篇

1. 心難氣
2. 氣難心
3. 理論心氣

1. 心難氣

此篇、主言釋氏修心之旨。以非老氏故、篇中多用釋氏之語。心者、合理
與氣、以爲一身神明之舍。朱子所謂虛靈不昧。以具眾理而應萬事者也。
愚以爲惟虛、故具眾理。惟靈、故應萬事。非具眾理則其虛也、漠然空無
而已矣。其靈也、紛然流注而已矣。雖曰應萬事、而是非錯亂、豈足爲神
明之舍哉。故言心而不言理。是知有其舍、而不知有其主也。

　　凡所有相、厥類紛總。惟我最靈、獨立其中。
　　凡所有相。用金剛經語。紛總、眾多之貌。我者、心自我也。靈卽所
謂虛靈也。此兩句、卽惠能所謂有一物長靈。上拄天下拄地。瞿曇所謂天
上天下、惟我獨尊之意。此爲心之自言。曰凡有聲色貌相盈於天地之間
者。其類甚多、惟我最爲至靈。特然獨立於庶類紛總之中也。

　　我體寂然、如鑑之空。隨緣不變、應化無窮。
　　心之本體寂然無眹、而其靈知不昧。譬則鏡性本空、而明無不照。蓋
隨緣者、心之靈而鏡之明也。不變者、心之寂而鏡之空也。是以、應感萬
變而無有窮盡。卽金剛經所謂應無所住、而生其心之意。蓋外邊雖有應變
之跡、而內則漠然無有一念之動。此釋氏之學第一義也。

　　**由爾四大、假合成形。有目欲色、有耳欲聲。善惡亦幻、緣影以生。
戕我賊我、我不得寧。**
　　爾、氣而言。四大、亦用釋氏語、所謂地水火風也。圓覺云。我今此
身、四大和合。又曰。六塵緣影、爲自心性。
　　此承上章而言心體本自寂然而已。但由爾四大之氣假托凝合、以成有
相之形。於是有目而欲見美色、有耳而欲聞善聲、鼻舌身意、亦各有欲。
順則以之爲善。逆則以之爲惡。是皆幻出、非有眞實。乃攀緣外境之影、
相續而生。凡此皆以戕賊我寂然之體。紛擾錯亂、使我不得而寧靜也。

絕相離體。無念忘情。照而寂寂、默而惺惺。爾雖欲動、豈翳吾明。

金剛經曰。凡所有相、皆是虛妄。惠能曰。一切善惡都莫思量。其後分爲無念、忘情、息妄、任性四宗。此言修心功夫。相言其形相。體言其理體。諸相非相、所當絕而去之。是體非體、所當離而棄之。我若常自寂然、無有一念之動、而常忘其起滅之情、則妄緣既斷、眞空自現。雖感照而體常寂寂。雖靜默而內自惺惺。蓋照而寂寂則非亂想也。默而惺惺則非昏住也。能如是則四大之氣、六塵之欲、雖欲投間抵隙、搖動於我。豈能掩翳以累我本體之明哉。此章言修心之要約而盡之矣。

2. 氣難心

此篇。主言老氏養氣之法。以非釋氏、故篇中多用老氏語。氣者、天以陰陽五行化生萬物、而人得之以生者也。然氣、形而下者。必有形而上之理、然後有是氣。言氣而不言理。是知有其末而不知有其本也。

予居邃古、窈窈冥冥。天 自然、無得而名。

予、氣自予也。邃古、上古也。老子曰、有物混成、先天地生。又曰。窈兮冥兮、其中有精、其精甚眞。又曰。天法道、道法自然。又曰。吾不知其名、字之曰道。老子之言。皆指氣而言者也。故此章本之以言氣居天地萬物之先。窈冥恍惚、自然而眞。不可得而言也。

萬物之始、資孰以生。我凝我聚、乃形乃精。我若無有、心何獨靈。

莊子曰。人之生、氣之聚也。此又本之、以言萬物之生、其始也是資何物以生成乎。其所資以有生者、非氣乎。惟氣妙合而凝聚、然後其形成而其精生、氣若不聚則心雖至靈、亦將何所附着乎。

嗟爾有知 禍之萌。思所不及、慮所未成。計利較害、憂辱慕榮。冰寒火熱、晝夜營營。精日以搖、神不得寧。

嗟。嘆息也。爾。指心也。此章言心所以害氣之事。嘆息而言心之有知覺者、乃衆禍之所由萌也。思其所不可及、慮其所未得成。計其利而欲得之、較其害而欲避之、憂其辱而懼陷焉、慕其榮而僥倖焉。畏則如冰之寒、怒則如火之熱。千端萬緒、交戰於胸中。晝夜之間、營營不息、使其精神日以搖蕩。漸就消耗而不得寧矣。

我不妄動、內斯靜專、如木斯槁、如灰不燃。無慮無 。體道之全。爾知雖鑿、豈害吾天。

此言養氣之功。莊子曰。形固可使如槁木。心固可使如死灰。又曰。無思無慮始知道。老子曰。道常無爲而無不爲。此章本此以立言也。

承上章言心之利欲、雖甚紛拏、氣得其養而妄動。以制於外、則其內亦有以靜定而專一。如木之槁、不復有春華之繁。如灰之死、不復有火燃之熾。心無所思慮、身無所營爲。以體其道沖漠純全之妙、則心之知覺、雖曰鑽鑿、豈能害我自然之天哉。此所謂道、指氣而言也。無慮無爲、體道之全八字、亦老氏之學最要旨也。

3. 理論心氣

此篇主言儒家義理之正、以曉諭二氏使知其非也。理者、心之所稟之德而氣之所由生也。

於穆厥理、在天地先。氣由我生。心亦稟焉。

於、嘆美之辭。穆、清之至也。此理純粹至善、本無所雜。故嘆而美之曰於穆。我者、理之自稱也。前言心氣直稱我與予、而此標理字以嘆美之。然後稱我者、以見理爲公共之道、其尊無對。非如二氏各守所見之偏而自相彼我也。

此言理爲心氣之本原、有是理然後有是氣。有是氣然後陽之輕清者上而爲天、陰之重濁者下而爲地。四時於是而流行、萬物於是而化生。人於其間、全得天地之理、亦全得天地之氣、以貴於萬物而與天地參焉。天地之理在人而爲性、天地之氣在人而爲形。心則又兼得理氣而爲一身之主宰也。故理在天地之先、而氣由是生。心亦稟之以爲德也。

有心無我、利害之趨。有氣無我、血肉之軀。蠢然以動、禽獸同歸。其與異者、嗚呼幾希。

蠢然、無知貌。幾希、少也。朱子曰。知覺運動之蠢然者、人與物同。仁義禮智之粹然者、人與物異。

此言人之所以異於禽獸者、以其有義理也。人而無義理則其所知覺者，過情欲利害之私而已矣。其所運動者、亦蠢然徒生而已矣。雖曰爲人、去禽獸何遠哉。此儒者所以存心養氣。必以義理爲之主也。若夫釋老之學、以清淨寂滅爲尚。雖彝倫之大、禮樂之懿、亦必欲屏除而滅絕之。是其胸中無欲與趨於利害者、疑若不同矣。然不知主天理之公。以裁制人欲之私。故其日用云爲、每陷於利害而不自知也。

且人之所欲無甚於生、所惡無甚於死。今以兩家之說觀之、釋氏必欲免死生是畏死也。老氏必欲求長生、是貪生也。非利害而何哉。又其中無義理之主、則枵然無得、冥然不知。是軀殼所存、亦不過血肉而止耳。此四句雖泛指眾人而言、中二家之實病。讀者詳之。

見彼匍匐惻隱其情。儒者所以不怕念生。

孟子曰。今人乍見孺子入於井、皆有怵惕惻隱之心。又曰。惻隱之心、仁之端也。此言惻隱之情本於吾心之固有、以明釋氏無念忘情之失。夫人得天地生物之心以生。所謂仁也是理實具於吾心。故見孺子匍匐入井、其惻隱之心油然自生而不可遏。推此心以擴充之、則仁不可勝用、而四海之內可兼濟也。故儒者、不怕念慮之生。但循其天理發見之自然、豈如釋氏畏怕情念之起。而強制之歸於寂滅而已哉。

可死則死、義重於身。君子所以殺己成仁。

論語曰。志士仁人無求生以害仁、有殺身以成仁。此言重義輕生之事以明老氏養氣貪生之失。蓋君子見得實理、則當其可死也、其身不忍一日安於生。是死生爲重乎。義理爲重乎。故儒者當救君親之難、有隕軀隕命以赴之者。非如老氏徒事修鍊以偷生也。

聖遠千載、學誣言厖。氣以 道、心以 宗。

厖。猶亂也。此言異端之說所以得熾者、以聖人之世既遠。而道學不明也。故老不知氣本乎理、而以氣爲道。釋不知理具於心而以心爲宗。此二家自以爲無上高妙、而不知形而上者爲何物。卒指形而下者而爲言。陷於淺近迂僻之中而不自知也。

不義而壽、龜蛇矣哉。瞌然而坐、土木形骸。

瞌然、睡貌。上二句責老、下二句責釋。卽前章有心無我、有氣無我之意。然前章泛言在眾人者。此章專指二氏而言也。

我存爾心、瑩徹虛明、我養爾氣、浩然而生。

孟子日。我善養吾浩然之氣。此言聖學內外交養之功。以義理存心而涵養之、則無物欲之蔽、全體虛明、而大用不差矣。集義養氣而擴充之、則至大至剛之氣浩然而自生、充塞天地矣。本末兼備、內外交養。此儒者之學、所以爲正、而非若二氏之偏也。

先聖有訓。道無二尊。心乎氣乎。敬受斯言。

胡氏引禮記天無二日、土無二王之語、以爲道無二致。欲道術之歸于一也。此言上文所論。皆本聖賢之遺訓、而非我之私言。其道之尊。無與爲二。非心氣之可比也。故於其終、特呼心氣以警之。其拳拳開示之意、至深切矣。

Appendix 2:
Pulssi chappyŏn
心氣理篇

1. 佛氏輪迴之辨 [*SBC* 1.75c]

人物之生生而無窮乃天地之化、運行而不已者也。原夫太極有動靜而陰陽生。陰陽有變合而五行具於是。無極太極之眞、陰陽五行之精、妙合而凝、人物生生焉。其已生者、徃而過。未生者來而續、其間不容一息之停也。佛之言曰人死、精神不滅、隨復受形。於是輪迴之說興焉。

 易曰、原始反終故知生死。又曰精氣爲物游魂爲變先儒解之曰、天地之化、雖生生不窮、然而聚必有散、有生必有死。能原其始而知其聚之生、則必知其後之必散而死。能知其生也、得於氣化之自然。初無精神寄寓於太虛之中、則知其死也、與氣而俱散無復更有形象。尚留於冥漠之內。

又曰、精氣爲物、游魂爲變天地陰陽之氣交合便成人物。到得魂氣歸于天、體魄歸于地。便是變了。精氣爲物、是合精與氣而成物。精魄而氣魂也。游魂爲變。變則是魂魄相離。游散而變、變非變化之變。既是變、則堅者腐、存者亡、更無物也。天地間如烘爐。雖生物、皆銷鑠已盡。安有已散者復合、而已往者復來乎。

今且驗之吾身、一呼一吸之間。氣一出焉、謂之一息。其呼而出者、非吸而入之也。然則人之氣息亦生生不窮。而往者過、來者續之理可見也。外而驗之於物、凡草木自根而幹而枝而葉而華實、一氣通貫。當春夏時、其氣滋至而華葉暢茂。至秋冬其氣收斂而華葉衰落。至明年春夏又復暢茂。非已落之葉、返本歸源而復生也。

又井中之水朝朝而汲之爨飲食者、火薰而盡之。濯衣服者、日曝[1]而乾之、泯然無跡。井中之泉、源源而出、無有窮盡。非已汲之水返其故處而復生也。且百穀之生也。春而種十石、秋而收百石。以至千萬其利倍蓰。是百穀亦生生也。

今以佛氏輪迴之說觀之、凡有血氣者、自有定數來來去去無復增損。然則天地之造物、反不如農夫之生利也。且血氣之屬不爲人類。則爲鳥獸魚鼈昆蟲其數有定。此蕃則彼必耗矣。此耗則彼必蕃矣。不應一時俱蕃、一時俱耗矣。

自今觀之、當盛世、人類蕃庶、當鳥獸魚鼈昆蟲亦蕃庶。當衰世、人物耗損鳥獸魚鼈昆蟲亦耗損。是人與萬物皆爲天地之氣所生。故氣盛則一時蕃庶。氣衰則一時耗損明矣。予憤佛氏輪迴之說惑世尤甚。幽而質諸天地之化、明而驗諸人物之生、得其說如是此。與我同志者、幸共鑑焉。

2. 佛氏因果之辨 [76d]

或曰、吾子辨佛氏輪迴之說至矣。子言人物皆得陰陽五行之氣以生。今夫人則有智愚賢不肖貧富貴賤壽夭之不同。物則有爲人所逐畜役勞苦、至死而不辭者。有未免網羅鈎弋之害、大小強弱之自相食者。天之生物、一賦一與。何其偏而不均如是耶。以此而言、釋子所謂生時所作善惡皆有報應者、不其然乎。且生時所作善惡、是之謂因。佗日報應、是之謂果。此其說不亦有所據歟。

曰、予於上論人物生生之理悉矣。知此則輪迴之說自辨矣。輪迴之說辨則因果之說不辨而自明矣、然子既有問焉。予敢不推本而重言之。夫所謂陰陽五行者、交運迭行參差不齊。故其氣也、有通塞偏正清濁厚薄高下長短之異焉。

而人物之生、適當其時、得其正且通者爲人。得其偏且塞者爲物。人與物之貴賤於此焉分。又在於人、得其清者智且賢。得其濁者愚不肖。厚

---

1. Actually 日*暴

者富而薄者貧。高者貴而下者賤。長者壽而短者夭。此大略也、雖物亦然。若麒麟龍鳳之爲靈、虎狼虺蛆之爲毒、椿桂芝蘭之爲瑞、烏喙菫茶之爲苦。是皆就於偏塞之中而又有善惡之不同。

然皆非有意而爲之。易曰、乾道變化各正性命。先儒曰、天道無心而普萬物是也。今夫醫卜小數也。卜者定人之禍福、必推本於五行之衰旺。至曰某人以木爲命。當春而旺、當秋而衰。其象貌靑而長、其心慈而仁。某人以金爲命。吉於秋而凶於夏。其象貌白而方。其心剛而明。曰水、曰火。莫不皆然。而象貌之醜陋、心識之愚暴、亦皆本於五行稟賦之偏。

醫者診人之疾病、又必推本於五行之相感。乃曰某之病寒乃腎水之證。某之病溫乃心火之證之類、是也。其命藥也、以其性之溫涼寒熱。味之酸醎甘苦分屬陰陽五行而劑之、無不符合。此吾儒之說以人物之生、爲得於陰陽五行之氣者。明有左驗無可疑矣。

信如佛氏之說、則人之禍福疾病無與於陰陽五行、而皆出於因果之報應。何無一人、捨吾儒所謂陰陽五行、而以佛氏所說因果報應、定人禍福診人疾病歟。其說荒唐謬誤、無足取信如此。子尚惑其說歟。

3. 佛氏心性之辨 [78a]

心者、人所得於天以生之氣。虛靈不昧以主於一身者也。性者、人所得於天以生之理。純粹至善、以具於一心者也。蓋心有知有爲、性無知無爲。故曰心能盡性、性不能知檢其心。又曰心統情性。又曰心者、神明之舍。性則其所具之理。觀此心性之辨可知矣。

彼佛氏以心爲性、求其說而不得。乃曰迷之則心、悟之則性。又曰心性之異名、猶眼目之殊稱。至楞嚴曰圓妙明心明妙圓性 (Interlinear Note: 按楞嚴經曰、汝等遺失本妙圓妙明心、寶明妙性。認悟中迷言。心則從妙起明。圓融照了。如鏡之光、故曰圓明妙心。性則卽明而妙。寂然寂湛、如鏡之體。故曰寶明妙性。) 以明與圓分而言之。

普照曰、心外無佛、性外無法。又以佛與法分而言之。似略有所見矣。然皆得於想象髣髴之中、而無豁然眞實之見。其說多爲遊辭而無一定之論、其情可得矣。吾儒之說曰、盡心知性。此本心以窮理也。

佛氏之說曰、觀心見性、心卽性也。是別以一心見此一心。心安有二乎哉。彼亦自知其說之窮。從而遁之曰、以心觀心如以口齕口。當以不觀觀之、此何等語歟。

且吾儒曰、方寸之間虛靈不昧、具衆理應萬事。其曰虛靈不昧者、心也。具衆理者、性也。應萬事者、情也。惟其此心、具衆理。故於事物之來、應之無不各得其當。所以處事物之當否、而事物皆聽命於我也。

此吾儒之學。內自身心、外而至事物、自源徂流、一以通貫、如源頭之水流於萬派、無非水也。如持有星之衡、稱量天下之物。其物之輕重與權衡之銖兩相稱。此所謂元不曾間斷者也。

佛氏曰、空寂靈知隨緣不變。 (Interlinear Note: 按佛氏以爲眞淨心隨緣是相、不變是性。如一眞金、隨大小器物等、是隨緣相也。本金不變是性也。一眞淨心隨善惡染淨等。是隨緣相也。本心不變、性也。) 無所謂理者具於其中。故於事物之來、滯者欲絶而去之、達者、欲隨而順之。

其絶而去之者、固已非矣。隨而順之者、亦非也。其言曰、隨緣放曠、任性逍遙。聽其物之自爲而已。無復制其是非而有以處之也。是其心如天上之月。其應也、如千江之影、月眞而影妄。其間未嘗連續。如持無星之衡、稱量天下之物、其輕重低昂。惟物是順而我無以進退稱量之也。故曰、釋氏虛、吾儒實。釋氏二、吾儒一。釋子間斷、吾儒連續。學者所當明辨也。

4. 佛氏作用是性之辨 [78d]

愚按佛氏之說、以作用爲性。龐居士曰、運水搬柴無非妙用是也。 (Interlinear Note: 按龐[2]居士偈曰、日用事無別。唯吾自偶諧。頭頭須取舍。處處勿張乖。神通幷妙用、運水及搬柴。)

蓋性者、人所得於天以生之理也。作用者人所得於天以生之氣也。氣之凝聚者、爲形質、爲神氣。若心之精爽、耳目之聰明、手之執、足之奔、凡所以知覺運動者皆氣也。

故曰、形旣生矣。神發知矣。人旣有是形氣、卽是理具於形氣之中、在心爲仁義禮智之性、惻隱羞惡辭讓是非之情。在頭容爲直。在目容爲端、在口容爲止之類。凡所以爲當然之則而不可易者、是理也。劉康公曰、人受天地之中以生所謂命也。故有動作威儀之則、以定命也。

其曰、天地之中者、卽理之言也。其曰威儀之則者、卽理之發於作用者也。朱子亦曰、若以作用爲性、則人胡亂執刀殺人敢道性歟。且理形而上者氣形而下也。佛氏自以爲高妙無上而反以形而下者爲說可笑也已。學者須將吾儒所謂威儀之則與佛氏所謂作用是性者、內以體之於身心、外以驗之於事物。則自當有所得矣。

5. 佛氏心跡之辨 [79b]

心者、主乎一身之中。而跡者、心之發於應事接物之上也。故曰、有是心必有是跡。不可判而爲二也。蓋四端五典萬事萬物之理、渾然具於此心之中。其於事物之來、不一其變。而此心之理、隨感而應各有攸當而不可亂也。

人見孺子匍匐入井便有怵惕惻隱之心。是其心有仁之性。故其見孺子

---

2. 龐

也、發於外者、便惻然心與跡、果有二乎。曰羞惡、曰辭讓、曰是非。莫不皆然。次而及於身之所接。見父則思孝焉。見子則思慈焉。至於事君以忠、使臣以禮、交友以信、是就使之然也。以其心有仁義禮智之性、故發於外者。

亦如此所謂體用一源、顯微無間者也。彼之學取其心、不取其跡。乃曰、文殊大聖遊諸酒肆、跡雖非而心則是也。侘如此類者、甚多。非心跡之判歟。程子曰、佛氏之學於敬以直內則有之矣。義以方外則未之有也。故滯固者、入於枯槁。疏通者、歸於恣肆、此佛之教。所以隘也、然無義以方外。其直內者、要之亦不是也。王通、儒者也、亦曰心跡判矣。蓋惑於佛氏之說而不知者也。故并論之。

6. 佛氏昧於道器之辨 [79d]

道則理也、形而上者也。器則物也、形而下者也。蓋道之大原出於天而無物不有、無時不然。卽身心而有身心之道。近而卽於父子、君臣、夫婦、長幼、朋友。遠而卽於天地萬物。莫不各有其道焉。人在天地之間、不能一日離物而獨立。是以凡吾所以處事接物者、亦當各盡其道。而不可或有所差謬也。此吾儒之學所以自心而身而人而物、各盡其性而無不通也。

蓋道雖不雜於器亦不離於器者也。彼佛氏於道、雖無所得、以其用心積力之久、髣髴若有見處。然如管窺天。一向直上去、不能四通八達。其所見必陷於一偏。見其道、不雜於器者。則以道與器歧而二之。乃曰、凡所有相、皆是虛妄。若見諸相非相、卽見如來 (Interlinear Note: 按此一段出般若經。言目前無法觸目皆如但知如是卽見如來)　必欲擺脫羣有、落於空寂。

見其道不離於器者、則以器爲道。乃曰善惡皆心、萬法唯識。隨順一切任用無爲猖狂放恣無所不爲。(Interlinear Note: 按。善心將生隨順一切任用無爲。惡心將生猖狂放恣、無所不爲。心之所有識乃爲之惟善惟惡。非心無識、非識無心。心識相對善惡生滅。)　此程子所謂滯固者入於枯槁、疏通者歸於恣肆者也。然其所謂道者、指心而言、乃反落於形而下者之器而不自知也。惜哉。

7. 佛氏毀棄人倫之辨 [80b]

明道先生曰、道之外無物、物之外無道。是天地之間、無適而非道也。卽父子而父子在所親。卽君臣而君臣在所嚴。以至爲夫婦爲長幼爲朋友無所爲而非道。所以不可須臾離也。然則毀人倫去四大 (Interlinear Note: 按四大受想行識)　其分於道遠矣。又曰、言爲無不周徧、而實則外於倫理。先生之辨盡矣。

8. 佛氏慈悲之辨 [80c]

天地以生物爲心、而人得天地生物之心以生。故人皆有不忍人之心。此卽所謂仁也。佛雖夷狄、亦人之類耳。安得獨無此心哉。吾儒所謂惻隱、佛氏所謂慈悲、皆仁之用也。其立言雖同、而其所施之方、則大相遠矣。

蓋親與我同氣者也。人與我同類者也。物與我同生者也。故仁心之所施、自親而人而物。如水之流盈於第一坎而後達於第二第三之坎。其本深故、其及者遠。擧天下之物、無一不在吾仁愛之中。故曰親親而仁民、仁民而愛物。此儒者之道。所以爲一爲實爲連續也。

佛氏則不然。其於物也、毒如豺虎、微如蚊虻、尚欲以其身、餧之而不辭。其於人也、越人有飢者、思欲推食之。秦人有寒者、思欲推衣。而衣之所謂布施者也。若夫至親如父子、至敬如君臣、必欲絶而去之。果何意歟。

且人之所以自重愼者、以有父母妻子、爲之顧藉也。佛氏以人倫爲假合。子不父其父、臣不君其君。恩義衰薄。視至親如路人、視至敬如辮髦。其本源先失。故其及於人物者、如木之無根、水之無源、易致枯竭。卒無利人濟物之效、而拔釰斬蛇虺。略無愛惜。

地獄之說、極其阿慘酷、反爲少恩之人。尚之所謂慈悲者、果安在哉。然而此心之天、終有不可得而昧者。故雖昏蔽之極、一見父母則孝愛之心油然而生。盍亦反而求之、而乃曰、多生習氣未盡除故、愛根尚在、執迷不悟。莫此爲甚。佛氏之教所以無義無理而名敎所不容者、此也。

9. 佛氏眞假之辨 [81a]

佛氏以心性爲眞常、以天地萬物假合。其言曰一切衆生種種幻化皆生如來圓覺妙心猶如空華及第二月 (Interlinear Note: 按此一段出圓覺經言衆生業識不知自身內如來圓覺妙心。若以智照用、則法界之無實如空華。衆生之妄相如第二月。妙心本月、第二月影也。)

又曰、空生大覺中、如海一漚發。有漏微塵國皆依空所立。 (Interlinear Note: 按此一段出楞嚴經、言大覺海中、本絶空有、由迷風飄鼓、妄發空漚而諸有生焉。迷風旣息、則空漚亦滅。所依諸有、遂不可得而空覺圓融復歸元妙。) 佛氏之言、其害多端。然滅絶倫理略無忌憚者。此其病根也、不得不砭而藥之也。

蓋未有天地萬物之前、畢竟先有太極而天地萬物之理。已渾然具於其中。故曰太極生兩儀、兩儀生四象。千變萬化皆從此出。如水之有源、萬派流注。如木有根、枝葉暢茂。

此非人智力之所得而爲也。亦非人智力之所得而遏也。然此固有難與初學言者。以其衆人所易見者而言之。自佛氏歿至今數千餘年、天之昆侖於上者。若是其確然也、地之磅礴於下者。若是其隤然也、人物之生於其間者。若是其燦然也、日月寒暑之徃來。若是其秩然也、是以天體至大、而其周圍運轉之度、日月星辰逆順疾徐之行。雖當風雨晦明之夕、而不能外於八尺之璣、數寸之衡。

歲年之積至於百千萬億之多、而二十四氣之平分。與夫朔虛氣盈餘分之積至於毫釐絲³忽之微、而亦不能外於乘除之兩策。孟子所謂天之高也、星辰遠也。苟求其故、千歲之日至、可坐而致者此也。

是亦孰使之然歟。必有實理爲之主張也。假者、可暫於一時、而不可久於千萬世。幻者可欺於一人而不可信於千萬人。而以天地之常久、萬物之常生謂之假且幻。抑何說歟。豈佛氏無窮理之學。求其說而不得歟。抑其心陋天地之大、萬物之衆不得容於其中歟。

豈樂夫持守之約、而厭夫窮理之煩、酬酢萬變之勞歟。張子曰明不能盡誣天地日月以爲###幻妄。則佛氏受病之處、必有所自矣。要之其所見蔽、故其言之詖如此。嗚呼、惜哉。予豈譊譊而多言者歟。予所言之而不已者。正惟彼心之迷昧爲可憐。而吾道之衰廢、爲可憂而已耳。

10. 佛氏地獄之辨 [82a]

先儒辨佛氏地獄之說曰、世俗信浮屠誑誘。凡有營事、無不供佛飯僧。云、爲死者滅罪資福、使生天堂受諸快樂。不爲者必入地獄剉燒舂磨受諸苦楚諜。不知死者形既朽滅、神亦飄散。雖有剉燒舂磨、且無所施。

又況佛法未入中國之前、人固有死而復生者。何故都無一人誤入地獄、見所謂十王者歟。此其無有而未足信也明矣。或曰、釋氏地獄之說、皆是爲下根之人。設此怖令爲善耳。程子曰至誠貫天地。人尚有不化。豈有立僞敎而人可化乎。

昔有僧問予曰、若無地獄人何畏而不爲惡乎。予曰、君子之好善惡惡如好好色、如惡惡臭。皆由中而出。無所爲而爲之。一有惡名至則其心愧恥。若撻于市、豈待地獄之說然後、不爲惡乎。其僧默然。於此幷書之、俾世之惑於其說者、知所辨焉。

11. 佛氏禍福之辨 [82b]

天道、福善而禍淫。人道、賞善而罰惡。蓋由人、操心有邪正、行己有是非、而禍福各以其類應之。詩曰、求福不回。夫子曰、獲罪於天無所禱也。蓋君子之於禍福。正吾心而已、修吾己而已。福不必求而至、禍不必避而自遠。故曰、君子有終身之憂無一朝之患。禍若有自外而至者、順而受之而已。如寒暑之過於前、而吾無所與也。

彼佛氏則不論人之邪正是非。乃曰、歸吾佛者、禍可免而福可得。是

3.　Actual ideograph is [絲+系(絲)]

雖犯十惡大憝者、歸佛則免之。雖有道之士、不歸佛則不免也。假使其說不虛。皆出於私心而非公道也、在所懲之也。況自佛說興至今數千餘年。祚之間事佛甚篤。如梁武唐憲者、皆不得免焉。韓退之所謂、事佛漸謹年代尤促者。此其說不亦深切著明矣乎。

12. 佛氏乞食之辨 [82c]

食之於人、大矣哉。不可一日而無食。亦不可一日而苟食。無食則害性命。苟食則害義理。洪範八政、食貨爲先。重民五教、惟食居首。子貢問政、則夫子以足食告之。此古之聖人知民之道。不可一日而無食。

故皆汲汲於斯、教以稼穡、制以貢賦。軍國有須、祭祀賓客有給、鰥寡老幼有養、而無匱乏飢餓之歎。聖人之慮民遠矣。上而天子公卿大夫、治民而食。下而農工商賈、勤力而食。中而爲士者、入孝出悌。守先王之道、以持後之學者而食。

此古之聖人、知其不可一日而苟食。故自上達下、各有其職、以受天養。其所以防民者至矣。不居此列者、姦民也。王法所必誅、而不赦者也。金剛經曰、爾時世尊食時着衣持鉢入舍衞城 (Interlinear Note: 按舍衞波斯國名)　乞食於其城中。夫釋迦牟尼者、以男女居室爲不義、出人倫之外、去稼穡之事、絕生生之本。

欲以其道、思以易天下、信如其道、是天下無人也。果有可乞之人乎。是天下無食也。果有可乞之食乎。釋迦牟尼者、西域王之子也。以父之位、爲不義而不居、非治民者也。以男耕女織、爲不義而去之。何勤力之有。無父子君臣夫婦則又非守先王之道者也。

此人雖一日食一粒、皆苟食也。信如其道、誠不食如蚯蚓、然後可也。何爲乞而食乎。且食在自力、則爲不義、而在乞則爲義乎。佛氏之言無義無理。開卷便見、故於此論而辨之。

13. 佛氏禪教之辨 [83c]

佛氏之說、其初不過論因緣果報、以誑誘愚民耳。雖以虛無爲宗、廢棄人事、尚有爲善得福、爲惡得禍之說。使人有所懲勸。持戒律不至於放肆。故人倫雖毀、義理未盡喪了。

至達摩入中國、自知其說淺陋、不足以感高明之士。於是曰、不立文字、言語道斷、直指人心、見性成佛。其說一出、捷徑便開、其徒轉相論述。或曰、善亦是心、不可將心修心。惡亦是心、不可將心斷心。善惡懲勸之道絕矣。

或曰、及淫怒癡皆是梵行、戒律持身之道失矣。自以爲不落窠臼、解縛去械、傲然出於禮法之外。放肆自恣、汲汲如狂、無復人理。所謂義理者、至此都喪也。

朱文公憂之曰、西方論緣業、卑卑喻羣愚流傳世代久。梯接凌空虛。

顧盼指心性、名言超有無。 (Interlinear Note: 按佛說大略有三。其初齋戒後有義學、有禪學。緣之名有十二。曰觸愛受取有生老死憂悲苦惱。業之名有三。曰身口意。指心性、謂卽心是佛、見性成佛。超有無、謂言有則云色卽是空[84a]言無則云空卽是色。)

捷徑一以開靡然世爭趨。號空不踐實。躓彼榛棘塗。誰哉繼三聖 (Interlinear Note: 按三聖謂禹周公孔子。) 爲我焚其書、甚哉。其憂之之深也。予亦爲之憮然三歎。

14. 儒釋同異之辨 [84a]

先儒謂儒釋之道。句句同而事事異。今且因是而推廣之。此曰虛。彼亦曰虛。此曰寂、彼亦曰寂。然此之虛、虛而有。彼之虛、虛而無。此之寂、寂而感。彼之寂、寂而滅。此曰知行、彼曰悟修。此之知、知萬物之理具於吾心也。彼之悟、悟此心本空無一物也。此之行、循萬物之理而行之、無所違失也。彼之修、絕去萬物而不爲吾心之累也。

此曰心具衆理。彼曰心生萬物。所謂具衆理者、心中原有此理。方其靜也、至寂而此理之體具焉。及其動也、感通而此理之用行焉。其曰、寂然不動。感而遂通天下之故、是也。

所謂生萬法者、心中本無此法。對外境而後、法生焉。方其靜也、此心無有所住。及其動也、隨所遇之境而生。其曰應無所住而生其心。 (Interlinear Note: 按此一段出般若經言。應無所住者、了無內外、中虛無物。而不以善惡是非介於胷中也。而生其心者、以無住之心應之於外而不爲物累也。謝氏解論語無敵無莫引此語。)

又曰、心生則一切法生。心滅則一切法滅 (Interlinear Note: 按出起信論。) 是也。此以理爲固有。彼以法爲緣起。何其語之同事之異如是耶。此則曰酬酢萬變。彼則曰隨順一切其言似乎同矣。

然所謂萬變者。其於事物之來、此心應之、各因其當然之則。制而處之、使之不失其宜也。如有子於此、使之必爲孝而不爲賊。有臣於此、使之必爲忠而不爲亂、至於物、牛則使之耕、而不爲牴觸。馬而使之載、而不爲踶齧。虎狼則使之設檻置阱而不至於齧人。蓋亦各因其所固有之理而處之也。

若釋氏所謂隨順一切者、凡爲人之子、孝者自孝、賊者自賊。爲人之臣、忠者自忠、亂者自亂。牛馬之耕且載者、自耕且載。牴觸踶齧、自牴觸踶齧。聽其所自爲而已。

吾無容心於其間。佛氏之學如此。自以爲使物而不爲物所使。若付一錢、則便沒奈何。佗此其事非異乎。然則天之所以生此人、爲靈於萬物。付以財成輔相之職者、果安在哉。

其說反復。頭緒雖多、要之、此見得心與理爲一、彼見得心與理爲二。彼見得心空而無理。此見得心雖空而萬物咸備也。故曰吾儒一、釋氏二。吾儒連續、釋氏間斷。然心一也、安有彼此之同異乎。

蓋人之所見、有正不正之殊耳。四大身中誰是主。六根塵裏孰爲精。

(Interlinear Note: 按地水火風四大、和合爲一身。而別其四大則本無主。色聲香味觸法六根塵、相對以生。而別其六根、則本無精。猶鏡像之有無也。) 黑漫漫地開眸看、終日聞聲不見形。 (Interlinear Note: 按以慧照用用[4]雖黑漫漫地開眸看、暗中有明。猶鏡光之暗中生明也。) 此釋氏之體驗心處。

　　謂有寧有跡。謂無復可存。惟應酬酢際。特達見本根。 (Interlinear Note: 按朱子詩) 此吾儒之體驗心處。且道心但無形而有聲乎。抑有此理存於心、爲酬酢之本根歟。學者、當日用之間、就此心發見處體究之。彼此之同異得失、自可見矣。

　　請以朱子之說、申言之。心雖主乎一身而其體之虛靈、足以管乎天下之理。理雖散在萬物、而其用微妙、實不外乎人之一心。初不可以內外精粗而論也。然或不知此心之靈、而無以存之、則昏昧雜擾、而無以窮衆理之妙。不知衆理之妙、而無以窮之、則偏狹固滯、而無以盡此心之全。此其理勢之相須、蓋亦有必然者。

　　是以聖人設教使人默識此心之靈。而存之於端莊靜一之中。以爲窮理之本、使人知有衆理之妙。而窮之於學問思辨之際、以致盡心之功。巨細相涵動靜交養。初未嘗有內外精粗之擇、及其眞積力久而豁然貫通焉。亦有以知其渾然一致、而果無內外精粗之可言矣。

　　今必以是爲淺近支離、而欲藏形匿影。別爲一種、幽淶恍惚、艱難阻絕之論。務使學者莽然措其心於文字言語之外。而曰道必如是、然後可以得之。則是近世佛學、詖淫邪遁之尤者、而欲移之。以亂古人明德新民之實學。其亦誤矣。朱子之言、反復論辨、親切著明。學者於此、潛心而自得之可也。

15. 佛法入中國 [85c]

漢明帝聞西域有神、其名曰佛。遣使之天竺得其書及沙門以來。其書大抵以虛無爲宗。貴慈悲不殺、以爲人死精神不滅、隨復受形。生時所作善惡皆有報應。故所貴修鍊、以至爲佛。善爲宏濶勝大之言、以勸誘愚俗。情於其道者、號曰沙門。於是中國始傳其術。圖其形像而王公貴人獨楚王英最先好之。

16. 事佛得禍 [86a]

梁武帝、中大通元年九月、幸同泰寺、設四部無遮大會。釋御服持法衣行清淨大捨。羣臣以錢一億萬、祈白三寶、奉贖皇帝、僧衆默然。上還內、

4.　Variant of 則

上自天監中、用釋氏法。長齋斷肉、日止一食、惟菜羹糲飯而已。多造塔公私費損。

時王侯子弟多驕淫不法、上年老厭於萬機。又專精佛戒、每斷重罪、則終日不懌。或謀叛逆事覺、亦泣而宥之。由是王侯益橫。或白晝殺人於都街、或暮夜公行剽掠。有罪亡命、匿於主家、有司不敢搜捕。上漸知其弊、而溺於慈愛、不能禁也。

中大同元年三月庚戌、上幸同泰寺。遂停寺省講三慧經。夏四月丙戌解講、是夜同泰寺浮屠災。上曰此魔也、宜廣為法事、乃下詔曰、道高魔盛、行善障生。當窮茲土木、倍增徃日、遂起十二層浮屠。將成、值侯景亂而止。及陷臺城、囚上於同泰寺。上口燥乾、求蜜於寺僧。不得、竟以餓死。

17. 舍天道而談佛果 [87a]

唐代宗始末甚重佛。宰相元載王縉皆好佛、縉尤甚。上嘗問、佛言報應、果有之耶。載等對曰、國家運祚靈長。非宿植福業、何以致之。福業已定。雖時有小災、終不能為害。所以安史皆有子禍。懷思出門病死。二虜不戰而退。此皆非人力所及、豈得言無報應也。上由是漸信之。常於禁中、飯僧百餘人。有寇至、厚加賞賜良田美利。多歸僧寺、載等侍上多談佛事、政刑日紊矣。

18. 事佛甚謹年代尤促 [87d]

元和十四年、迎佛骨于京師先是功德使上言鳳翔寺塔、有佛指骨相傳。三十年一開、開則歲豐人安。來年應開、請迎之。上從其言、至是、佛骨至京師留禁中三日。歷送諸寺。王公士民瞻奉捨施、如恐不及。

刑部侍郎韓愈上表諫曰、佛者夷狄之一法耳。自黃帝至禹湯文武、皆亨壽考、百姓安樂。當是時、未有佛也。漢明帝時、始有佛法。其後亂亡相繼、運祚不長。宋齊梁陳元魏以下、事佛漸謹年代尤促。唯梁武在位四十八年。

前後三捨身[5]竟為侯景所逼、餓死臺城。事佛求福乃反得禍。由此觀之、佛不足信可知矣。佛本夷狄之人、與中國、言語不通、衣服殊製。不知君臣父子之情。假如其身尚在、來朝京師。陛下容而接之。不令惑眾也。況其身死已久。枯槁之骨豈且以入宮禁。乞付有司、投諸水火永絕禍本。上大怒、將加極刑、宰相裴度崔羣等言。愈雖狂發於忠懇。宜寬容以開言路。乃貶潮州刺史。

---

5. Han Yu's original text has 前後三度、捨身施佛。

19. 闢異端之辨 [88b]

堯舜之誅四凶以其巧言令色方命圮族也。禹亦曰何畏乎巧言令色。蓋巧言
令色、喪人之心方命圮族。敗人之事、聖人所以去之、而莫之容也。湯武
之征桀紂也、一則曰、予畏上帝、不敢不正。一則曰予不順天、厥罪惟
均、天命天討。非已之所得而辭也。

　夫子曰、攻乎異端斯害也已。害之一字、讀之令人凜然。孟子之好
辯、所以距楊墨也、楊墨之道不距、聖人之道不行。故孟子以闢楊墨爲已
任。其言曰、能言距楊墨者、亦聖人之徒也。其望助於人者至矣。墨氏兼
愛、疑於仁。楊氏爲我、疑於義。其害至於無父無君。此孟子所以闢之之
力也。

　若佛氏則其言高妙、出入性命道德之中、其惑人之甚。又非楊墨之比
也。朱子曰、佛氏之言、彌近理而大亂眞者。此之謂也、以予惛庸、不知
力之不足、而以闢異端己任者。非欲上繼六聖一賢之心也、懼世之人、惑
於其說、而淪胥以陷。人之道至於滅矣。嗚呼。亂臣賊子、人人得而誅
之、不必士師。邪說橫流、壞人心術。人人得而闢之、不必聖賢。此予之
所以望於諸公。而因以自勉焉者也。

Appendix 3:
Hyŏnjŏng non
顯正論

1. Prologue [*HPC* 7.217a5]

體非有無而通於有無。本無古今而通於古今者、道也。有無因於性情也。古今因於生死也。性本無情、迷性生情。情生智隔、想變體殊。萬象所以形也、生死所以始也。

夫情也、有染淨焉、有善惡焉。淨與善、聖之所以興也。染與惡凡之所以作也。故知情若不生、則凡之與聖悉無得而興焉。菩薩性、雖已覺、而情猶有所未盡。故稱之云覺有情也。菩薩尚爾、況餘二乘乎。三乘尚爾況餘人天異類乎。佛則覺滿而智無不周。淨極而情累已盡。故情之言、不可加於佛也。唯佛一人之外、皆稱有情者、以此。

夫三乘五乘、皆所以治其情也。人天乘所以治其染垢。三乘所以治其淨垢也。染淨垢盡然後、方親造大覺之境矣。五戒所以生人道也。十善所以生天道也。諦緣所以成二乘也。六度所以成菩薩也。竊觀三藏指歸、只要令人去情顯性而已。

情生於性、猶雲起於長空。去情顯性猶雲開而現大淸也。情有薄者焉、有厚者焉。猶雲有淡者焉、有濃者焉。雲有濃淡之異、而掩天光則一也。情有厚薄之殊、而礙性明則同也。雲起也、日月收照而天下暗然也。雲開也光被大千而宇宙廓如也。

佛教比之、則若淸風之掃浮雲也。欲所見之廓如、而厭淸風者惑矣。欲自他之淸泰、而厭吾道者失矣。若教人人依此而修之、則心可得而正矣。身可得而修矣。可以齊家、可以治國、可以平天下矣。

2. Distinctions in Levels of Teaching [*HPC* 217b11]

機之利者、可以爲菩薩、可以爲聲聞、可以爲緣覺。機之劣者、可以生天、可以成善人矣。苟如是而世不治、未之有也。何則。厭罪報則應斷諸惡。諸惡雖不斷盡、而足以去一惡矣。去一惡則息一刑。一刑息於家、萬刑息於國矣。忻福緣則應修諸善。諸善雖未盡修而足以行一善矣。行一善則得一慶。一慶興於家、萬慶興於國矣。

夫五戒十善教中之最淺者也。本爲機之最下者而設也。苟能行之則足以誠於身、利於人矣。況於諦緣乎。況於六度乎。儒以五常而爲道樞。佛之所謂正戒、卽儒之[217c]所謂五常也。不殺、仁也。不盜、義也。不婬、禮也。不飲酒、智也。不妄語、信也。

但儒之所以教人者、不以德行、卽以政刑也。故云導之以政、齊之以刑、民免而無恥。導之以德、齊之以禮、有恥且格。夫導之以德齊之以禮、非聖人不能。故云默而成之、不言而信存乎德行。導之以政齊之以刑、則未免有賞罰分明。故云賞罰國之大柄也。

夫默而成之、不言而信、固吾佛之化也、而兼以因果示之。示之以賞罰則或不過面從而已。[218a]　示之以因果則服、乃心服也。今於世上目覩其然也。何則。若勸之以賞禁之以罰、則止惡者、畏其威而止之。爲善者、利其賞而爲之。故其從化也面從而已。非心服也。

若人欲知今之所以窮達者、則示之以宿種。欲知後之禍福者、則示之以現因。則達者忻前世之種善而益勤。窮者悔前世之不修而自勉。且邀福於後世者、則孜孜於爲善。避禍於後世者、則必愼於爲惡。此則不服則已。服則心服而未嘗有面從者也。

雖然安得使人人皆可以心服也。其未能心服者、則姑以賞罰而導之。使駸駸然心悅而誠服也。故示之以因果之外、亦有賞罰之訓存焉。所謂應攝受者而攝受之、應折服者而折服之、是也。此則近於儒也。所以儒與釋、皆不可廢也。

佛之將化也、以其法、付之君、付之臣。盖欲以其道導天下而爲治世之大助、而令共蹈乎修眞之路也、吾佛之教不論在家出家。只要令人不違道用而已。不必剪其髮異其服然後爲也。所以云隨方解縛假名三昧。又云無有定法名阿耨菩提。佛之心如此、豈小通哉。

[218b]然若無忍力者、則居塵不染、在家成道難矣。所以教人出家、令修遠離行也。儒之言曰、男有室女有家、以嗣家業不絕厥祀可謂孝矣。今浮圖氏絕婚姻去人倫、長往山林、永絕後嗣。豈可謂孝乎。昏定晨省、承顏順色。出必告、反必面。今浮圖氏不告父母、自許出家。一自出家、終身不返。生不奉甘旨、死不計厚葬。豈非不孝乎。

3. The Constant and the Expedient [*HPC* 7.218b10]

試嘗論之曰。經權爲道之大要也。非經無以守常。非權無以應變。經以守常、權以應變、然後得夫道之大全、而無所徃而不可也。不知守常、無以正人心。不知應變、無以成大事。夫人也、托父母而受生。寄君國以得存。入孝出忠固臣子之所當爲也。又婚姻祭祀亦人倫之大經也。非婚、生生之理絕。非祀、追遠之法廢。

然爲臣子而盡忠孝者難矣。婚姻而終身守正、奉祀而盡心致齊者、又其難矣。盡忠盡孝、而謹守其職守正致齊、而終身不輟然後生不失善名。死、得生人道。此經以守常之效也。

4. Śākyamuni's Attainment of Freedom from Attachment [*HPC* 7.218b23]

然生得善名而已、斷愛欲者幾希。死、生人道而已、免輪廻者難矣。愛爲輪[218c] 廻之本、欲爲受生之緣。夫人者、既未免妻子之累、愛欲其可斷乎。苟未斷於愛欲、則輪回其可免乎。欲免輪回、先斷愛欲。欲斷愛欲、先去妻子。欲去妻子、須出塵寰。不出塵寰、不去妻子、斷愛欲、免輪回、大聖垂慈大權示迹之外。庸人凡俗、其可得乎。

夫如是者。億億世而難遇、萬萬人而難得。夫愛緣、如磁石與鐵偶相似。無忍力者、居塵世而難免。如本師釋尊居兜率而稱爲護明菩薩、降王宮而名曰悉達。此豈無忍力者哉。可謂玄曦慚其照遠、上界惡以緣銷者也。

雖涉愛緣、應不爲愛緣所染也。將欲爲後世垂範、以金輪之嫡子。不告父母而辭入雪山。輕生苦節、安忍不動、待其情累蕩盡。眞明朗發然後、返鄉而覲父、登天而訪母。爲說法要、皆令度脫。此聖人之所以權以應變而反常合道者也。

5. Societal Obligations [*HPC* 7.218c19]

且佛者、三明六通而悉備、四智八解而圓具。其德播天下後世而使天下後世。稱其父母曰大聖人之[219a]父母。以其姓姓一切姓使出家者、皆稱之曰釋子。豈不謂之大孝乎。孔不云乎、立身行道、揚名於後世、以顯父母

孝之終也。以其道、導天下後世、而使天下後世聞其風、感其化。隨其機
之大小稟其法而得度。豈不謂之大慈乎。孔不云乎、一日克已復禮天下歸
仁。

　　曰、人生斯世、當盡忠於君、傾誠輔國。今浮圖氏不朝天子、不事王
侯。高棲遐舉、坐觀成敗。豈可謂忠乎。曰、教中使爲君者、先受戒品、
潔淨身意。然後方登寶位。又令凡出家者。莫不朝焚夕點而祝君祝國。可
不謂之忠乎。

　　且、君者爵祿以勸善、刑罰以禁惡之外、吾佛示之以爲善招慶爲惡招
殃。人之聞者、自然收其惡心、發其善意。吾佛之教不假爵賞之勸、刑罰
之威。今人靡然趨化。豈無輔於君國乎。

6. Harming Life [*HPC* 7.219a20]

曰、人食物、物給人、固其自然也。而七十者、非肉不飽、故養老者不可
不以此供之。又春蒐夏苗秋猫冬狩、乃先王之所以爲民除害。順時立法、
不可易也。且犧牲從古于今、奉祀之禮物。尤不可[219b]廢也。今浮圖親
老而食不甘、不供之以肉。教人亦廢先王之制、犧牲之禮。豈非過歟。

　　曰、暴殄天物、聖人之所不與也。況天道至仁豈令人殺生以養生哉。
書云、惟天地萬物父母、惟人萬物之靈。亶聰明作元后、元后作民父母。
天地既爲萬物之父母、則生乎天地之間者、皆天地之息也。天地之於物
也、猶父母之於子也。子有愚智之殊、猶人與萬物之有明昧也。父母之於
子也、雖愚不肖、亦愛而憫之。猶恐不得其養焉。況其加害乎。

　　殺生養生、如殺同息以自養也。殺同息以自養、則於父母之心爲如何
哉。子之相殺、非父母之心也。人物之相殘、豈天地之意乎。人與萬物既
同得天地之氣。又同得天地之理、而同生於天地之間。既一氣一理之所
賦、焉有殺生養生之理哉。如云天地與我同根萬物與我一體。此釋氏之言
也。仁者以天地萬物爲一己。此儒者之言也。爲行一如其言然後、方盡仁
之道矣。

7. The Meaning of Humaneness [*HPC* 7.219b22]

醫書以手足痿痺爲不仁。蓋手足一身之微者也。雖微病焉則氣不通矣。仁
也者、天地萬物融 [219c] 爲一體、而無所間然之謂也。深體此理者、則雖
微物未嘗有所加害也。可謂得仁人之道矣。

　　如鵝珠草繫比丘、蓋其人矣。不如是則人與物氣[人+彡]而不叺理礙而
不通。如手足之痱也。醫書所云可謂善狀其仁矣。

　　詩云、一發五犯。論語云、釣而不綱、弋不射宿。孟子云、君子遠庖
廚也。聞其聲、不忍食其肉。又云數罟不入汚池、魚鼈不可勝食。此皆爲
仁而未盡其道也。何不契於一己之言乎。中庸云、言顧行行顧言、君子胡
不慥慥爾。今何至此乎。此儒者之所以善論爲仁之道而未盡善也。既要殺

少、何必發矢。旣憐其宿、何射不宿。旣遠庖廚、何必食肉。小旣傷殘、
何須害大。

佛於大戒以不殺居先。又慈心因緣不食肉經云、如佛所說、食肉者、
此人行慈不滿足。常受短命多病身、迷没生死不成佛。又、教中所以教持
漉囊者、恐傷微命也。昔有二比丘、同欲見佛、行於曠野。渴遇蟲水。一
人云但得見佛、飲之何罪。卽飲。一人云、佛戒殺生。若破佛戒、見佛
[220a]何益。忍渴不飲。死生天上、先見於佛得佛讚嘆。此乃仁人之眞語
實行、而冥相契於一己之言、惓惓之訓也。

餘未出家。有釋曰海月者。讀論語於豫。「至博施濟衆堯舜其猶病
諸」註云「仁者、以天地萬物爲一己之言。」置卷而問豫曰、孟子仁者
乎。曰、然。鷄豚狗彘彘萬物乎。曰、然。曰、仁者以天地萬物爲一己。
此眞稱理之談也、孟子苟爲仁者。而鷄豚狗彘又爲萬物則何以云鷄豚狗彘
之畜無失其時、七十者可以食肉乎。豫於是辭窮而未能答。考諸經傳、而
無有殺生稱理之論。博問先知、而無有釋然決疑之者。

常蘊此疑久未能決。越丙子許游三角山、到僧伽寺、與一老禪夜話話
次。禪云、佛有十重大戒、一不殺生。豫於是釋然心服而自謂此眞仁人之
行也。而深體乎仁道之語也。從此不疑於儒釋之間、而遂有詩云。素聞經
史程朱毅、未識浮圖是與非、反復潛思年已遠、始知眞實却歸依。

夫巢知風穴知雨。蜘蛛有布網之巧、蜣蜋有轉團之能。物皆如是、同
禀靈明。至於好生惡殺之情、亦何嘗異於人哉。方其磔然奏刀[220b]愬然就
死之時、盻盻然視、卣卣然鳴。豈非含怨結恨之情狀也。而人自昧耳。所
以人與物、相作而不覺、相償而無休。安有仁人、見其如是而忍爲之哉。

以我之嗜味、較彼之忍痛。苦樂皎然、而輕重可忖。報應之說、如其
妄也、則一任其作。如其不妄、來苦難當。可不愼歟。夫春蒐夏苗秋獮冬
狩、雖先王之法制、今有大山之中、海嶋之間、畋所不及之處。人與物各
遂其生、各安其所而善終天年者。以此觀之、則夫民也、何必因其獵而遂
其生也。

古人教以不合圍不掩群。此知其殺之不可、而事出乎不得已也。大抵
不得已底事。或中而不必合理也。旣不合理、何以爲大經乎。易云、古之
聰明睿智神武而不殺夫。蓋四時之畋、聖人托此、示之以神武、預防其外
寇爾。豈以殺爲心哉。此乃爲天下者之大權者爾。

以此觀之、則夫畋也、正同嫂溺援之以手之義。嫂溺手援暫時之用
爾。何以爲人間之常法也。至於犧牲、則人居平日、以肉爲甘旨。則其死
也、以其所嗜、祭之宜也。然潑水添冰、罪必加矣。昔人有殺羊祭先、其
先[220c]托夢而禁之。此其驗也、迹此觀之、則犧牲、雖曰盛禮亦廢之可
也。

8. Drinking Alcohol [*HPC* 7.220c3]

曰、酒所以合歡之藥也。調和血脈以却風冷。又於祭祀酒令降神。不可無
也。今浮圖設戒以禁不酤不飲。豈非過歟。

曰、酒爲亂神敗德之本、而尤害於道也。故律中指其過曰三十有六。
儒博亦明其失、云、「內昏其心志、外喪其威儀。」斯言善明、爲過之甚
也。內昏其心志故、妨其自修也。外喪其威儀故、妨其化道也。非惟無益
於自他、亦乃招殃禍於無窮也。由是儀狄獻之而致踈於禹、羅漢飲之而見
呵於佛。

夫禹之所以踈儀狄、佛之所以責羅漢者、豈非以酒之爲害。當使人婬
荒迷亂、至於滅身、敗道、亡國、失位者乎。禮將有事於天地鬼神、必先
數日齋、然後行一日祭。齋者、不茹薰葷酒、專誠而致潔也。以誠不專潔
不至、則神不享矣。佛之齋戒也、誠則長誠[221a]而無雜。潔則終身而不
汚。若以數日比之、天地何遠。既知齋之爲是、何必數日而已哉。數日之
外無祭之時、其可放緩乎。此儒之所以與佛有間者也。

9. Making Offerings [*HPC* 7.221a5]

曰、珍財人之所賴以生。當用之有節、畜而不費、以遺夫子孫、令不墜其
宗祀、不見其窮露。今浮圖、逃於四民之外、不事王事。亦已足矣。更誇
人以布施報應、令人盡持奉佛、而經至於飢寒窮露。豈非過歟。

曰、珍財長貪取禍之具也。布施清心致福之方也。儒博豈不云乎、財
聚則民散、財散則民聚。佛之所以勸人行施者、非爲自利而然也。只要令
人破除慳貪以淨心田而已。佛誡比丘、三常不足。三不足者、衣食睡眠皆
不足也。既以此誡其徒也、豈爲衣食於人、而勸之以施乎。若以衣食爲
心、則佛之教豈到今日。

10. Defense of the Doctrine of Karma and Rebirth [*HPC* 7.221a19]

至於報應之說、則豈獨吾教乎。易云、積善有餘慶、積惡有餘殃。又如洪
範、人合乎皇極、則天應之以五福。違、則應之以六極。此非報應歟。形存
而其應已然。及其死也、形雖謝而神存。善惡之應、豈不然乎。佛之言曰、
假饒[221b]百千劫、所作業不亡。因緣會遇時、果報還自受。豈欺人哉。

曰、人之生也、陰以稟其質、陽以稟其氣。一陰一陽、配爲魂魄而成
形。及其死也、魂昇魄降而就盡。夫人之所以有知覺者以其心也。心也
者、魂魄之合而一身之主也。其死也、與氣俱散、而更無有形、神尚留於
冥漠之中。誰更受福受殃。今浮圖、忻之以天堂怖之以地獄、令人致惑。
天是蒼蒼、而所有者、日月星辰而已。地是土石、而所載者、人與萬物而
已。謂之不亡者存、而感天堂地獄者、豈非妄乎。

曰、陰陽、固人之所賴以生者也。陰陽合而受生。陰陽散而就死。若
固有之眞明、則不隨形生、不隨形謝。雖千變萬化而湛然獨存也。夫心有
二。曰堅實心、曰肉團心。肉團心者、魂魄之精也。堅實心者、眞明之謂
也。今所謂心者、眞明也、非肉團也。

夫心者、身之主也。形者、心之使也。善惡等事、心君命之、形臣作
之。至於報應、生、則君臣等受。死、則形臣已謝、而心君獨受。詩云、
文王陟降在帝左右。陟降之者、豈非在天之靈乎。

昔有秀[221c]才曰王淮之。自小不信佛法。一日死而復蘇曰、向者自
謂形神俱滅。今始知佛之所謂形謝而神存、信不誣矣。

又宋人李源、與僧圓澤交。相約世世無相棄。一日同遊澤見夫人之汲
者、曰、此婦姓王氏。吾當爲其子。十二年後、杭州天竺寺外、須公相
見、以明交義。至暮澤果死。源果十二年、赴其約、聞葛洪川畔有牧童扣
牛角而歌、曰、三生石上舊精魂。賞月吟風、不要論。慚愧情人遠相訪。
此身雖異性長存。及相見、曰、李公眞信士也。而又歌、曰、身前身後事
茫茫、欲話因緣恐斷腸。吳越山川尋已徧、却回煙棹上瞿塘。

至如羊祜爲李氏之子、王子爲蔡氏之孫。餘曾觀此傳、爲羊李頌云。
羊李只一人、往復非異環。誰知七歲子、滅已五年還。爲王蔡頌云。昔日
王家子、今爲蔡氏孫。不因一點墨、同異議紛紜。

觀此數事、則足知靈明之不隨形變也。謂之人死、而形神俱滅、豈非
昧乎。至於天獄、則非是實然固有。乃人之業感自然如是也。孔子嘗曰。
吾不復夢見周公久[222a]矣。蓋夢者、人之神游、非形之使然也。夫子之
所以夢與周公見者、蓋平日心存周公之道、專而行之故。其精神自然相感
而然也。

人亦如是。日於善惡、爲之旣專。則善者夢見其榮。惡者夢見其辱。
所以然者、善者亹亹然、惟義是從。惡者恈恈然、惟利是求。善者惟義是
從、故事事而適宜。惡者惟利是求、故事事而違義。善者事事而適宜、故
人必善之。惡者事事而違義、故人必惡之。善者人善之、故自達於上、而
加之以爵祿。惡者人惡之故、自達於上、而加之以刑罰。由是善者與與忻
致其榮。惡者錯愕謀避其殃。

善惡之習、忻厭之情、蘊在情神。故、其於夢也、亦見榮見辱。其神
往而不返、則便是來生。此善者之所以感天堂、惡者之所以感地獄者也。
天堂地獄設使無者。人之聞者、慕天堂而趨善。厭地獄而沮惡。則天獄之
說之於化民。利莫大焉。果其有者、善者必昇天堂、惡者必陷地獄。故使
之聞之則善者自勉而當享天宮、惡者自止而免入地獄。何必斥於天獄之
說、而以爲妄耶。

11. Defense of the Buddhist Practice of Cremation [*HPC* 7.222a24]

曰、夫送死。人間世之大事者也。故丁父[222b]母之喪者、不可不以爲重
也。聖人垂厚葬追遠之訓、所以示其重也。所以令厚葬者、如木根深則枝
葉扶疎而實多。根淺則枝葉夭閼而無實。夫父母之於子也、如木之於實
也。子之於父母、猶實之於木也。故云、父之傳於子、猶木之傳於實也。
由是遇其喪者、要須擇其地、得其宜、深其穴、厚其葬、茂其林、貯其
水。令陰深而畜氣、土厚而不澆。致令子孫繁衍、而厥祀綿綿。

今浮圖、不顧此理而妄設火化之法、令人無後而絕嗣。豈非過也。況
方其火化之際、人子之心其可忍視乎。以是惑、人過犯漫天。

曰、夫人者、有形焉、有神焉。形比則如屋、神比則如主。形謝而其
神往焉、猶屋倒而主不得住焉。夫屋也、成以土木嚴以雜穢。人以爲己
有、貪湎其中而不知其陋也。雖見其倒、未能頓忘而不能遠去也。

夫身也。水土以搆其形、火風以持其質。中含雜穢、不淨流溢、人之
護之甚於金玉。何嘗有厭離之情也。及其死也、火風先去而地水猶存。其
爲地水前所愛護故、不能頓忘而隨往無礙也。智者焚其地水、而指其往生
之[222c]路。其神更無稽滯之情、卽同膠葛而淸昇也。

由是吾佛世尊、丁父之喪躬自執爐。四天舉棺、羅漢採薪而闍維。今
其父之神、淸昇而生天。黃蘗運公之度母也陳懷白佛、隔江擲炬。其母於
火焰中、化爲男子。身乘大光明、上昇天宮。兩岸皆見咸以爲奇。江名福
川、官司改福川爲大義渡。

以是觀之、則火化之法、令人去穢而就淨、神淸而遐邇、舉堪。爲薦
往之助道、垂世之洪規。若以火化爲不忍、方其穴土而埋之。其可忍也。
今有大山之麓、大野之原、多有古墳、盡爲農者之所耕。頭骨星散。日煮
風飄、無人顧護。其初莫不立石栽松以嚴其地、以圖子孫之繁衍、厥祀之
綿綿。今何至此乎。

但、生前五蘊皆空、六根淸淨。一念無生者、則雖寓形宇內、而常棲
神於物表、故澄澄合空。湛湛如水。猶以有身爲幻也、由是及其化也、如
決疣去垢。如解懸脫枷。如鳥出籠、如馬出閑。洋洋乎、于于乎、逍遙自
適也、去留無礙也。其於地水安有稽滯之情[223a]哉。

此人分上、沈之可也、露之可也。鑿石而藏之、穴土而坑之、以至爲
野火之所燒、蟲蟻之所食。無所施而不可也。故達磨葬於熊耳山、六祖全
身留世、普化搖鈴騰去、淸凉命飴[1]　林獸。此皆達人遺世之高蹤、忘我之
勝迹者也。自餘則未能忘形無我故、須經火化然後其神淸昇而無滯也。有
人客死他鄉、收其骨而火之而其後德望高於世、寵望歸於己。子孫振振而
厥祀綿綿。謂之火化而利不及後者、私憂過計之甚也。毋以無稽之談、枉
招冥龜之報。

曰、人之生死、卽人之始終也。故孔子只言生死而未嘗言其前後也。
今浮圖言其前後而幷其死生之間、謂之三世。夫生前死後、非耳目之所
接。孰親視之乎。以之惑人豈非誕也。

曰人之生死、猶晝夜之代謝。既有代謝則自成前後。晝、則以去夜爲
前、來夜爲後。夜、則以去日爲前、來日爲後。幷其晝夜自成三際。晝夜
既爾、歲月亦然。歲月既爾、生死亦然。已往之無始未來之無窮、亦由是
而可知也。易云、彰往察來。明失得之報。往來之言、豈非[223b]所謂前
後乎。以三世之說爲誕者、未之思也。

1.　*HPC* offers the alternative of 飴.

12. Refutation of the Complaint against Buddhism as a Foreign Religion [*HPC* 7.223b3]

曰、天下之可遵者、五帝三王之道而已。故孔聖祖述而羣賢相傳載諸方策而列國皆遵。此道可求之於中國、不可求之於夷狄也。佛西夷之人也。豈以其道流行於中國也。漢明帝、求其法於西域昧也非明也。

曰、道之所存、是人之所歸也。五帝三王既道之所存故、爲人之所歸、而王於華夏也。佛之興天竺而爲法輪王、亦復如是。華夏之指天竺爲西、猶天竺之指華夏爲東也。若取天下之大中、則當午無影爲中、天竺乃爾。佛之所以示生於彼者、豈非以其天下之大中也。

所謂東西者、蓋彼此時俗之相稱爾。非占其中而定其東西也。苟以佛爲夷、而不遵其道、則舜生於東夷、文王生於西夷。可夷其人而不遵其道乎。所出迹也、所行道也。但觀其道之可遵不可遵也、不可拘其所出之迹也

前不云乎。道之所存、是人之所歸也。春秋以徐伐莒而夷狄之。狄人與齊人、盟于邢而中國之。夫徐以中國而受夷狄之名、以其不義也。狄人[223c]受中國之稱、以其有義也。凡於襃貶之間、但觀人之明昧。事之當否。豈以其所出、而議其人乎。如不求其迹、而求其所行之道。則但五戒十善之道、可無愧於五帝三王之道矣。況諦緣六度等法乎。若使五帝三王遇之、則必合掌跪膝而聽受矣。明帝之求不其宜乎。

13. Refutation of the Accusation of Buddhism as a Harbinger of Calamity [*HPC* 7.223c8]

曰、自佛法入中國以來、世漸澆漓飢饉荐臻。民多失所爲瘋日甚。其爲害也。不亦大哉。

曰、堯、舜、禹、湯、以天下之大聖、而尚未免水旱之災。桀、紂、幽、厲、以天下之人主而未免爲獨夫。周衰而人民已匱。秦作而天下大亂。以孔子之大聖、而未免於絕粮。顏回之亞聖、而未免於夭折。原憲之大賢、而未免於家貧。此亦以佛而然歟。佛興天竺正當周昭。至漢明帝法流東土。三代以前、佛未之作。孔顏之時、名亦未聞。彼時當無災孼。亦無飢饉。堯何有九年之水、湯何有七年之旱。孔顏何窮、而原憲何貧乎。

唐太宗與 [224a] 魏徵、李淳風等、協心同德、混一天下兆民咸熙、率土來賀。新羅眞德王、自製大平歌、織錦爲文而獻之。其略曰「大唐開洪業、巍巍皇猷昌、止戈戎威定、修文契百王、深仁諧日月、撫運邁虞唐。以至云、維嶽降宰輔、惟帝任忠良、五三成一德、昭我唐家皇。」又新羅太宗春秋公與金庾信、同心勠力、一統三韓。有大功於社稷。

彼時、年豐穀賤、民樂無憂。皆謂之聖代。若是佛法使不昇平、此當佛法盛行之時也、何其昇平、至於如是之極乎。趙州稔禪師、生經七百甲

子。五臺山開法師、生存三百餘載。若是佛法令人夭折、彼旣佛子何其命也、至於如是之壽乎。古今、治亂、脩短、苦樂、大關時運之盛衰、亦是衆生之業感。以世不昇平、民不聊生、歸咎於佛法、亦未之思也。

14. Refutation of the Accusation of Monks being Parasites [*HPC* 7.224a19]

曰爾浮圖輩逸爲遊民。不蠶不耕、而衣食於人、故民被其惱、屢至於窮。其爲廢也、不亦大哉。

曰、僧之任在弘法利生。弘法而令慧命不斷。利生而使人人自善、是僧之務也。苟能如是。則可無愧於爲人之所奉矣。[224b]苟不能然、是其人之罪也。豈佛之過歟。孟子曰、於此有人焉入則孝出則悌、守先王之道、以待後之學者。不得食於子。子何尊梓匠輪輿而輕爲仁義者哉。

此豈非以守道利人而可衣食於人乎。夫人之貧富、各自有素分。宿有善種者、則雖日費而有餘。宿無善種者、則雖日聚而不足。世有人焉、見佛不禮、見僧呵毀。終身而不施一錢。衣不蔽形、食不充口。此亦因僧而致然歟。

15. Refutation of the Charge of Decadence in the *Saṃgha* [*HPC* 7.224b11]

曰、清淨寡欲、爲法亡軀、多聞強記、接引後來、固釋子之行也。今浮圖輩、不修其行、反汚師法。人問其道、如立面墻。褊販如來資養身命。廬其居、人其人。以充乎四民之數、而令輔弼乎。君國可也。

曰、麒麟鸞鳳族不成羣。尺璧寸珠市不可求。孔門三千稱哲人者、十人而已。如來海會稱第一者、亦不過十人而已。況今去聖愈遠、根機微劣。安得使人人如迦葉之淨行、阿難之多聞乎。孔顏之後千載之下、如顏淵閔子騫者、亦未之聞也。夫僧之爲僧、具五德脩六和然後、方稱其名也。然名實相符[224c]者、蓋難其人矣。林有不材之木、田有不實之禾。縱有不能如法奉行者、不可疾之甚也。但令因其形服、漸薰成性、不失其道而已。豈得因其失而廢其法也。

16. Refutation of the Charges of Nihilism and Antinomianism [*HPC* 7.224c6]

曰、考其爲書、務於虛遠、崇於寂滅。其功倍於小學而無用。其高過於大學而無實。不可以爲修己治人之方也矣。

曰、書者、載道之具也。弘化之方也。見其書則知其道之可遵不可遵。知其禮之可慕不可慕也。其道可遵、其禮可慕、則豈以非吾所習而可棄之也。君不聞乎。天下無二道、聖人無兩心。夫聖人者、雖千里之隔、萬世之遠、其心未嘗有異也。孔夫子之言曰、毋意毋必毋固毋我。易又云、艮其背、無我也。行其庭、無人也。無我無人、何垢之有。釋迦老之言曰、無我無人修一切善法、卽得菩提。此聖人之所以異世而同其心也。

　　所謂虛遠寂滅之言、三藏十二部中、據何典而言歟。大戒云、孝順至道之法[225a]孝名爲戒、亦名制止。一向謂之虛遠可乎。圓覺云、心花發明、照十方剎。一向謂之寂滅可乎。若欲驗其眞僞、必先審其書也。不審其書而妄排之、則必爲達者之所嗤矣。

　　君不聞乎。未盡天下文章、不得雌黃古今。孔之言曰、夫孝天之經也、地之義也、民之行也。豈非至道之謂乎。感而遂通天下之故、豈非明照之謂乎。儒之所謂明德、卽佛之所謂妙精明心也。所謂寂然不動、感而遂通、卽佛之所謂寂照者也。所謂有善於己、然後可以責人之善、無惡於己、然後可以正人之惡者、與吾教所謂斷惡修善、饒益有情者、何以異乎。

17. The Unity of the Three Teachings [*HPC* 7.225a14]

所言之理旣同、而所教之迹、何以異乎。專己略人、是此非彼、人之常情也。通人達士唯義是從。豈以人我彼此而是非者乎。使人不待爵賞之勸而靡然從化者、三教之中、佛教能然也。蓋以吾佛大聖大慈之所感也。舜好問而好察邇言、隱惡而揚善。禹拜昌言。若使舜禹遇佛之化、則豈不歸美乎。而以爲不可爲修己治人之方者、亦未之思也。

　　曰老與儒釋、同異優劣如何。

　　[225b]曰、老之言曰、無爲而無不爲。當有爲而無爲。釋之言曰、寂而常照、照而常寂。孔之言曰、夫易無思也無爲也。寂然不動、感而遂通。夫寂然者、未嘗無感、卽寂而常照也。感通者、未嘗不寂、卽照而常寂也。無爲而無不爲、卽寂而常感也。有爲而無所爲。卽感而常寂也。據此則三家所言、冥相符契、而如出一口也。若履踐之高低、發用之同異、則洗盡心垢、廓淸慧目、然後看盡大藏儒道諸書。參於日用之間、生死禍福之際、則不待言而自點頭矣。吾何強辨以駁君聽。

Notes

Introduction

1. Recently the rendering of "authenticity" has become popular for *sŏng*, but this seems to me to be a move toward unhelpful abstraction. Compare "I just met Jack for the first time — a real *sincere* fellow" with "I just met Jack for the first time — a real *authentic* fellow." What would we make of "authentic" in this case? In my translation choices I prefer real-language feeling over philosophical abstraction wherever possible.

2. In the earliest period of the translation of the Chinese classics into English, *ŭi* was rendered with the Christian-sounding "righteousness," while in recent decades this seems to have given way to a preference for "rightness" among most scholars of Confucianism. But the main implication in the *Analects* and *Mencius* is that of a sense of fairness in dealing with subordinates, thus my general preference is a "(sense of) justice." *Ŭi* refers to our capacity to give other persons and things their proper due, putting aside our own desires or interests. In the *Analects* and the *Mencius,* it is commonly seen contrasted with the notion of personal profit (K. *yi,* Ch. *li* 利) and is a defining component of the character of the exemplary person (K. *kunja,* Ch. *junzi* 君子). The rendering of this concept into English as "due-giving" was suggested to me by the noted scholar of Islam William Chittick, who in noting it as a standard attribute of the character of Sufi sages, points out that it bears great resemblance to this fundamental Confucian concept. See Chittick, *Sufi Path of Knowledge,* 174.

3. Numerous passages in the *Analects* attest to this essence-function relationship between humaneness and the other Confucian values. For example, in *Analects* 1:2, "Yuzi said, 'There are few who have developed themselves filially and fraternally who like offending their superiors. Those who do not like to offend their superiors are never troublemakers. The noble man concerns himself with the fundamentals. Once the fundamentals are established, the proper Way appears. Are not filial piety and obedience to elders fundamental to the enactment of humaneness?'" Scores of similar examples exist. See Muller, "Tiyong and Interpenetration in the Analects," for an elaboration of this position, along with other examples.

4. For example, in *Daode jing,* chap. 48: "In studying, each day something is gained. // In following the Way, each day something is lost. // Lost and again lost. // Until there is nothing left to do." Muller, *Daode jing.*

5. For a more complete discussion of this point, see Muller, "Essence-Function (*t'i-yung*)."

6. In rendering the title of the *Dasheng qixin lun* as "Awakening of Mahāyāna Faith," as opposed to Hakeda's "Awakening of Faith in Mahāyāna," I am following the argument made by Sung Bae Park in chap. 4 of his *Buddhist Faith and Sudden Enlightenment*. He argues there that the inner discourse of the text, along with the basic understanding of the meaning of *mahāyāna* in the East Asian Buddhist tradition, does accord with a Western theological "faith in…" subject-object construction, but instead according with an indigenous East Asian essence-function model. Thus, *mahāyāna* should not be interpreted as a noun-object but as a modifier that characterizes the *type* of faith.

7. Although this sutra first appeared with the Indian title *Vajrasamādhi-sūtra* attached, it was clearly composed in East Asia. Scholars such as Robert Buswell have argued that it may well have even been composed in Korea. See Buswell, *Formation of Ch'an Ideology* and *Cultivating Original Enlightenment*.

8. The extensive mutual influence that occurred between Buddhism and Daoism is examined in depth in Sharf, *Coming to Terms with Chinese Buddhism*.

9. Charles Hartman's *Han Yü and the T'ang Search for Unity* provides an excellent study of Han's life and works.

10. A translation by Bryan Van Norden is online at http://faculty.vassar.edu/brvannor/Phil210/HanYu/On the Origin of the Way.pdf.

11. Translated in many anthologies. See, for example, de Bary, *Sources of Chinese Tradition*, 583–585. Chŏng Tojŏn makes extensive use of these two essays in the final passages of the *Pulssi chappyŏn*.

12. See Gregory, *Inquiry into the Origin of Humanity*, 35–36.

13. Some Western scholars have come to question the blanket use of this term, citing important differences in various Confucian-based doctrinal systems that appeared at this time. See, for example, Joseph Adler, *Reconstructing the Confucian Dao*, 11–12.

14. See de Bary, *Message of the Mind*, 17.

15. The point is often made in present-day Chan historical scholarship that despite Chan's anti-textual rhetoric, its adherents ended up composing a voluminous literature that would be studied by succeeding generations. While this is true, we must still pay due attention to the actual message of this literature, which points to a Buddhist teaching emphasizing simplicity, intuitiveness, and directness in daily activity and that invariably casts "sutra lecturers" in an inferior role to Chan masters of the "great function."

16. The Four Books are the basic texts of Confucian learning selected by Zhu Xi as a core curriculum during the Song period. They are the *Analects*, the *Mencius*, the *Great Learning*, and the *Doctrine of the Mean*.

17. This canon was authorized by the emperor in 51 BCE and included the *Shijing* 詩經 (Book of Poems), the *Shujing* 書經 (Book of Documents; also called the Book of History), the *Yijing* 易經 (Book of Changes), the *Chunchiu* 春秋 (Spring and Autumn Annals), and the *Liji* 禮記 (Record of Ritual).

18. Along with Michael Kalton, I take the Neo-Confucian *li-qi* pair to be a rather obvious influence from the Huayan *li-shi* paradigm. As Kalton says, "The most prominent development of the concept of *li* was also under Buddhist auspices, notable in the Hwa Yen school" as part of the "Taoist and Buddhist ambience [that] contributed its own notes to this surge of Neo-Confucian vitality and creativity" (*The Four-Seven Debate*; xvii). That is to say, I don't think it is any more necessary to track down a direct association between the Cheng brothers or Zhu Xi with a Huayan scholar than it would be to find a direct relationship with Derrida in a modern scholar who shows the influences of deconstruction. For an effort at tracking down direct personal connections in Huayan, see, for comparison, Adler, *Reconstructing the Confucian Dao*, 104.

19. For a thorough and insightful study of Zhou Dunyi, especially in the all-important context of his relationship to Zhu Xi, see Adler, *Reconstructing the Confucian Dao*.

20. The works of these two scholars are available in Chinese, but so far very little is available in English translation except in small selections contained in anthologies, the largest of which is that in Wing-tsit Chan's *Source Book* (518–571).

21. *Analects* 12:1 reads, "Yan Yuan asked about the meaning of humaneness. The Master said, 'To completely overcome selfishness and keep to propriety is humaneness. If for a full day you can overcome selfishness and keep to propriety, everyone in the world will return to humaneness. Does humaneness come from oneself, or from others?'" See Muller, *Analects*.

22. See Wing-tsit Chan, *Source Book*, 554–555.

23. See Morrison, *Power of Patriarchs* (esp. 95–100 for Qisong's dealings with Confucianism.

24. In using the term "exclusivism" here, I refer especially to the landmark work done on this topic by John Goulde in his 1984 Ph.D. dissertation, "Anti-Buddhist Polemic in Fourteenth and Fifteenth Century Korea: The Emergence of Korean Exclusivism." In this work Goulde traces the developments of the Neo-Confucian polemic from their Chinese roots, through their failures and successes in Korea, to their final culmination in the creation of the Chosŏn dynasty (1392–1910). Nothing has been published subsequently in English to surpass Goulde's dissertation in terms of discussion of this critical episode in Korean history.

25. Wang Yangming was a Ming-dynasty Neo-Confucian thinker who argued against some of the fundamental aspects of the philosophy of Zhu Xi and espoused the doctrine of the "unity of knowledge and action." He would become especially influential in Japan, where there was a strong interest in Lu-Wang philosophy among the samurai class of the Edo period. His ideas were largely rejected in Korea. For a complete study of the life and thought of Wang, see Julia Ching, *To Acquire Wisdom*.

26. See Goulde, "Anti-Buddhist Polemic," 166–192, for a detailed description of the lives and works of the five above-mentioned figures, and others.

27. For a comprehensive treatment of Chŏng Tojŏn, see Han Yŏng'u, *Chŏng Tojŏn sasang ŭi yŏn'gu*. In English, see Chai-shik Chung, "Chŏng Tojŏn: 'Architect'

of Yi Dynasty Government." Also see the discussion of Chŏng in the chapter "The Ideology of Reform" in Duncan, *The Origins of the Chosŏn Dynasty*.

28. Translated into English a few times, the most recent and authoritative is Peter Gregory's 1995 translation entitled *Inquiry into the Origin of Humanity*. My own translation of this text is forthcoming from the Numata BDK series.

29. For a full study of the Chinese doctrinal classification systems, see Chanju Mun's *History of Doctrinal Classification in Chinese Buddhism*.

30. This sutra is not extant but is cited in many old texts. It is a Chinese indigenous sutra composed by Tanjing 曇靖 of the Northern Wei dynasty during the reign period of Emperor Xiaowu of the Liu-Song dynasty (453–464). Makita Tairyō reconstructed the text based on Dunhuang manuscripts: Pelliot 3732 and Stein 2051 and the citation found in the *Fayuan zhulin* (T 2122.53.932b–933a). See Makita *Gikyō kenkyū*, 184–206. The text takes its name from its two main protagonists, the merchants Trapuṣa and Bhallika. In the *Diwei jing,* these two fellows are described as well versed in knowledge of yin and yang, divination using tortoise shells, and the *Yijing*. They meet the Buddha immediately after his awakening, and he teaches them that those who keep the five precepts will be reborn as humans while those who do the ten good deeds will be reborn in a heaven as gods (hence the name of the teaching, *rentian jiao* 人天教, for which the text was known in the doctrinal taxonomies of the period); persons who commit misdeeds will be born into the unfortunate destinies. The five wholesome practices are correlated with the five Confucian virtues (Ch. *wuchang* 五常); they are also correlated with various other sets of five, after the manner of the tradition of correlative cosmology native to Chinese culture.

31. The present-day Sŏngyun'gwan University in Seoul traces its roots to this academy.

32. A reference to Zhou Gongdan 周公旦 and Shao Gong 召公, two worthies who cooperated in the establishment of the Zhou dynasty. This passage is from the biographical sketch of Kihwa entitled "Hamhŏ tang Tŭkt'ong hwasang haengjang," *HPC* 7.250c6–11.

33. This is a common trope of hagiographies of East Asian Buddhist scholar-monks, one that establishes the scholar's command of the Confucian teachings while at the same time showing that he found them to be inadequate. And like many earlier Chinese and Korean scholars, it is clear that Kihwa's persistent interest in Confucianism was such that we might even say that he continued to some extent to be a Confucian. As Morrison points out, this pattern can be seen in a number of Chinese monks of the late Tang and early Song, including Zanning 贊寧 (919–1001), the Tiantai master Zhiyuan 智圓 (976–1022), and Qisong (*Power of Patriarchs*, 115–120).

34. Kihwa's extant writings are contained in volume 7 of the *Collected Works of Korean Buddhism* (*Han'guk Pulgyo chŏnsŏ*). One of his major works, his commentary on the *Sutra of Perfect Enlightenment,* is translated and published by Muller under the same title; his *Hyŏnjŏng non* is translated in this volume. In terms of Kihwa's connection with Zongmi, the *Sutra of Perfect Enlightenment* is of some sig-

nificance, as it was Zongmi's favorite text, on which he commented extensively. In Korea, it was Kihwa who wrote the definitive commentary on the sutra. Thus, Kihwa and Zongmi are closely linked in terms of mutual interest in this sutra, in the unity of study and practice, in Huayan, the in the *Awakening of Mahāyāna Faith,* and so forth.

35. I stress this point in view of the fact that Han Young-woo has explicitly stated that "the *Hyŏnjŏng non* is *not* a refutation of the *Pulssi chappyŏn.*" See Han's *Chŏng Tojŏn,* 53, n. 1. I see Han's view as accurate only in a very strict sense. It may be true that Kihwa did not sit down upon the publication of the *Chappyŏn* and write an immediate point-by-point rebuttal. In 1398, when Chŏng wrote the *Chappyŏn,* Kihwa would have been twenty-two, a mere novice in Buddhism. Yet even though Kihwa never directly names Chŏng or his treatise, the fact that Chŏng was a faculty member of the Sŏngyun'gwan at the time that Kihwa was a student would make it a virtual impossibility for Kihwa not to have read the text. Furthermore, in the *Hyŏnjŏng non* Kihwa directly replies to all of the *Chappyŏn*'s accusations, using mimicry that directly alludes to Chŏng's rhetorical style.

36. Since these works are now available in digital form, it would be instructive to do an n-gram analysis of them to glean some actual statistics. I have not attempted to identify every single citation here, as it would be an endless task. I do, however, attempt to note citations of relatively well-known phrases from these two major sources.

37. On the matter of the paramount importance of consistency and continuity for Zhu Xi, see Adler, *Reconstructing the Confucian Dao,* 33–50.

38. The Chinese line 體用一原、顯微無間 is probably cited here from Zhu Xi's *Chuanxilu* 傳習録, but is originally from Cheng Yi's commentary on the *Yijing.* See *Henan Er Cheng yishu* 18, Cheng Yi, Scripta Sinica.

39. From the *Vimalakīrti-nirdeśa-sūtra,* T 475.14.539a29.

40. "Correcting the internal with reverence, correcting the external with justice" is a repeated aphorism found in the texts of the Cheng brothers, Zhu Xi, and many other Neo-Confucian writers, originally drawn from the *Yijing,* in the text of *kun* 坤, the second hexagram. See Wilhelm, *I-Ching,* 393.

41. *Henan Er Cheng yishu,* 15. Also see Wing-tsit Chan, *Sourcebook,* 530, sec. 11. This particular citation comes from the same section of the Cheng's *Yishu* that contains most of the philosophical arguments that form the basis for Chŏng's arguments in the *Pulssi chappyŏn.*

42. *Analects* 7:27 says, "When fishing, the Master would not use a net; when hunting, he would not shoot at a perched bird."

43. *Mencius* 1A:7 says that "The noble man keeps his distance from the butchery, for if he hears the screams of beasts being slaughtered, he cannot stand to eat their meat."

44. For the first phrase, see Muller, *Daode jing,* chap. 37.

45. *Zongjing lu,* T 2016.48.528a1.

46. *Xici zhuan,* pt. 1.

47. A solid treatment of this issue can be found in Vermeersch, "Yi Seong-

gye and the Fate of the Goryeo Buddhist System." I also recommend the excellent summary of the later history of Korean Buddhism provided in the first chapter of Hwansoo Kim's *Empire of the Dharma*, which makes this point eminently clear.

48. English translation by Yong-ho Lee in "The Ideal Mirror of the Three Religions."

49. Those familiar with the influential little book *The Secular as Sacred*, written a generation ago by Herbert Fingarette, will recognize that I am here disagreeing with the central tenet expressed in that work: that it is the concept of propriety that is most fundamental to the worldview of the Confucian classics, with *ren* having only secondary significance. Fingarette has been duly praised for his insightful analyses regarding the pervasiveness of the unconscious uses of propriety, not only in ancient Chinese society but in society in general. But in his prioritization of *li* over *ren,* he ignores a mountain of evidence in the Confucian classical texts that belies his position; the textual evidence in the *Analects* that points to a greater "psychological interiority" for *ren* than the other virtues of the sage, or noble person (*junzi*), is overwhelming. And to merely state that *ren* is more internal, deeper than the other virtues is to stop short, as the relationship between *ren* and the other virtues is quintessentially *ti-yong* in nature.

50. It is noteworthy that in traditional East Asian thought, the relationship of black and white is markedly different from the common association seen in the West, where black tends to be associated with evil and white with good. From the earliest periods of East Asian history, black (also written with the ideograph *xuan* 玄) has the connotations of depth, profundity, mastery, etc., while white tends to be associated with superficiality.

51. This Chinese concept of *pu,* which has connotations of simplicity and naiveté, is the origin of the A. A. Milne character, the beloved Winnie the Pooh. See Benjamin Hoff, *The Tao of Pooh.*

52. On the role of *li* in Chinese thought, see Ziporyn, "Ironies of Oneness and Difference."

53. In his commentary to the *Daode jing,* entitled *Laozi zhu* 老子注. See especially his commentary to chap. 38 (translated by Lynn, *Classic of the Way and Virtue*). The evidence that Wangbi was the first to actually use this construction is not fully conclusive.

54. *American Heritage Dictionary,* 2nd College ed.

55. *Webster's New World Dictionary.*

56. *American Heritage Dictionary,* 2nd College ed.

57. See the opening section of my translation of *Great Learning.*

58. For an in-depth study and translation of the documents of this debate, see Kalton, *The Four-Seven Debate* and Chung, *The Korean Neo-Confucianism of Yi T'oegye and Yi Yulgok*

59. Even though it is not defined specifically with the ideographs *ti* and *yong* until the early third century CE, an essence-function type of framework can be seen operating ubiquitously in the earliest Chinese classics. See my discussion in Muller "Key Operative Concepts."

60. Once we understand the essence-function structure as a tool for describing the dynamics of spiritual training, we can begin to make a distinction between approaches that tend to be more "essence-oriented" and those that are more "function-oriented." For example, we might observe that the Confucian tendency to focus on forms of behavior in the social context—training oneself through propriety, filial piety, loyalty, and so forth—results in a tendency to approach the matter of personal cultivation through *function*. On the other hand, a typical Daoist approach that recommends a "return" to one's original nature—or points to the invisible virtue possessed by someone who otherwise shows no special talents (such as the ugly Ai-tai To introduced by *Zhuangzi*)—could be characterized as an essence-oriented approach.

61. The locus classicus for this term is the Councils of the Great Yu 大禹謨 chapter of the *Shang shu* 尚書. "The human mind is precarious; the mind of *dao* is subtle" 人心惟危、道心惟微 (Scripta Sinica).

62. Although a strong monastic system developed in East Asia, the practice of leaving home never became as culturally widespread as it had in India, and many East Asian monastic forms of practice (most notably in Chan) came to place strong emphasis on involvement in phenomenal activity such as farming, physical exercise, and so forth.

63. See, for example, the *Linji lu*, T 1985.47.495b16.

64. The noted scholar of Sufism, William Chittick, told me of a similar attitude in the Islamic tradition about the need to balance the mystical and everyday dimensions of experience, which goes something like this: A disciple came on his camel to visit with his master. Neglecting to properly tie his camel to a stake outside, the disciple came out afterward to find the camel was gone. He lamented to his master, saying, "I put my faith in Allah!" To this the master replied, "Put your faith in Allah, but don't forget to tie up your camel!"

65. See Sharf, *Coming to Terms with Chinese Buddhism.*

66. See, for example, Wing-tsit Chan translation: "If a man (the ruler) can for one day master himself and return to propriety, all under heaven will return to humanity" (*Source Book,* 38).

This rendering assumes that the only way to make the people "humane" is through the enforcement of political power. There is no doubt that Confucius himself sought to place himself in the services of a good king to help bring peace to the world. But at the same time there is no indication that he is speaking to a king here, nor does the word *wang* appear in the sentence. James Legge in his translation says, "If a man can for one day subdue himself and return to propriety, all under heaven will ascribe virtue to him" (*Analects,* 250). Legge's rendering weakens the force of the passage even further by interpreting the word *gui* (which clearly means "return" in Chinese) as "ascribe to him," a thoroughly unnatural reading. D. C. Lau stays fairly close to Legge when he translates, "If for a single day a man could return to the observance of rites through overcoming himself, then the whole Empire would consider benevolence to be his" (*Analects,* 112).

67. In *Analects* 12:19, Zhi Kangzi asked Confucius about government, saying,

"Suppose I were to kill the unjust in order to advance the just. Would that be all right?" Confucius replied, "In governing, what is the need of killing? If you desire good, the people will be good. The nature of the noble man is like the wind; the nature of the inferior man is like the grass. When the wind blows over the grass, it always bends."

68. See Nakamura Hajime, *Bukkyōgo daijiten,* 971a.

69. The importance of recognizing the value of the mutual influences of study and practice was one of the predominant themes in the discourse of Kihwa, whose work we will read below, a matter that is elaborated at length in his *Commentaries of Five Masters on the Diamond Sutra (Ogahae sŏrui)*. I have examined Kihwa's discussions on this topic in Muller, "Gihwa's Analysis."

70. It is no doubt because of this understanding that memorization played such a central role in the instruction of all three major thought systems. We also might note that even in the so-called bibliophobic streams of meditational Buddhism in East Asia, meditation sessions and various other rituals include, right up to modern times, memorized chanting of seminal texts such as the *Heart Sutra* and *Diamond Sutra.*

71. While there were occasional thinkers in East Asian history (such as Mencius' contemporary, Xunzi) who did not subscribe to this view of "innate sagehood," they remain a small minority.

Translation 1: On Mind, Material Force, and Principle (*Simgiri p'yŏn*)

1. I.e., the description of a mind that lacks the limitations of private concerns, which is equanimous and yet capable of penetrating everywhere. This comes from Zhu Xi's commentary on the *Great Learning,* on the section on "Illuminating Virtue" *Daxue zhangju,* Mingde, Zhuzbu 大學章句, 明德, 朱注. http://mokusai-web .com/shushigakukihonsho/daigaku/daigaku.html.

2. Referring to its characteristic of non-obstruction.

3. E.g., T 235.8.749a24.

4. From the *Liuzu tanjing* (Platform Sutra of the Sixth Patriarch), T 2008. 48.359b29–359c1. Translated by John McRae: "One day the master announced to the assembly, 'I have a thing without head or tail, without name or title, without front or back'" (McRae, *Platform Sutra of the Sixth Patriarch,* 78).

5. This statement by Śākyamuni, which it is said he uttered shortly after being born, is well known and can be found throughout the Buddhist canon. This particular rendition is only found in Chan texts, e.g., the *Biyan lu* (Blue Cliff Record), T 2003.48.146c16. Chan Buddhists would probably not have readily supported this equivalence, as it sounds too much like eternalism, but this is all part of Chŏng's rhetorical strategy.

6. "Its numinous intelligence is not dulled": *ling zhi bu mei* 靈知不昧 is a common Chan term. See, for example, *Zongjing lu,* T 2016.48.417c11.

7. T 235.8.749c22–23. See Muller's translation of the *Diamond Sutra.*

8. The "four gross elements" are the four main sensory aspects of matter, of which, in Indian Buddhism, all physical substances are composed. They are: (1) the earth element (Skt. *pṛthivī dhātu*), which has the basic quality of hardness and the function of protection; (2) water (Skt. *ab-dhātu*), which has the function of gathering and storing wetness; (3) fire (Skt. *teja-dhātu*), which is the nature of heat and has the function of warming; (4) wind (Skt. *vāyū-dhātu*), which has the function of giving motion to all living things, motion being that which produces and maintains life. It was thought that these four together produce material substance.

9. I know of no Buddhist text that teaches that the four elements arise from material force — the psycho-physical "stuff" of the universe — and therefore speculate that this may be a Neo-Confucian interpolation based on the phrase cited in the next sentence from the *Sutra of Perfect Enlightenment* and its surrounding context.

10. T 842.17.914b22; see Muller, *Sutra of Perfect Enlightenment*, 103.

11. Chŏng is misquoting, whether intentionally or not, as the line in the sutra is 六塵緣影爲自心相, which translates as "*characteristics* of the mind" (T 842.17.913b25), not *nature* of the mind. This apparently minor misquote is of critical importance in light of the fact that the specific Buddhist notion being critiqued in this section is that of nature (*sŏng* 性). This is one of several places in this text where Chŏng makes minor textual changes that tend to lend support to his arguments.

12. The above paragraph is also derived from the same section of the *Sutra of Perfect Enlightenment* (T 842.17.913b23–29); see Muller, *Sutra of Perfect Enlightenment*, 103.

13. Chŏng is paraphrasing common Sŏn characterizations of Buddhist meditative practice but then questioning their validity. In terms of the importance of the essence-function paradigm in Neo-Confucian thought, the disconnection from characteristics and essence would be to imply that Buddhism is chaotic, without an organizing principle. Once again, it is unlikely that Buddhists — even Sŏn Buddhists — would accept such a characterization. When one searches the term "free from essence" 離體 in the Buddhist canon, virtually all appearances of the term are in the phrase "not free from essence" 不離體, with the phrase "function is not separate from essence" 用不離體 being notably frequent.

14. T 235.8.749a24; Muller, *Diamond Sutra*.

15. *Platform Sutra*, T 2008.48.360a13.

16. These appear to be related to four typical Chan approaches. The three of *wunian* 無念, *wangqing* 忘情, and *xiwang* 息妄 are found in Zongmi's *Chan Preface* (*Chan yuanquan xu*, T 2015), one of the more popular hermeneutical Chan texts in the Koryŏ.

17. *Diamond Sutra*, T 235.8.749a24.

18. The five phases (*wuxing* 五行) of early Chinese cosmology — wood 木, fire 火, earth 土, metal 金, and water 水 — are first seen in the "Great Plan" 洪範 chapter of the *Shujing*.

19. The ontological priority of principle over material force (as opposed to simultaneity) was to be the subject of later debate between T'oegye, Yulgok, and

their followers. See Michael Kalton's *Four-Seven Debate* and Edward Chung's *The Korean Neo-Confucianism of Yi T'oegye and Yi Yulgok* for a full studies of this topic.

20. Or, knowing the "function" and not knowing the "essence."

21. An allusion to the language of the *Daode jing*. See, for example, *Daode jing*, chap. 56, at http://www.acmuller.net/con-dao/daodejing.html.

22. Ibid., chap. 25.

23. Ibid., chap. 21.

24. Ibid., chap. 25.

25. Ibid., chap. 25.

26. It is quite unlikely that a bona fide Daoist philosopher would accept Chŏng's assertion that material force is the subject here. The Daoist scholar would certainly say that it is the *dao* itself that is the subject and that the *dao* is certainly ontologically and logically prior to material force.

27. Zhuangzi, "Knowledge Wandered North." Watson renders the passage as "Man's life is a coming-together of breath" (*Complete Works*, cited from online version at http://terebess.hu/english/chuangtzu2.html).

28. Again, we need to be careful in following Chŏng's interpretation, as the cited source text does not actually say that *ki* is a "source."

29. The metaphor of "boring" (or "drilling") as a function of intelligence that robs life comes from the *Zhuangzi*: "The emperor of the South Sea was called Shu [Brief], the emperor of the North Sea was called Hu [Sudden], and the emperor of the central region was called Hun-tun [Chaos]. Shu and Hu from time to time came together for a meeting in the territory of Hun-tun, and Hun-tun treated them very generously. Shu and Hu discussed how they could repay his kindness. 'All men,' they said, 'have seven openings so they can see, hear, eat, and breathe. But Hun-tun alone doesn't have any. Let's trying boring him some!' Every day they bored another hole, and on the seventh day Hun-tun died" (Watson, *Chuang Tzu: Basic Writings*, 95).

30. Watson, *Basic Writings*, 31.

31. Watson, from the chapter "Knowledge Wandered North," translates this passage as "Only when there is no pondering and no cogitation will you get to know the Way" (*Complete Works*, http://terebess.hu/english/chuangtzu2.html#22).

32. *Daode jing*, chap. 37.

33. Once again, there can be little doubt that a Daoist scholar would reject Chŏng's equivocation of the Way and material force here.

34. In other words, the ideograph *wo* 我 as it is used here should be distinguished from the Buddhist Sanskrit concept of *ātman*, the principal object of Buddhist deconstructive rhetoric. Chŏng's usage here is closer to the Freudian sense of ego, a center point of self-awareness with which one faces the outside world.

35. According to Mencius, all human beings are endowed at birth with the four potentialities of humaneness (K. *in*), justice (K. *ŭi*), propriety (K. *ye*), and wisdom (K. *chi*).

36. Zhu Xi's commentary on the Mencius, chapter on Gaozi. *Mengzi jizhu*, Gaozi

zhangju (孟子集註, 告子章句), http://mokusai-web.com/shushigakukihonsho/ moushi/moushi_06.html.

37. *Mencius* 2A:6. All translations from the *Mencius* are my own. See http:// www.acmuller.net/con-dao/mencius.html.

38. Ibid., 2A:6.

39. *Analects* 15:9. All translations of the *Analects* are my own, published at http://www.acmuller.net/con-dao/analects.html.

40. *Liji*, "Four Regulations for Funeral Clothing" 喪服四制, Scripta Sinica.

Translation 2: An Array of Critiques of Buddhism (*Pulssi chappyŏn*)

1. In rendering *taiji* as "supreme polarity," I follow Joseph Adler, who points out that the connotations of the term are not those of a "great ultimate" or "apex," etc., but rather a way of describing the great tension between yin and yang that exists before actual differentiation into heaven and earth. Thus, the origin of myriad phenomena. See the chapter titled "*Taiji* as Supreme Polarity" in Adler, *Reconstructing the Confucian Dao*, 111–135.

2. The above passage appears to be a reference to Zhou Dunyi's *Diagram of the Supreme Polarity* (*Taiji tu shuo* 太極圖說), which summarizes the standard classical Chinese account of how various phenomena come into being based on yin-yang cosmology, which extends back to the *Yijing*. The five phases of early Chinese cosmology—wood, fire, earth, metal, and water—are first seen in the "Great Plan" chapter of the *Book of History*.

3. Both of these citations are from the same passage in the *Yijing*'s "Xici zhuan," pt. 1. See Legge, *I Ching*, 353; Wilhelm, *I-Ching*, 293.

4. Here and in the passages that follow, Chŏng is taking issue with the Buddhist doctrine of transmigration, which explains that when living beings pass away, some part of the mind exists in a non-material realm and subsequently enters into another body upon rebirth. Chŏng says that when something dies, it utterly disappears. When living beings are born, they are born spontaneously, with no prior transcendent history.

5. From the *Liji*, "Animals for the Heavenly Sacrifice" ("Jiaotesheng" 郊特牲). Scripta Sinica.

6. But in fact leaves *do* decompose to become part of the soil, eventually to be reabsorbed into the roots, something that one would think the ancients must have also been able to figure out.

7. From a present-day scientific standpoint Chŏng is of course mistaken, since it is in fact the case that after evaporation, water is re-assimilated into the water table to be used again. Again, one wonders if this scientific fact was not known at the time.

8. The Buddhists do not say that the number of living beings is "fixed." The Buddhist notion of "neither increase nor decrease" is based on a perception of infinity rather than fixity.

9. That is, as causes and effects with the special connotation of (*hetu-phala*) as understood in Buddhist karmic theory.

10. The *qilin* 麒麟 is a mythical hoofed and horned animal considered to be the greatest of all the beasts.

11. The camellia and cassia are known for their longevity. The bracket fungus and epidendrum have a beautiful fragrance and medicinal properties.

12. Crowsbeak (also called monkshood or wolfsbane) is a poisonous plant of the crowfoot family; it is shaped like the beak of a crow.

13. From the main text of the first hexagram *qian* 乾. See Wilhelm, *I-Ching*, 314.

14. The two compound words *shenshui* 腎水 and *xinhuo* 心火 are technical terms in traditional Chinese medicine for certain types of sickness. They also indicate the basic traditional Chinese physiological understanding of the affinity of the kidneys with the phase of water and the heart with the phase of fire.

15. The term *xuling bumei* 虛靈不昧 comes from Zhu Xi's commentary on the *Great Learning* (*Daxue zhangju*). It describes a mind free of the limitations of private concerns, a mind that is equanimous and yet capable of penetrating everywhere.

16. *Yan* 眼 and *mu* 目 are synonyms that mean "eye."

17. *HPC* 4.746c113, Chinul says 非此心外有佛可成也.

18. *HPC* 4.742b10–11. Chinul's actual text says 心性之外無一法可得.

19. This quote comes from the *Zhuzi yulei*, fasc. 9, Xuesan, Lunzhixing 學三, 論知行, but is originally derived from a line in the *Mencius*: 盡其心者, 知其性也 (*Mencius* 7A:1). The *Zhuzi yulei*, or *Sayings of Master Zhu*, is a record in 140 fascicles of the discussions between the Neo-Confucian master Zhu Xi and his disciples. It was compiled by Li Jingde 黎靖德 of the Southern Song seventy years after the passing away of Zhu Xi.

20. From the *Zongjing lu*, T 2016.48.656b7.

21. This is a teaching of Chan, but as Zongmi points out in his Chan Preface, only one type of teaching. Zongmi says, "Chan can be analyzed more finely into three types of teachings: The first is that of stopping falsity and cultivating the mind. The second is that of completely effacing without a trace. The third is directly expressing the nature of the mind. When teaching these three, the hidden meaning of the first type is that of explaining characteristics based on the nature. The hidden meaning of the second is effacing characteristics to express the nature. The hidden meaning of the third is that the direct manifestation of the true mind *is* the nature" (T 2015.48.402b16–19). Chŏng here is referring to the third, most direct type of teaching.

22. 方寸之間, 事事物物皆有定理矣. *Zhuzi yulei*, fasc. 14, no. 280.

23. Also from Zhu Xi's commentary on the *Great Learning* (*Daxue zhangju*). The full line says: 明德者, 人之所得乎天, 而虛靈不昧, 以具眾理而應萬事者也。禪家則但以虛靈不昧者爲性, 而無以具眾理以下之事.

24. For a fuller discussion of the range of connotations of *chŏng* in Buddhist-Confucian discourse, see note 2 in the first passage of the translation of Kihwa's *Hyŏnjŏng non* below.

25. A *zhu* 銖 is one-twelfth of the weight of a *liang* 兩. The implication here

is that if you place them on a scale, there will be no doubt whatsoever about their weight or value.

26. Phrases like *kongji lingzhi* 空寂靈知 and *suiyuan bubian* 隨緣不變 abound throughout the *Zongjing lu* (T 2016), but Chŏng could just as well have gotten this general idea from any number of East Asian Buddhist texts that were readily available to him.

27. This phrase appears twice in the *Sayings of Layman Pang* as well as in case 42 of the *Biyan lu* (T 2003.48.179b28–c2). Also see T 2037.49.832a14. For an English translation of this work, see Sasaki, *Man of Zen*.

28. The nature-principle and function-material force pairs here are analogs of essence and function (*ti* and *yong*), as discussed in the final part of this book's introduction.

29. From Zhou Dunyi's *Explanation of the Diagram of the Supreme Polarity*. Much of Chŏng's argument in this section is derived from Zhou's theories of human nature here and in other places in his writings.

30. As defined in *Mencius* 2A:6, the latter four pairs respectively represent the germinative potentialities for the prior four positive mental functions. This is dealt with more fully two passages below.

31. *Chunqiu Zuo Chuan zhengyi* 春秋左傳正義, fasc. 27, year 13, Zhenggong 成公: 「劉子曰吾聞之民受天地之中以生所謂命也。是以有動作禮義威儀之則以定命也。」 (Scripta Sinica). This is an oft-cited passage in the writings of Zhu Xi and other Neo-Confucian philosophers.

32. I have not been able to find this passage in Zhu Xi's works or elsewhere.

33. The "four potentialities" taught in *Mencius* 2A:6 are four basic good tendencies assumed to be the natural property of all human beings and capable of being enhanced and developed. The feeling of concern for the well-being of others (*ch'ŭg'ŭn* 惻隱) is the beginning of humaneness (K. *in* 仁). The sense of shame and disgust (K. *su'ak* 羞惡) is the beginning of justice (K. *ŭi* 義); the sense to treat others with courtesy and respect (K. *cirang* 辭讓) is the beginning of propriety (K. *ye* 禮). The sense of right and wrong (K. *sayang* 是非) is the beginning of wisdom (K. *chi* 知).

34. In Confucianism, these are the five ways of proper interaction in human relationships: justice (K. *ŭi* 義), compassion (K. *cha* 慈), friendship (K. *u* 友), respect (K. *gong* 恭), and filial piety (K. *hyo* 孝).

35. Chŏng is here alluding to the famous passage in the *Mencius* that claims that humaneness is the basic constituent of the mind of all people, since any person, no matter who, will spontaneously move to rescue a child that is about to fall into a well. See *Mencius* 2A:6.

36. See *Analects* 3:19.

37. The Chinese line 體用一原、顯微無間 is probably cited here from Zhu Xi's *Chuanxilu* 傳習錄, but is originally from Cheng Yi's commentary on the *Yijing*. See *Henan Er Cheng yishu* 18, Cheng Yi, Scripta Sinica.

38. See T 475.14.539a29.

39. "Correcting the internal with reverence, correcting the external with due-

giving" is an aphorism repeated in the texts of the Cheng brothers, Zhu Xi, and many other Neo-Confucianism writers. It is drawn from the *Yijing,* in the text of *kun* 坤, the second hexagram. See Wilhelm, *I-Ching,* 393.

40. Wang Tong (584–618) was a Confucian scholar of the Sui from Longmen. Styled Zhongyan 仲淹, he was posthumously named Wenzhong zi 文中子. He was the grandfather of Wangbo 王勃 and the teacher of Fang Xuanling 房玄齡 and Weizheng 魏徵 of the Tang. His extant works include the *Zhongshuo* 中説 and the *Wenzhongzi* 文中子.

41. *Yijing,* "Xici zhuan," pt. 1, chap. 12.

42. 道之大原出於天 is from the *Han Shu* 漢書, by Dong Zhongshu 董仲舒.

43. From the *Diamond Sutra,* T 235.8.749a24–25.

44. The first part of this phrase, "Good and evil [phenomena] are all mind" 善惡皆心, is actually not found in the canon, with the more common rendering being "the three realms are nothing but mind" 三界唯心. The latter part of this phrase, "the myriad phenomena are nothing but consciousness" 萬法唯識, is found in many Taishō texts, for example at T 2016.48.477a27.

45. Cheng Hao, "Selected Sayings," no. 32. Wing-tsit Chan, *Source Book,* 535–536.

46. Ming Dao was the style of Cheng Hao.

47. *Doctrine of the Mean,* chap. 1.

48. *Chengshi yishu* 程氏遺書, fasc. 5, online in Mokusai web in Cheng Hao, "Selected Sayings," no. 32. Wing-tsit Chan, *Source Book,* 535.

49. Ibid.

50. *Zhuzi youlei,* fasc. 1, "The Supreme Polarity, Heaven and Earth," pt. 1 太極天地, 上.

51. This is one of Mencius' most influential pronouncements. *Mencius* 2A:6.

52. This is a basic approach to the brand of philosophy espoused by Confucius and Mencius that caring for people is not something done indiscriminately or equally (as Mozi taught) but is prioritized. One is supposed to pay the greatest degree of attention to one's parents, then one's family members and relatives. After practicing humaneness adequately with family, one can extend oneself to strangers. Chŏng is pointing out the difference between this and the Buddhist notion of compassion, one of the main characteristics of which is that it does not discriminate.

53. *Mencius* 7A:45. Mencius said, "The noble man cares about creatures but does not love them as if they are people. He loves people as people but not in the intimate way he loves his family. He loves his family intimately and is humane to people. He is humane to people and cares about creatures."

54. The stories of the past lives of the Buddha and great bodhisattvas contain episodes of them giving up their lives to feed hungry tigers and so forth.

55. That is, a total stranger.

56. Donation (Skt. *dāna*) is the first of the six basic Mahāyāna Buddhist practices.

57. Referring to monks who abandon society in favor of monastic life, including the Buddha himself, who left his family to seek enlightenment.

58. A reference to a story in the *Shiji* wherein a group of soldiers led by a drunken commander traveling a path at night hastily draw their swords to kill a snake that later turns out to be a boy. *Shiji*, Gaozu benji 高祖本紀, no. 8.

59. This could be a reference to the idea expressed in various passages of the *Sutra of Perfect Enlightenment*, for example at T 842.17.916b6–10 or 919c28, yet the phrase *zhimi buwu* 執迷不悟 itself, Buddhistic as it sounds, does not appear even once in Taishō.

60. From the *Sutra of Perfect Enlightenment*, 91–92 (T 842.914a10) and 78 (T 842.913b25).

61. An oft-cited line from the *Śūraṃgama-sūtra*, T 945.19.130a21.

62. "Xici zhuan." See Legge, *I Ching*, 373, and Wilhelm, *I-Ching*, 318.

63. These two tropes of fount-streams and roots-branches are commonly used to express the theme of essence and function in Confucian, Daoist, and Buddhist literature.

64. The turntable (or gear) and crossbar are parts of an ancient Chinese device, called a *xuanji yuheng* 璇璣玉衡, used for astronomical charting and calculation.

65. *Mencius*, 3B:26.

66. From the Daxin 大心 (seventh) chapter of Zhang Zai's *Zhengmeng* 正蒙 (Youthful Ignorance) (http://mokusai-web.com/shushigakukihonsho/seimou/seimou.html). In this passage Zhang Zai is making a similar criticism of the Buddhists: that they do not fully look into the principles of things.

67. These are the ten kings who guard the dark realms of the dead, mentioned in such texts as the *Guanding jing* 灌頂經 (T 1331.21.495b28ff.).

68. http://mokusai-web.com/kougiroku/shougaku/kagen/kagen23_28.html; 嘉言 26.

69. This kind of characterization was made by Zongmi in his *Origin of Humanity*. In the opening portion of that treatise, where he introduces the "teaching for men and gods," he says:

> The Buddha, for the sake of beginners, at first set forth the karmic retribution of the three periods of time [i.e., past, present, and future] and the causes and effects of good and bad [deeds]. That is to say, [one who] commits the ten evils in their highest degree falls into hell upon death, [one who commits the ten evils] in their lesser degree becomes a hungry ghost, and [one who commits the ten evils] in their lowest degree becomes an animal. (Gregory, *Inquiry into the Origin of Humanity*, 115; T 1886.45.708c15–16)

70. *Chengshi yishu*, fasc. 5. http://mokusai-web.com/shushigakukihonsho/niteizensho/niteizensho_14.html.

71. From the *Great Learning*, chap. 6, verse 1.

72. *Mao Shi* 毛詩, Daya 大雅, Wenwang zhi shi 文王之什, Hanlu 旱麓, Scripta Sinica.

73. *Analects*, 3:13.

74. Originally found in the *Liji*, Tangong 檀弓, pt. 1; cited by Mencius (*Mencius* 4B:29).

75. The ten crimes are killing, stealing, debauchery, lying, flattery, insult, slander, coveting, becoming angry, and holding false views.

76. The demise of Emperor Wu in spite of his Buddhist faith is given account by Han Yu. See n. 77 below.

77. *Liezhuan* 列傳 fasc. 176, Han Yu 韓愈, Scripta Sinica. Or, the *Han Changli wenshi* 韓昌黎文集, fasc. 39, Lunfogubiao 論佛骨表 (Memorial on the Buddha's Bone). Changli 昌黎 was Han's home region, and he used it as one of his pen names.

78. *Hongfan* (Great Standard) is the title of a section of the *Shujing* (Book of History), or book 4 of the *Zhoushu* 周書. It consists of nine chapters said to be taken from the Luo Text 洛書 that Yu 禹 obtained and is considered the original authoritative text for the formation of classical policy and morality. Legge translates the title as "The Great Plan." The eight essentials for governing is a subsection of this. According to Legge's translation: "Third, of the eight objects of government: the first is called food; the second, commodities; the third, sacrifices; the fourth, the minister of works; the fifth, the minister of instruction; the sixth, the minister of crime; the seventh, the entertainment of guests; the eighth, the army" (*Shoo King*, 327).

79. 重民五教, 惟食喪祭. From the chapter entitled "The Successful Completion of the War" 武成 in the *Shujing*. Legge translates: "[King Wu] attached great importance to the people's being taught the duties of the five relationships of society, and to take care of food, for funeral ceremonies, and for sacrifices." *Shangshu* 尚書, Zhoushu 周書, Wusheng 武成 (Scripta Sinica).

80. *Analects* 12:7.

81. T 235.8.748c21–23.

82. *Sutra of Perfect Enlightenment*, 162; T 842.17.917b5.

83. Although in slightly different phrasing, this message is expressed in the same passage from the *Sutra of Perfect Enlightenment*, ibid.

84. A very rough listing of the twelve links of dependent arising.

85. Although this is only the fourteenth of the nineteen sections, it can be regarded as Chŏng's actual summation of the philosophical, doctrinal, and practical arguments against Buddhism. That is to say, in this and the preceding sections, the formation of the critique has been based largely on the writings of Zhu and the Cheng brothers, whereas the subsequent sections tend to be composed of anecdotal references from the earlier, philosophically less-sophisticated writings of anti-Buddhist literati such as Han Yu, which criticize Buddhism on the basis of its being a foreign religion, a harbinger of calamity, and so forth. This is also the section that Kihwa takes up for his most extensive refutation in the concluding passages of the *Hyŏnjŏng non*, with a comparison of the respective passages offering the clearest evidence that Kihwa indeed composed the *Hyŏnjŏng non* as a response to the *Pulssi chappyŏn*.

86. *Yijing*, "Xici zhuan," pt. 1, Scripta Sinica.

87. T 235.8.749c23.

88. Xie is apparently the name of a Confucian commentator, which I have not yet identified.

89. The *Awakening of Faith* says: 以心生則種種法生。心滅則種種法滅. T 1666.32.577b22.

90. The notion of "sympathetic resonance," especially the extent to which it can be found pervasively in the various East Asian philosophical traditions, is explored in depth by Robert Sharf in chapter 2 ("Chinese Buddhism and the Cosmology of Sympathetic Resonance ") of his *Coming to Terms with Chinese Buddhism*.

91. *Caicheng fuxiang* 財成輔相 is derived from the *Yijing*, Commentary on the Hexagram Tai 泰, which says, 天地交泰，后以財成天地之道，輔相天地之宜，以左右民。 "The interaction of heaven and earth results in tranquility. The emperor manages and produces the Way of heaven and earth, and assists in the harmonization of heaven and earth, in order to help the people" (Scripta Sinica).

92. See *Sutra of Perfect Enlightenment*, 78; T 842.17.914b25–28.

93. For one account of this, see case 86 of the *Biyan Lu* (Blue Cliff Record), T 2003.48.211c26–28.

94. *Zhuzi yulei*, fasc. 18. See http://mokusai-web.com/shushigakukihonsho/daigaku/daigaku_wakumon.html.

95. See *Mencius* 2A:2. Mencius said, "When I hear glib speech, I know what it is covering up. When I hear lewd speech, I know its pitfalls. When I hear tricky speech, I know where it departs from the truth. When I hear evasive speech, I know its emptiness."

96. From the *Great Learning*.

97. I have not been able to identify this text or its author.

98. *Śramaṇa* is a Sanskrit term meaning "a Buddhist monk" (or nun), a wanderer, or world-renunciant religious practitioner striving for liberation. Originally in India, *śramaṇa* was a general term for a person who had shaved his head, renounced his worldly status and possessions, and trained his mind and body in the attempt to cease doing evil acts and instead strive for the good. It originally referred to non-Buddhist practitioners such as the Jains, who based their beliefs on the Vedas and Upanishads.

99. Chu Wangying was the installed name of Liuying of the latter Han. Born as the sixth son of the emperor Guangwu, in his young adulthood Chu led the life of an itinerant knight, engaging in acts of chivalry in defense of the oppressed. In his later years, he became an adherent of Daoism and Buddhism. See *Hou Han Shu* 後漢書, sec. 72, Scripta Sinica.

100. A temple located in the northeastern part of the Jiangning area of Jiangsu. Built under the auspices of Emperor Wu of the Liang in the ninth lunar month of 521, the original temple had a nine-story pagoda. It became a favorite temple of the emperor, and there were held many large Dharma convocations concerning such scriptures as the *Prajñāpāramitā* sutras, the *Nirvana Sutra,* etc. After the passing of Wu, the temple fell into decline but was rebuilt again in the Song, with the new name of Fabaosi 法寶寺. This temple would again later fall into ruin.

101. The four groups are monks, nuns, laymen, and laywomen.

102. The *Sanhui jing* in one fascicle (T 768), translated during the Eastern Jin by a presently unknown figure. It consists of a list of sixty-plus items intended as a guide for practice and seems to be a compilation of pieces culled from other scriptures.

103. Emperor Taizong of the Tang (727–779), reign name of the ninth Tang emperor, Li Yu 李豫 (r. 762–779).

104. An Lushan and Shi Siming were the notorious usurpers who carried out the An Lushan rebellion (755–763), only to be murdered by their own sons.

105. The two invaders are the non-Chinese tribes of Huihe 回紇 and Tufan 吐蕃, both of which are said to have backed down on their own without fighting.

106. Of course this is a rhetorical device. Chǒng is saying that the Buddhists claim that these events were beyond human control, when everyone knows that they were in fact brought about directly by various types of strategy and intrigue.

107. This refers to Famensi in the region of Fengxiang.

108. The original text from Han Yu says: 不過宣政一見、禮賓一設、賜衣一襲、衞而出之於境。不令惑衆也。"He would not exceed the standard single audience at Xuanzheng palace; he would offer a single reception as is proper for guests; he would present him with a single set of clothes; he would protect and guide his departure from the realm. He would not allow him to delude the people."

109. Pei Du 裴度 (765–839) was a famous minister of the Tang dynasty, originally from Wenxi in Shanxi. He worked mainly during the reigns of Xianzong and Wenzong. He later abandoned his political career and cultivated a friendship with Bai Juyi and Liu Yuxi.

110. According to Morohashi, Cui Qin 崔羣 (d.u.) was a Tang-period government official, originally from Wucheng. He was said to be of exceptional intelligence, passing the highest rank government examinations before reaching the age of adulthood. During the reign of Muzong 穆宗 he served as military commissioner and as an imperial secretary in charge of personnel.

111. For an online English translation of Han Yu's text, see http://acc6.its .brooklyn.cuny.edu/~phalsall/texts/hanyu.html.

112. The "four villains" during the era of Emperor Shun were: Gong Gong 共工, Huan Dou 驩兜, San Miao 三苗, and Gun 鯀. See the *Shujin*, Shundian 舜典, Scripta Sinica.

113. *Zhushu* 尚書, Shangshu 商書, Tangshi 湯誓, Scripta Sinica.

114. *Analects* 2:16.

115. According to the Mencius, the teachings of Yang and Mo were extremely popular at the time. See *Mencius* 3B:9. Mo Di, commonly known as Mozi 墨子, was a philosopher of the Warring States period. He was famous for his theories of universal love, rejection of war, and his disregard for Confucian teachings on ritual and music, believing deeply in the merits of hard work and frugality. His teachings are referred to as Mohism. Yang Chu 楊朱 was a thinker of the same period famous for teaching a doctrine of "every man for himself." Both were sharply criticized by Mencius.

116. *Mencius* 3B:9.

117. Preface to the Commentary on the *Doctrine of the Mean,* from the Commentary on the Four Books (*sishu zhangju jizhu,* "zhongyong zhangju xu") 四書章句集注, 中庸章句序. http://mokusai-web.com/kougiroku/chuuyou/chuuyou00 _2shoujo.html.

Translation 3: Exposition of Orthodoxy (*Hyŏnjŏng non*)

1. The original text contained in the *HPC* does not include this kind of thematic breakdown and headings. I have added them as an aid to understanding the text and to help juxtapose it with the *Pulssi chappyŏn.*

2. The term being translated here as "feelings," *chŏng* 情, should be understood in a negative sense in the Buddhist context. In Buddhism it is a broad concept that embraces such notions as "discrimination" and "affliction" in addition to the commonsense understanding of being capable of "feeling." But its richness and complexity are greatly compounded when it is invoked by a scholar with a rich Confucian background such as Kihwa, who is thus keenly aware of its central role in the long Confucian discourse going back to the *Doctrine of the Mean* (*Zhongyong*), where it refers to the disparate human emotions, or feelings, that arise derivatively from the originally pure nature. In the *Doctrine of the Mean,* however, while emotions do not have a negative connotation in themselves, they are understood as containing a potential for disharmony. The relationship between them and the original pristine nature of the human mind is taken up repeatedly in Confucian and Neo-Confucian discourse. This is another analogue of the essence-function model and can be overlaid on the East Asian Buddhist notion of a pure (Buddha) nature that functions imperfectly in the discriminating and afflicted mind of sentient beings. Kihwa is thus tying the two traditions together in a single paradigm of discourse right from the start. In the ensuing passages, the reader should be aware that the term translated as "feelings" is packed with these connotations of imperfection, discrimination, and affliction, to the extent that it is *almost* possible to translate it consistently as "mental disturbances" — except that such a rendering would lose some impact at certain points and pull us away from the Confucian connotations of the term.

3. The term 覺有情 (K. *kak yujŏng*) is one way of translating the Sanskrit *bodhisattva,* being used in a positive way to indicate enlightened beings who experience feelings of compassion and are thus motivated to aid sentient beings. See Yuanzhao's *Commentary on the Amitâbha Sutra* 阿彌陀經義疏, T 1761.37.358c27.

4. "Two vehicles" is a term that appears in Mahāyāna Buddhist texts and is usually disparaging in its connotations, referring to two kinds of practitioners who selfishly focus on their own liberation. Included here are *śrāvaka*s (a buddha's direct disciples who hear his sermons) and *pratyekabuddha*s ("solitary realizers," those who attain liberation on their own without the aid of a teacher, subsequently abiding in isolation without a special concern for teaching others). In Mahāyāna

Buddhism, both are considered to be inferior to the bodhisattvas, who dedicate their efforts toward the spiritual improvement of others rather than seeking their own blissful liberation.

5. To be born as a human or god is considered to be relatively fortunate in Buddhism, better than being reborn as an *asura* (titan), animal, hungry ghost, or hell-dweller.

6. The five vehicles are five teachings conveying a karmic reward, which differs according to the vehicle: (1) rebirth among men conveyed by observing the five precepts; (2) rebirth among the gods by the ten forms of good action; (3) among the *śrāvaka*s by adherence to the four noble truths; (4) rebirth among *pratyekabuddha*s by contemplation of twelvefold dependent arising; (5) rebirth among the buddhas and bodhisattvas by practicing the six perfections. These are well-known in Buddhist literature, but elaborated in detail in Zongmi's *Inquiry,* a text in which Kihwa was well-versed.

7. The five basic Buddhist precepts, discussed extensively below, are not killing, not stealing, not lying, not engaging in sexual excesses, and not drinking alcohol.

8. The ten virtues are the ten basic precepts to be followed by monks and nuns. They start with the above five basic precepts and then include the additional five of not eating after noon; not watching dancing, singing, and shows; not adorning oneself with garlands, perfumes, and ointments; not using a high bed; and not accepting gold and silver.

9. In Sanskrit the six perfections, *pāramitā*s, are charity, moral behavior, tolerance, vigorous effort, meditation, and wisdom. They are said to be transcendent in that each practice is supposed to be informed by an attitude of relinquishment of karmic merit, based on one's compassion for others, and an insight into the empty nature of persons and things.

10. A reference to the *Great Learning,* which teaches that the broad goal of ruling a peaceful country begins with the ruler's own spiritual cultivation: "When the mind is corrected, the self is cultivated; when the self is cultivated, the clan is harmonized; when the family is harmonized, the country is well governed; when the country is well governed, there will be peace throughout the land. See http://www.acmuller.net/con-dao/greatlearning.html for a full translation.

11. In classifications of the teaching such as that constructed by Zongmi in his *Inquiry,* the Buddhist teachings are ranked in terms of profundity into five levels. In the first level, the most elementary, people are taught about the law of karmic retribution, wherein moral activity brings good retribution and immoral activity brings evil retribution. The five precepts and ten virtuous forms of behavior represent the codification of moral behavior.

12. This correlation of the five Confucian virtues with the five lay precepts is something that was carried out very early in the period of assimilation of Buddhism into China, when it was common to render new Buddhist concepts in terms similar to those used in Confucianism and Daoism. See Wright, *Buddhism in Chi-*

nese History, 37; Sharf, *Coming to Terms with Chinese Buddhism*, 98; Gregory, *Inquiry into the Origin of Humanity*, 97.

13. *Analects* 2:3.

14. *Zhouyi* 周易, "Xici zhuan" 繫辭, pt. 1, sec. 24, Scripta Sinica.

15. Neither the Scripta Sinica text database nor Chinese Text Project contained this line as of 2014/07/08. In the Dushu.com text database it is identified as a quote from the *Zhou Li*. 《周禮》曰：刑賞以馭其威。賞罰，國之大柄也。 http://big5.dushu.com/showbook/100921/1028618.html.

16. From the *Yijing*, "Xici zhuan", pt. 1, Scripta Sinica. It is instructive, but not especially surprising, that Kihwa would cite a line from the "Xici zhuan" and claim that it is characteristically Buddhist. Kihwa cites extensively from the "Xici zhuan" throughout his works, most notably in the introduction to his commentary on the *Yuanjue jing*, where he uses passages from the "Xici zhuan" to explain the connotations of Mahāyāna.

17. From the *Śrīmālā-sūtra*: 應折伏者而折伏之。應攝受者而攝受之。　T 353.12.217c11–12.

18. After first criticizing the superficiality of the Confucian teaching of guiding through reward and punishment, Kihwa tries to show that it can be seen as an expedient method that is useful in the right situation. This is one of the earlier clear marks of the difference in tone to be seen between Chŏng and Kihwa, in that Kihwa is really not seeking to discredit the Confucian teaching but to show how, when properly understood, Confucian and Buddhist teachings can be applied together in harmonious fashion. This approach is reminiscent of that of the great Silla-period scholar Wonhyo (617–686), whose approach rarely pronounced a specific form of teaching to be entirely unuseful. He rather tended to see all kinds of teachings as expedients that could be fit into the larger whole and be understood properly in their particular contexts.

19. *Platform Sutra*, T 2008.48.358c4.

20. *Diamond Sutra*, T 235.8.749b15.

21. *Zuo Chuan* 左傳, "Huangong zhuan" 桓公傳, Year 18, Scripta Sinica; also paraphrased in *Mencius* 3B:3.

22. *Zhou li* 周禮, "Dasitu" 大司徒 (Minister of Education), Scripta Sinica.

23. I have found this phrase cited in numerous Confucian and Buddhist texts but have not yet been able to identify the locus classicus.

24. *Liji*, "Quli" 曲禮, pt. 1, Scripta Sinica.

25. This phrase is usually seen in the form of 入孝出弟, "When at home be filial, when out in society be fraternal." It appears in Zhu Xi's works in various forms. The locus classicus is the *Liji*, which says 入孝弟, 出尊長養老, "When at home be filial and fraternal; when out in the world, respect and support your elders." *Liji*, "Xiangyinjiu yi" 鄉飲酒義, Scripta Sinica.

26. Within the five cardinal relationships, ministers are expected to manifest loyalty to their ruler and children are expected to show love and respect to their parents.

27. Here Kihwa is drawing from a section in the *Sutra of Perfect Enlightenment*

that analyzes the role of attached love and desire in the propulsion of cyclical existence. See T 842.17.916b4–15 and the *Sutra of Perfect Enlightenment*, 141–142.

28. For example, in the *Mahāvairocanâbhisaṃbodhi-sūtra*, in Tuṣita Heaven the Buddha is named Prabhāpāla, "Guardian of Light." T 848.18.12c4.

29. *Chanzong Yongjia ji*, T 2013.48.393a15.

30. The three awarenesses are (1) the power of divine vision, wherein the buddhas can observe the full course of passage by sentient beings through the six destinies; (2) the power of the knowledge of previous lifetimes, whereby they know the events of countless kalpas of previous lifetimes experienced by themselves as well as all the beings in the six destinies; (3) the power of the extinction of contamination, whereby they completely extinguish all the afflictions of the three realms and thus are no longer subject to rebirth in the three realms.

31. The six superknowledges possessed by a buddha include the prior three awarenesses, plus (4) unimpeded bodily action; (5) the power of divine hearing, with which buddhas are able to hear all the words of suffering and joy experienced by living beings in the six destinies; and (6) the power of awareness of the minds of others, whereby they know the thoughts of all the beings who pass through the six destinies.

32. In the Buddhist scriptures we can find a number of varying sets of the four kinds of wisdom. One set includes the four kinds of wisdom that cut off delusion: (1) the wisdom that extinguishes the production of the notion of self, (2) the wisdom of establishing pure works, (3) the wisdom of doing what should be done, (4) the wisdom that keeps this existence from being reborn.

33. There are also various sets of the eight gates to liberation, but their variance is usually just limited to one or two items. For example: (1) liberation when subjective desire arises, by examination of the object, or of all things and realization of their filthiness; (2) liberation when no subjective desire arises, by still meditating as above. These two are deliverance by meditation on impurity, the next six on purity: (3) liberation by concentration on the pure to the realization of a permanent state of freedom from all desire; (4) liberation in realization of the infinity of space, or the immaterial; (5) liberation in realization of infinite knowledge; (6) liberation in realization of nothingness; (7) liberation in the state of neither associative thought nor non-associative thought; (8) liberation by means of a state of mind in which there is final extinction, nirvana, of both sensation and associative thought.

34. *Xiaojing* 孝經 (Classic of Filial Piety), Kaizong mingyi 開宗明義, chap. 1, Scripta Sinica.

35. *Analects* 12:1, discussed in detail in the introduction.

36. See *Mencius* 1A:3 for this discussion.

37. We can notice that here and above Kihwa is mimicking the rhetorical style used by Chŏng in the *Pulssi chappyŏn* in presenting the opponent's argument in a sensible-sounding fashion and then refuting it.

38. This translation follows Legge, *Shoo King*, 283–284.

39. *Zongjing lu*, T 2016.48.915a8.

40. *Henan Er Cheng yishu*, 15. Also see Wing-tsit Chan, *Source Book*, 530, sec. 11.

41. "Non-humaneness (K. *pur'in* 不仁) is a Chinese medical term for paralysis or palsy, still in use today.

42. This is a reference to a Buddhist story about a monk in ancient India who was exemplary in his practice of the precepts. This monk, while traveling, came to an inn where a royal jeweler was also staying. The jeweler happened to leave a gem on a table, whereupon it was eaten by a goose. Upon becoming aware of the missing gem, the jeweler blamed the monk, who was aware that it was actually the goose who stole the gem. Fearful that exposure of the truth would result in the slaughter of the goose, the monk kept silent and was therefore bound and beaten severely. The goose, who returned to drink the blood of the bleeding monk, was killed by the jeweler, who cut it open and found the jewel inside. From the *Da zhuangyan jing lun* 大莊嚴經論 (*Kalpanā maṇḍitikā*), T 201.4.319a24.

43. In ancient India, a monk was mugged by a thief, who restrained him by tying him up in the live grass. The monk, not wanting to violate the prohibition against taking life, remained lying tied up in the grass rather than ripping the grass up. A king, passing by, found the monk and was so moved by this scene that he converted to Buddhism. Ibid., T 201.04.268c10.

44. From the fourteenth section of the Shaonan 召南 chapter of the *Book of Odes* 詩經, Scripta Sinica. See Legge, *Shoo King*, 36.

45. *Analects* 7:27.

46. *Mencius* 1A:7.

47. *Mencius* 1A:3.

48. See Muller, trans., *Doctrine of the Mean*, commentary, sec. 13.

49. T 183.3.458c3–4. A story of a previous life of the bodhisattva Maitreya. In the ancient past, while Maitreya was still an omniscient Brahman, he came upon Śākyamuni giving a sermon. At first he debated with the Buddha, but recognizing the Buddha's wisdom, he became his disciple. He then aroused the mind of determination for enlightenment and vowed to become Maitreya Buddha in the future. While practicing single-minded concentration, he was caught in the middle of a continuous heavy downpour during which he could not beg for food. Thus he went hungry for a week. Seeing a mother and child pair of rabbits, he caught and began to cook them, but since killing and eating meat is against the Buddhist precepts, he took the meat out of the fire and threw it away. On this occasion, the rabbit is Śākyamuni and the Brahman is Maitreya Bodhisattva, who will become the Buddha fifty-six million years after Śākyamuni's passing away.

50. *Analects* 6:28.

51. *Mencius* 1A:3.

52. *Liji*, "Quli" 曲禮, pt. 2, Scripta Sinica.

53. "Xici zhuan" 繫辭傳, pt. 1, Scripta Sinica. For alternative translations, see Wilhelm, *I-Ching*, 317; and Legge, *I Ching*, 372.

54. 嫂溺不援是豺狼 "To not pull your older brother's wife out of the water is to be an animal." This line comes from *Mencius* 3B:17, where Mencius is giving a teaching reminiscent of Jesus' "follow the spirit of the law rather than the letter

of the law." Ancient Chinese rules of propriety strictly prohibited the physical contact between man and woman outside of one's own marital relationship. This passage is Mencius' reply to a question about whether, in this kind of emergency situation, it is against the rules of propriety for a younger brother-in-law to make physical contact with his elder sister-in-law. Mencius replies with this line.

55. Although this passage is cited in numerous Confucian commentaries, I have not been able to identify its locus classicus.

56. In Buddhist texts, we can regularly find the compound word 茹葷, whereas 茹薰 does not appear in Taishō even once. Given the graphical and phonetic resemblance of 薰 and 葷, along with the fact that replacement of the latter makes perfect sense, I am inclined to see 薰 as a printing error.

57. Commentary to the *Great Learning,* chap. 10.

58. *Yijing,* hexagram 2 (Ch. *kun* 坤), Scripta Sinica.

59. The five blessings are to live a long life, to have wealth, not to suffer from sickness or calamity, to enjoy morality, to fulfill one's destiny. These are elucidated in the Hongfan 洪範 section of the *Shujing* 書經.

60. The Hongfan discusses five kinds of good fate 五福 that are the result of good behavior and six kinds of evil fate 六極 that are the result of evil behavior. See Legge, *Shoo King,* 340–341. The six extremes, or six misfortunes, experienced by people who don't follow the leadership of sage-emperors in the *Book of History* are short life 凶短折, sickness 疾, anxiety 憂, poverty 貧, evil 惡, and weakness 弱.

61. T 310.11.335b14. This verse is found in the *Ratnakūṭa-sūtra* (*Da baoji jing* 大寶積經), but it is recited repetitiously—almost like a mantra—in a number of Vinaya texts, such as the *Mūlasarvâstivāda-vinaya-vibhaṅga* (*Genben shuo yiqieyoubu pinaiye yaoshi* 根本說一切有部毘奈耶, T 1448).

62. Meaning only physically existent phenomena like plants and animals, not disembodied spirits.

63. From the *Shujing, Daya* 大雅, "Wenwang" 文王, Scripta Sinica. Translation adapted from Legge, *Shoo King,* 428.

64. Morohashi's *Dai kanwa jiten* (20823-2190) lists a Wang Huaizhi who lived during the Southern Song dynasty, a scholar renowned for his expertise in the transmission of ritual practices. During the Song, *xiucai* 秀才 was an unofficial designation for all candidates in a metropolitan examination (*xingshi* 省試) in the civil service recruitment examination sequence. See Hucker, *Dictionary of Official Titles,* 248.

65. This is a summary of the passage contained in the *Fayuan zhulin* 法苑珠林, T 2122.53.875a14.

66. Li Yuan's story appears in Morohashi, 6: 5797, col. 3; Yuanzi's story is in Morohashi, 3: 2370, col. 4.

67. This story appears in a few places in the Buddhist canon, varying in the facts and in completeness. The most complete version I have been able to locate is in the *Lebang yigao* 樂邦遺稿, T 1969B.47.238a2–17. The gist of the story is that Yuanze vows to be reborn as a son of Ms. Wang and to meet his friend Liyuan again, which he does. This text—and a number of others in the canon—offers numerous

accounts such as this, which are cited as factual evidence of reincarnation. Qutang 瞿塘 is the name of one of the three famous gorges through which the Yangtze River passes. Its steep walls are said to be breathtaking as one passes through by boat.

68. Yang Hu of the Qin was in his former life a man named Li 李 in the clan of Lin 鄰 who died prematurely. In his new life, at the age of five, he was obsessed by a ring owned by his nursemaid that had been his in his prior lifetime. See T 670.16.479b16–20; also see Morohashi 28425-60.

69. This reincarnation story is also told in the *Lebang yigao* 樂邦遺稿, T 1969B.47.245c29–246a3.

70. *Analects* 7:5

71. *Mencius* 8:13.

72. This metaphor is from the *Han Shu* 漢書, *Yangxiong zhuan* 揚雄傳, pt. 2, Scripta Sinica, 虛擧而上升、則不能攦膠葛騰九閎.

73. *Jingde zhuandeng lu* 景德傳燈錄, T 2076.51.220b4.

74. T 2002.48.362b4–18.

75. Puhua, one of Linji's cohorts, was known as a mischievous prankster who was fond of tinkling bells. After he passed away, the sound of tinkling bells was mysteriously heard in the village streets. *Linji lu*, T 1985.47.503b20–24.

76. I have not been able to locate the source of this story.

77. Confucius was known for his reluctance to discuss otherworldly phenomena such as the afterlife, spirits, and such. See *Analects* 11:11: "Zhi Lu asked about serving the spirits. Confucius said, 'If you can't yet serve men, how can you serve the spirits?' Lu said, 'May I ask about death?' Confucius said, 'If you don't understand what life is, how will you understand death?' "

78. From the "Xici zhuan" pt. 2, Scripta Sinica. English translation following Wilhelm, *I-Ching*, 344. Also see Legge, *I Ching*, 396. Kihwa seems to be citing the second line out of context here.

79. From the commentary to the *Chunqiu gongyang chuan* 春秋公羊傳 (Spring and Autumn Annals, "Biography of Gongyang") 公羊傳注疏, 4th year of Ding Gong 定公四年, Scripta Sinica. The phrase 以春秋之義 is found extensively throughout the thirteen classics.

80. Yan Hui, whose name appears in a number of places in the *Analects*, was Confucius' favorite disciple, surpassing all the rest in terms of wisdom and humility. He died young, about the age of thirty, his passing greatly lamented by his teacher. See *Analects* 6:3.

81. One of Confucius' disciples from the state of Lü, more commonly known by the nickname Zi Si 子思. He is known for his forgetting of material comforts in his enjoyment of the Way.

82. (r. 58–75 CE). Emperor Ming, the second emperor of the Latter Han. As the son of Emperor Guangwu 光武帝, he further solidified the rule of the dynasty and brought about the golden age of the Latter Han. In 65 CE, he sent the monk Cai Yin 蔡愔 and others to the western regions (India and Central Asia) in search of Buddhist sutras. They returned two years later for an official introduction of Buddhism to China.

83. The Three Dynasties of antiquity were the Xia 夏, Yin 殷, and Zhou 周. This was the period praised by Confucians as the age of sage kings.

84. Queen Jindeok (r. 647–654), the twenty-eighth ruler of Silla, composed this poem, embroidered it, and sent it together with a piece of silk brocade to the Tang emperor in China. See Ha and Mintz, *Samguk Yusa*.

85. *Mencius* 3B:4. In this passage, Mencius is engaged in debate with a ruler named Bang Gang 彭更, who has criticized Mencius and his followers, insinuating that they are parasites on society because all they do is go around lecturing people without performing a specific type of labor or trade. Mencius replies that a well-functioning society must have people in many different types of roles in order to achieve a balance, and that their worth must be measured in terms of their overall intentions rather than of mere material production. See Legge, *Works of Mencius*, 269–271.

86. Min Ziqian (536–487) was one of Confucius' leading disciples, known for his exemplary practice of filial piety. He was from the state of Lu and was fifteen years Confucius' junior.

87. *Xunzi* 荀子, "Jiebi" 解蔽, Scripta Sinica. 天下無二道、聖人無兩心.

88. *Analects* 9:4.

89. *Yijing*, hexagram 52, interpreted by Wilhelm (*I-Ching*) as "keeping still." What Kihwa offers here is quite different from what appears in the standard version of the *Yijing* text. It is not clear whether Kihwa is just paraphrasing or working with a text or commentary of which we are not aware. The Chinese from the text in question reads: 艮其背不獲其身。行其庭不見其人。无咎。象曰、艮止也。時止則止、時行則行、動靜不失其時、其道光明。

90. Paraphrase of the *Diamond Sutra*, T 235.8.751c25–27.

91. For those familiar with the context of these citations in the *Analects* and *Yijing*, it is obvious that Kihwa is stretching things a bit here, as neither of these non-Buddhist intimations of "no-self" comes close in connotation to the Buddhist notion of *anātman*. He does do a bit better in his final comparison, however, in drawing a correspondence among the three teachings in terms of a common understanding of the integration of movement and stillness—a way of expressing the Buddhist emptiness.

92. *Sutra of Brahmā's Net* 梵網經, T 1484.24.1004a24. English translation from Muller, *Exposition of the Sutra of Brahmā's Net*, 246–247.

93. T 842.17.920b13; HPC 7.165a4. *Sutra of Perfect Enlightenment*, 220.

94. From the *Xiaojing; Sancai* chapter 三才章, no. 7, Scripta Sinica.

95. *Yijing*, "Xici zhuan," pt. 1, Scripta Sinica.

96. Ibid.

97. Source not found.

98. Although this precise phrasing is not found, its point is made repeatedly in a number of Yogâcāra texts, as in the following from the *Mahāyāna-saṃgraha*: 菩薩戒有三品別。一律儀戒。二攝善法戒。三饒益有情戒。 (T 1594.31.146b11–12).

99. Commentary to the *Doctrine of the Mean*, chap. 6.

100. *Shujing*, "Dayumo" 大禹謨 ("The Counsels of the Great Yu"), Scripta Sinica. See Legge, *Shoo King*, 64.

101. For the first phrase, see Muller, *Daodejing*, chap. 37.

102. *Zongjing lu* (Record of the Axiom Mirror), T 2016.48.528a1.

103. "Xici zhuan," pt. 1, Scripta Sinica.

104. This constitutes the bottom line of Kihwa's understanding of the fundamental philosophical unity of the three teachings. It is within the realms of "empty yet not empty" or what Buddhism calls the "middle path" that Kihwa finds their unifying principle. The position of "empty yet existent" reflects a metaphysical understanding that is guided by interpenetration, in that there should not be either a physical or conceptual obstruction between emptiness and existence. They mutually contain each other; they are neither the same nor different.

Bibliography

Abbreviations

HPC = *Hanguk Pulgyo chŏnsŏ* 韓國佛教全書
SBC = *Sambong chip* 三峯集
T = *Taishō Shinshū Daizōkyō* 大正新脩大藏經

Online Digital Text Corpora

Citations from the *Analects, Great Learning, Doctrine of the Mean, Mencius,* and *Daode jing* were found in the digital versions on http://www.acmuller.net/con-dao.

Citations from the Five Classics, Chinese Histories, and other Daoist works were found in the Scripta Sinica Text Database at http://hanchi.ihp.sinica.edu.tw/ihp/hanji.htm and the Chinese Text Project at http://ctext.org.

Citations for Neo-Confucian works of Zhou Dunyi, Zhang Zai, and Zhu Xi were found in the Mokusai Web archives at http://mokusai-web.com and the Chinese Philosophical Etext archive at http://sangle.web.wesleyan.edu/etext/index.html.

Citations for the Taishō Canon were found through the SAT Daizōkyō Text Database at http://21dzk.l.u-tokyo.ac.jp/SAT/ddb-bsk-sat2.php

Classical Texts

Amituojing yishu 阿彌陀經義疏 (Commentary on the Amitābha Sutra). Yuanzhao 元照, ed. T 1761.

Baoxing lun 佛性分別大乘究竟要義論 (*Ratnagotravibhāga-mahāyānôttaratantra-śāstra*). T 1611.

Biyan lu 碧巖錄 (Blue Cliff Record). Xuedou Zhongxian 雪竇重顯 and Yuanwu Keqin 圜悟克勤, eds. T 2003.

Chanzong Yongjia ji 禪宗永嘉集 (Collection of Yongjia of the Chan School). Xuanjue 玄覺. T 2013.

Chengshi yishu 程氏遺書 (Remaining Writings of the Chengs), Mokusai Web.

Chunqiu Zuo Chuan zhengyi 春秋左傳正義 (Spring and Autumn Annals, Commentary to the "Biography of Zuo"). Scripta Sinica.

Chunqiu gongyang chuan 春秋公羊傳 (Spring and Autumn Annals, "Biography of Gongyang"). Scripta Sinica.

Da ban niepan jing 大般涅槃大般涅槃經 (*Mahāparinirvāṇa-sūtra*). Dharmakṣema 曇無讖, trans. T 374.

Da baoji jing 大寶積經 (*Ratnakūṭa-sūtra*). Bodhiruci 菩提流志, trans. T 310.

Da Piluzhena chengfo shenbian jiachi jing 大毘盧遮那成佛神變加持經 (Sutra on the Miraculous Powers and Grace of Mahāvairocana Buddha). Śubhakarasiṃha 善無畏 and Yijing 一行, trans. T 848.

Da zhuangyan jinglun 大莊嚴經論 (*Kalpanā maṇḍitikā*). Attrib. to Aśvaghoṣa 馬鳴菩薩; trans. Kumārajīva 鳩摩羅什. T 201.

Dafangguang yuanjue xiuduluo liaoyi jing 大方廣圓覺修多羅了義經 (Sutra of Perfect Enlightenment). T 842.

Dasheng qixin lun 大乘起信論 (Treatise on Awakening of Mahāyāna Faith). T 1666.

Daxue zhangju, Mingde, Zhuzbu 大學章句, 明德, 朱注 (Zhu Xi's commentary on the *Great Learning*, on the section on "Illuminating Virtue"). http://mokusai -web.com/shushigakukihonsho/daigaku/daigaku.html.

Er Cheng ji 二程集 (Collected Works of the Two Chengs). Beijing: Zhonghwa shu ju, 1981.

Fanwang jing 梵網經 (Sutra of Brahmā's Net). Trans. attrib. to Kumārajīva 鳩摩羅什. T 1484.

Fayuan zhulin 法苑珠林 (Dharma Garden Jewel Forest). Daoshi 道世. T 2122.

Genben shuo yiqieyoubu pinaiye yaoshi 根本說一切有部毘奈耶藥事 (*Mūlasarvâstivāda-vinaya-vibhaṅga*). Yijing 義淨, trans. T 1448.

Guanding jing 灌頂經 (Consecration Sutra). Trans. attrib. to Śrīmitra 帛尸梨蜜多羅. T 1331.

Hamhŏ tang Tŭkt'ong hwasang haengjang 涵虛堂得通和尚行狀 (The Life of Reverend Hamhŏ Tŭkt'ong). HPC 7.250–252.

Hamhŏ tang Tŭkt'ong hwasang ŏrok 涵虛堂得通和尚語録 (Record of the Teachings of the Reverend Hamhŏ Tŭkt'ong). HPC 7.226–250.

Han Shu 漢書 (History of the Han Dynasty). by Dong Zhongshu 董仲舒. Scripta Sinica.

Henan Er Cheng yishu 河南二程遺書 (Remaining Writings of the Two Chengs of Henan). Taipei: Guoxue zhiben shu-cong si bai zhong, Taiwan shangwu yinshu kuan 45. Most citations located in Scripta Sinica.

Hou Han Shu 後漢書 (History of the Latter Han). Scripta Sinica.

Hyŏnjŏng non 顯正論 (Exposition of Orthodoxy). Kihwa. HPC 7.217–225.

Jingang bore boluomi jing 金剛般若波羅蜜經 (*Vajracchedikā-prajñāpāramitā-sūtra* [Diamond Sutra]). Kumārajīva 鳩摩羅什, trans. T 235.

Jingang sanmei jing 金剛三昧經 (*Vajrasamādhi-sūtra*). T 273.

Jingde chuandeng lu 景德傳燈錄 (Record of the Transmission of the Lamp Published in the Jingde Era). Daoyuan 道原, ed. T 2076.

Kisillon so 起信論疏 (Commentary to the Awakening of Faith). Wǒnhyo 元曉. HPC 1.698–722; T 1844.

Lebang yigao 樂邦遺稿 (Manuscripts Bequeathed from Paradise). Zongxiao 宗曉, ed. T 1969b.

Liezhuan 列傳 (Transmission of Lie). Scripta Sinica.

Liji 禮記 (Record of Ritual). Scripta Sinica.

Linji lu 臨濟錄 (Record of Linji). T 1985.

Liuzu tanjing 六祖壇經 (Platform Sutra of the Sixth Patriarch). T 2008.

Mao Shi 毛詩 (Book of Odes). Scripta Sinica.

Mengzi jizhu, Gaozi zhangju 孟子集註, 告子章句 (Zhu Xi 's commentary on the Mencius, chapter on Gaozi). http://mokusai-web.com/shushigakukihonsho/moushi/moushi_06.html.

Miaofa lianhua jing 妙法蓮華經 (Lotus Sutra). T 262.

Sanhui jing 三慧經 (Sutra on the Three Kinds of Wisdom). T 768.

Shang shu 尚書 (Book of Historical Documents). Scripta Sinica.

She dasheng lun 攝大乘論 (*Mahāyānasaṃgraha-śāstra*). Attrib. to Asaṅga 無著. Paramârtha 眞諦, trans. T 1593.

Shengman shizi hu yisheng da fangbian fangguang jing 勝鬘師子吼一乘大方便方廣經 (*Śrīmālādevī-siṃha-nāda-sūtra*). Guṇabhadra 求那跋陀羅, trans. T 353.

Shiji 史記 (Record of History). Scripta Sinica.

Shujing 書經 (Book of History). Scripta Sinica.

Sishu zhangju jizhu ([Zhu Xi's] Commentary on the Four Books). Mokusai Web.

Taebanggwang wŏngak sudara youĭgyŏng sŏrŭi 大方廣圓覺修多羅了義經説誼 (Commentary on the *Sutra of Perfect Enlightenment*). Kihwa 己和. *HPC* 7.122–169.

Taesŭng kisillon pyŏlgi 大乘起信論別記 (Expository Notes to the Awakening of Faith). Wŏnhyo 元曉. *HPC* 1.677–697; T 1845.

Taesŭng kisillon so pyŏlgi hoebon 大乘起信論疏別記會本 (Combined Edition of Wŏnhyo's Commentary and Expository Notes to the Awakening of Faith). *HPC* 1.733–788.

Xiaojing 孝經 (Classic of Filial Piety). Scripta Sinica.

Xunzi dong shi. Taipei: Guoxue zhiben shu-cong si bai zhong, Taiwan shangwu yinshu kuan 34.

Yijing 易經 (Book of Changes). Scripta Sinica.

Yiqiezhi guangming xianren cixin yinyuan bushirou jing 一切智光明仙人慈心因緣不食肉經 (Sutra on the Omniscient Luminous Sages Who Possess the Causes and Conditions of Compassion in Not Eating Meat). Unknown, trans. T 183.

Yuanjue jing 圓覺經 (Sutra of Perfect Enlightenment). T 842.

Yuanren lun 原人論 (Inquiry into the Origin of Humanity). Zongmi 宗密. T 1886.

Zhengmeng 正蒙 (Youthful Ignorance). Mokusai Web.

Zhou li 周禮 (Rites of Zhou). Scripta Sinica.

Zhuzi yulei (Sayings of Master Zhu). Confucian Etext Archive, http://sangle.web.wesleyan.edu/etext/song-qing/song-qing.html.

Zongjing lu 宗鏡錄 (Record of the Axiom Mirror). Yanshou 延壽, ed. T 2016.

Zuo Chuan 左傳 (Transmission of Zuo). Scripta Sinica.

Secondary Sources

Adler, Joseph A. *Reconstructing the Confucian Dao: Zhu Xi's Appropriation of Zhou Dunyi*. Albany: State University of New York Press, 2014.

An Kyehyŏn. *Han'guk pulgyo sasang sa yŏngu* (Studies in the History of Korean Buddhist Thought). Seoul: Dongguk University Press, 1982.

Buswell, Robert E., Jr. *Cultivating Original Enlightenment: Wŏnhyo's Exposition of the Vajrasamādhi-Sūtra (Kŭmgang Sammaegyŏng Non)*. Honolulu: University of Hawai'i Press, 2007.

———. *The Formation of Ch'an Ideology in China and Korea*. Princeton, NJ: Princeton University Press, 1989.

Chan, Wing-tsit, ed. *Neo-Confucian Terms Explained*. New York: Columbia University Press, 1986.

———, trans. *Reflections on Things at Hand: The Neo-Confucian Anthology Compiled by Chu Hsi and Lu Tsu-ch'ien*. New York: Columbia University Press, 1967.

———. *A Source Book in Chinese Philosophy*. Princeton, NJ: Princeton University Press, 1969.

Ch'en, Kenneth. *Buddhism in China: A Historical Survey*. Princeton, NJ: Princeton University Press, 1964.

Ch'ien, Edward T. "The Neo-Confucian Confrontation with Buddhism: A Structural and Historical Analysis." *Journal of Chinese Philosophy* 15 (1988): 347–348.

Ching, Julia. *To Acquire Wisdom: The Way of Wang Yang-Ming*. New York: Columbia University Press, 1976.

Chittick, William C. *The Sufi Path of Knowledge: Ibn Al-'arabi's Metaphysics of Imagination*. Albany: State University of New York Press, 1989.

Cho Myŏnggi, ed. *Han'guk pulgyo sasang sa* (Pak Kilchin Festschrift). Seoul: 1975.

Choi, Min Hong. *A Modern History of Korean Philosophy*. Seoul: Sŏng Moon Sa, 1978.

Ch'ong P'yongjo. *Han'guk chonggyo sasangsa* (A History of Korean Religious Thought). Seoul: Yonsei University Press, 1991.

Chong Tojŏn. *Sambong chip*. Seoul: Kuksa p'yŏnch'an ŭi wŏn hoe, 1971.

———. *Sambong chip*. Seoul: Minjok munhwa ch'ujinhoe, 1977.

———. *Sambong chip*. 2 vols. Seoul: Gyŏngin munhwasa, 1987.

Chung, Chai-shik. "Chŏng Tojŏn: 'Architect' of Yi Dynasty Government and Ideology." In *The Rise of Neo-Confucianism in Korea*, edited by Wm. Theodore de Bary, 59–88. New York: Columbia University Press, 1985.

Chung, Edward Y. J. *The Korean Neo-Confucianism of Yi T'oegye and Yi Yulgok: A Reappraisal of the "Four-Seven Thesis" and Its Practical Implications for Self-Cultivation*. Albany: State University of New York Press, 1995.

Cleary, Thomas. *Entry into the Inconceivable: An Introduction to Hua-yen Buddhism*. Honolulu: University of Hawai'i Press, 1982.

Cleary, Thomas, and J. C. Cleary, trans. *The Blue Cliff Record*. Boulder: Shambhala, 1978.

Cook, Francis. *Hua-yen Buddhism: The Jewel Net of Indra*. University Park: University of Pennsylvania Press, 1977.

de Bary, Wm. Theodore, ed. *The Message of the Mind in Neo-Confucianism*. New York: Columbia University Press, 1989.

———, ed. *The Buddhist Tradition*. New York: Modern Library, 1969.

———, ed. *Sources of Chinese Tradition*. New York: Columbia University Press, 1960.

de Bary, Wm. Theodore, and Jahyun Haboush Kim, ed. *The Rise of Neo-Confucianism in Korea*. New York: Columbia University Press, 1985.

Duncan, John B. *The Origins of the Chosŏn Dynasty*. Seattle: University of Washington Press, 2000.

Fingarette, Herbert. *Confucius: The Secular as Sacred*. New York: Harper and Row, 1972.

Fu, Charles. "Morality or Beyond: The Neo-Confucian Confrontation with Mahayana Buddhism." *Philosophy East and West* 23 (1973): 390–391.

Goulde, John Isaac. "Anti-Buddhist Polemic in Fourteenth and Fifteenth Century Korea: The Emergence of Confucian Exclusivism." Ph.D. dissertation, Harvard University, 1984.

Gregory, Peter N. *Inquiry into the Origin of Humanity: An Annotated Translation of Tsung-mi's Yuan jen lun with a Modern Commentary*. Honolulu: University of Hawai'i Press, 1995.

———. *Tsung-mi and the Sinification of Buddhism*. Princeton, NJ: Princeton University Press, 1991.

Ha, Tae-hung, and Grafton K. Mintz, trans. *Samguk Yusa*. Seoul: Yonsei University Press, 1972.

Han Kidu. *Han'guk sŏn sasang yŏn'gu* (Studies in Korean Sŏn Thought). Seoul: Ilsasa, 1991.

———, ed. *Sungsan Pak Kilchin Paksa hwagap kinyŏm: Hanguk pulgyo sasang sa* (Pak Kiljin Festschrift). Seoul: 1975.

Han Yŏng'u. *Chŏng Tojŏn sasang ŭi yŏn'gu*. Seoul: Seoul National University Press, 1985.

———. "Chŏng Tojŏn ŭi in'gan kwa sahoe sasang." *Chindan hakpo* 50 (1980): 123–135.

Hartman, Charles. *Han Yü and the T'ang Search for Unity*. Princeton, NJ: Princeton University Press, 1986.

Hoff, Benjamin. *The Tao of Pooh*. New York, Penguin Books, 1983.

Hucker, Charles O. *A Dictionary of Official Titles in Imperial China*. Stanford, CA: Stanford University Press, 1985.

Kalton, Michael. *The Four-Seven Debate: An Annotated Translation of the Most Famous Controversy in Korean Neo-Confucian Thought*. Albany, NY: SUNY Press, 1994.

Kamata Shigeo. *Chōsen bukkyōshi*. Tokyo: Tokyo University Press, 1987.

———. *Chūgoku Kegon shisōshi no kenkyū*. Tokyo: Tokyo University Press, 1965.

———. *Shūmitsu kyōgaku no shisōshiteki kenkyū*. Tokyo: Tokyo University Press, 1975.

Keel, Hee-Sung. *Chinul: The Founder of the Korean Sŏn Tradition*. Berkeley Buddhist Studies Series 6. Berkeley, CA: Regents of the University of California, 1984.

Kim, Hwansoo Ilmee. *Empire of the Dharma: Korean and Japanese Buddhism, 1877–1912*. Cambridge, MA: Harvard University Asia Center, 2012.

Kim Young Tae and U Chŏngsang. *Han'guk pulgyo sa* (A History of Korean Buddhism). Seoul: Sinhŭng Ch'ulp'ansa, 1969.

Kwŏn Kijong. "Chosŏn chŏngi ŭi sŏngyo kwan" (The Sŏn-Kyo Standpoint of the Early Chosŏn). In *Han'guk sŏn sasang yŏn'gu*, 245–282. Seoul: Minjok munhwa sa, 1994.

Lau, D. C. *The Analects*. Harmondsworth, UK: Penguin Books, 1979.

Lee, Kibaik. *A New History of Korea*. Cambridge, MA: Harvard University Press, 1984.

Lee, Peter H., ed. *Sourcebook of Korean Civilization*. Vol. 1. *From Early Times to the 16th Century*. New York: Columbia University Press, 1993.

Lee, Young-ho (Ven. Jinwol). "The Ideal Mirror of the Three Religions (*Samga Kwigam*) of Ch'ŏnghŏ Hyujŏng." *Buddhist-Christian Studies* 15 (1995): 139–187.

Legge, James, trans. *Analects, Great Learning and Doctrine of the Mean*. New York: Dover Publications, 1971.

———, trans. *I Ching: Book of Changes*. New York: Random House, 1996.

———, trans. *The She King or Book of Poetry*. Taipei: SMC Publishing, 1991.

———, trans. *The Shoo King*. Taipei: SMC Publishing, 1991.

———, trans. *The Works of Mencius*. New York: Dover Publications, 1970.

Lynn, Richard John, trans. *The Classic of the Way and Virtue: A New Translation of the Tao-te Ching of Laozi as Interpreted by Wang Bi*. New York: Columbia University Press, 1999.

Makita Tairyō. *Gikyō kenkyū*. Kyoto: Kyōto Daigaku Jinbun Kagaku Kenkyūjo, 1976.

McRae, John R., trans. *The Platform Sutra of the Sixth Patriarch*. Berkeley, CA: Numata Center for Buddhist Translation and Research, 2000.

Morrison, Elizabeth. *The Power of Patriarchs: Qisong and Lineage in Chinese Buddhism*. Leiden: Brill, 2010.

Muller, A. Charles, trans. *The Analects of Confucius*. http://www.acmuller.net/con-dao/analects.html, 2012.

———. "The Buddhist-Confucian Conflict in the Early Chosŏn and Kihwa's Syncretic Response: The Hyŏn jŏng non." *Review of Korean Studies* 2 (1999): 183–200.

———. "The Centerpiece of the Goryeo-Joseon Buddhist-Confucian Confrontation: A Comparison of the Positions of the *Bulssi japbyeon* and the *Hyeonjeongnon*." *Journal of Korean Buddhist Seminar* 9 (2003): 23–47.

———. "The Composition of Self-Transformation Thought in Classical East Asian Philosophy and Religion." *Bulletin of Toyo Gakuen University* 4 (1996): 141–152.

———, trans. *Daode jing*. http://www.acmuller.net/con-dao/daodejing.html, 2009.

————, trans. *Diamond Sutra*. http://www.acmuller.net/bud-canon/diamond _sutra.html, 2012.

————, trans. *Doctrine of the Mean*. http://www.acmuller.net/con-dao/docofmean .html, 2012.

————. "East Asian Buddhist Apocrypha: Their Origin and Role in the Development of Sinitic Buddhism." *Bulletin of Toyo Gakuen University* 6 (1998): 63–76.

————. "Essence-Function (*t'i-yung*): Early Chinese Origins and Manifestations." *Bulletin of Toyo Gakuen University* 7 (1999): 93–106.

————. *Exposition of the Sutra of Brahmā's Net*. Vol. 11 of *The Collected Works of Korean Buddhism*. Seoul: Jogye Order of Korean Buddhism, 2012.

————. "Gihwa's Analysis of the Relationship between the Worded and Wordless Teachings: The *Ogahae seorui*." *Bulletin of Toyo Gakuen University* 12 (2004): 1–16.

————. "The Great Confucian-Buddhist Debate." In *Religions of Korea in Practice*, edited by Robert E. Buswell, 177–204. Princeton, NJ: Princeton University Press, 2007.

————, trans. *The Great Learning*. http://www.acmuller.net/con-dao/ greatlearning.html, 2012.

————. *Hamhŏ Kihwa: A Study of His Major Works*. Albany, NY: SUNY Press, 1993.

————. "The Key Operative Concepts in Korean Buddhist Syncretic Philosophy: Interpenetration and Essence-Function in Wŏnhyo, Chinul, and Kihwa." *Bulletin of Toyo Gakuen University* 3 (1995): 33–48.

————, trans. *Mencius (Selections)*. http://www.acmuller.net/con-dao/mencius .html, 2014.

————. *The Sutra of Perfect Enlightenment: Korean Buddhism's Guide to Meditation*. Albany, NY: SUNY Press, 1999.

————. "Tiyong and Interpenetration in the Analects of Confucius: The Sacred as Secular." *Bulletin of Toyo Gakuen University* 8 (2000): 93–106.

Mun, Chanju. *The History of Doctrinal Classification in Chinese Buddhism: A Study of the Panjiao System*. Lanham, MD: University Press of America, 2005.

Nakamura Hajime, ed. *Bukkyōgo daijiten*. Tokyo: Tokyo Shoseki, 1975.

Palais, James B. "Han Yong-u's Studies of Early Chosŏn Intellectual History." *Journal of Korean Studies* 2 (1984): 199–224.

Park Chong Hong. *Han'guk sasang sa: Pulgyo sasang pyŏn*. Seoul: Min'ŭmsa, 1976.

Park, Sung Bae. *Buddhist Faith and Sudden Enlightenment*. Albany, NY: SUNY Press, 1982.

Rhi Kiyong. *Han'guk pulgyo yŏn'gu* (Studies in Korean Buddhism). Seoul: Han'guk pulgyo yon'guwŏn, 1982.

Sasaki, Ruth Fuller, et al. *A Man of Zen: The Recorded Sayings of Layman P'ang*. New York: Weatherhill, 1976.

Sharf, Robert H. *Coming to Terms with Chinese Buddhism: A Reading of the Treasure Store Treatise*. Honolulu: University of Hawai'i Press, 2002.

Shim, Jae Ryong. *The Philosophical Foundation of Korean Zen Buddhism: The Integra-*

tion of Sŏn and Kyo by Chinul (1158–1210). Honolulu: University of Hawai'i Press, 1979.

Shimada Kenji. *Shushigaku to yomeigaku*. Tokyo: Iwanami Shoten, 1967.

Song Ch'ŏn'ŭn. "Kihwa ŭi sasang " (Kihwa's Thought). In *Han'guk pulgyo sasang sa* (Pak Kiljin Festschrift). Iri: Wŏn Pulgyo Sasang Yŏn'guwŏn, 1975.

Song Hwan'gi. *Hamhŏ Tŭkt'ong hwasang yŏn'gu* (A Study of the Reverend Hamhŏ Tŭkt'ong). Seoul: Dongguk University Press, 1974.

Vermeersch, Sem. "Yi Seong-Gye and the Fate of the Goryeo Buddhist System." *Korea Journal* 53, no. 2 (2013): 124–154.

Watson, Burton, trans. *Chuang Tzu: Basic Writings*. New York: Columbia University Press, 1964.

———. *The Complete Works of Chuang-tzu*. New York: Columbia University Press, 1968. Citations in this book are from the online version at http://terebess .hu/english/chuangtzu2.html.

Wilhelm, Richard. *The I-Ching*. Princeton, NJ: Princeton University Press, 1973.

Wright, Arthur F. *Buddhism in Chinese History*. Stanford, CA: Stanford University Press, 1959.

Wu Joung-Sang. *Chosŏn chŏngi pulgyo sasang sa yŏn'gu* (Studies of the Buddhist Thought of the Early Chosŏn). Seoul: Dongguk University Press, 1966.

Yi, Chaech'ang, ed. *Hanguk sŏn sasang yŏn-gu* (Studies in Korean Sŏn Thought). Seoul: Dongguk University Press, 1984.

Yun Sasun. "Chŏng Tojŏn sŏngnihak ŭi t'ŭksŏng kwa keu p'yŏngga munje." *Chindan hakpo* 50 (1980): 151–160.

Ziporyn, Brook. *Ironies of Oneness and Difference: Coherence in Early Chinese Thought: Prolegomena to the Study of Li*. Albany, NY: SUNY Press, 2012.

———. "Li (Principle, Coherence) in Chinese Buddhism." *Journal of Chinese Philosophy* 30, nos. 3–4 (2003): 501–524.

Index

abhijñā, 39
accordance with affairs, 75
affliction, 3, 73, 159
ahiṃsā, 24, 26
alchemy, 7
alcohol, 95
altruism, 63. *See also* humaneness (*in*)
An Lushan, 79
Analects, 3, 10, 25, 30, 38, 39, 40, 52, 74, 91,
    92, 140, 142, 143, 145, 146, 147, 151,
    153, 155, 156, 158, 161, 162, 163, 165,
    166
Ānanda, 108
antinomianism, 108, 109, 110
asaṃskṛta, 5
ātman, 31
Avataṃsaka-sūtra, 37
Awakening of Mahāyāna Faith, 5, 6, 15, 21, 23,
    40, 74, 142

begging, 71, 72
benevolence. *See* humaneness
bodhi, 5
Bodhidharma, 102
bodhisattvas, 83, 84
Book of History, 90
Book of Odes, 70, 91, 98
broad learning, 41
Buddha Nature, 5
Buddha's bone, 79
Buddhism: corruption in, 12, 24; criticized
    for being a foreign religion, 16; di-
    verse in doctrines, 23; as escapist, 20;
    as essential teaching, 28; as incoher-
    ent, 66, 149; Kihwa turns to, 93; in
    the Koryŏ, 12, 13, 14; as nihilistic, 61;
    as one of the three teachings, 110;
    precepts in, 93; sacred-secular integra-

tion in, 42; Sinicized, 6; spread in East
    Asia, 3, 7; translation into Chinese
    idiom, 5

cause and effect, 1
Chan, 6, 7, 8, 9, 10, 11, 13, 15, 18, 22, 36, 42,
    45. *See also* Sŏn
Cheng Hao, 9, 10, 12, 14, 22, 24, 25, 34, 63,
    65, 69, 93; as source for Chŏng Tojŏn,
    21
Cheng Yi, 9, 10, 12, 14, 22, 93; as source for
    Chŏng Tojŏn, 21
ch'e-yong, 3. *See also* essence-function
Chindŏk, 106
Chinese medicine, 21
Chinul, 14, 15, 21, 60
Chittick, William, 147
Cho In'ok, 13
chŏng. See feelings
Chŏng Ch'ong, 13
Chŏng Mongju, 13
Chŏng Tojŏn, 10, 16, 18, 19, 21, 24, 26, 28,
    142, 143, 145; main themes of works,
    14; writings, 13; and Yi Sŏnggye, 13
Chu Wangying, 78
clothing, 1, 66, 96, 107
compassion, 22; criticized by Chŏng, 65
Confucianism, 1, 2, 3, 7, 8, 10, 15, 16, 21,
    24, 26, 34, 35, 36, 40, 61, 75, 85, 86, 93,
    96, 140, 143, 144; canon, 9; coherent,
    27; as coherent, 23, 66; as functional
    teaching, 28; interpreted by Zongmi,
    18; as one of the three teachings, 110;
    philosophical stagnation in, 7; rejected
    by Kihwa, 93; sacred-secular integra-
    tion in, 42; as understood by Kihwa,
    19, 24
Confucius, 6, 16, 18, 24, 25, 27, 70, 89, 105;

About the Translator

A. Charles Muller is professor in the Graduate School of Humanities and Sociology, University of Tokyo. His main work lies in the fields of Korean Buddhism, East Asian Yogâcāra, East Asian classical lexicography, and online scholarly resource development. Among his major book-length works are *The Sūtra of Perfect Enlightenment: Korean Buddhism's Guide to Meditation* (1999) and *Wŏnhyo's Philosophy of Mind* (2012). He has also published over two dozen articles on Korean and East Asian Buddhism. He is the editor and primary translator of three volumes published in the *Collected Works of Korean Buddhism,* and is the publication chairman for the Numata BDK sutra translation project. Among the online digital projects he has initiated are the *Digital Dictionary of Buddhism (http://www .buddhism-dict.net/ddb)* and the H-Buddhism Buddhist Scholars Information Network *(http://www.h-net.org/~buddhism)*.

Korean Classics Library: Philosophy and Religion

Salvation through Dissent: Tonghak Heterodoxy and Early Modern Korea
George L. Kallander

Reflections of a Zen Buddhist Nun
Kim Iryŏp, translated by Jin Y. Park

A Handbook of Buddhist Zen Practice
translated by John Jorgensen

Korea's Great Buddhist-Confucian Debate: The Treatises of Chŏng Tojŏn (Sambong) and Hamhŏ Tŭkt'ong (Kihwa)
translated and with an introduction by A. Charles Muller

Korean Classics Library: Historical Materials

Reclaiming Culture: Selected Essays on Korean History, Literature, and Society from the Japanese Colonial Era
edited by Christopher P. Hanscom, Walter K. Lew, and Youngju Ryu

Production Notes for Muller / *Korea's Great Buddhist-Confucian Debate*
Jacket design by Guy Horton
Composition by Wanda China with display type in Lucida Sans and Scala
Sans Pro and text in Book Antiqua
Printing and binding by Maple Press
Printed on 55 lb. natural offset, 360 ppi.